Reflections on Risk
Volume VI

ASA Institute for Risk and Innovation

Edited by Emily Hayes
Annie Searle, Executive Editor

Printed in the United States of America
First edition: February 2022
Tautegory Press, Seattle, Washington USA

Printing History
All research notes here were previously published as "ASA Research Notes" in ASA Newsletters ©Annie Searle & Associates LLC and at its website www.anniesearle.com between September 2019 and September 2021.

Library of Congress Control Number: 2012931422
ISBN: 979-8-9850101-0-7

Cover design by Jesse Brown

CONTENTS

FORWARD

Just as technology has undergone remarkable transformation over the past ten years, ASA's Institute for Risk and Innovation has evolved to provide both immediate and longer-term access to research notes that reflect the most urgent issues of our time. Early on, we focused on risks around our nation's critical infrastructure and public-private partnerships because those areas represented our advisory practice. More recently, we have published more research around the impact on society of social media and sophisticated cyber-tools. As a result, research has focused not only on critical infrastructure risks or public-private partnerships, but also around information ethics and policy, privacy, disinformation, artificial intelligence, surveillance and cryptocurrency. My own time is spent primarily in the classroom, but also working on policy issues around regulation, disaster recovery and advocacy for privacy regulation.

Special thanks to Emily Oxenford Hayes, editor of this and five other volumes of *Reflections on Risk*. Emily is also the editor of our monthly newsletter, *ASA News & Notes*, where these research notes first appear.

Each research note is published first in our monthly publication, *ASA News & Notes*, then housed on the ASA website until we have 24 or so research notes to gather into a volume like this one. We have streamlined our processes for publication somewhat over the years, but the principles from which we publish remain the same. The primary source of research notes is from courses I teach at the University of Washington's Information School, most of which focus on risk, cybersecurity and information ethics, policy and law. I read all the papers that my students submit, as does my teaching assistant, so students get two sets of comments on their work. Papers that I offer to publish must meet a high bar: not only must they be well organized and well written, but they must contain original analysis and cutting-edge recommendations for managing the risks as well. The papers that become research notes are meant to provide executives and practitioners alike with a short but accurate lens through which to view increasingly complex issues driven by information and technology. I hope you find this sixth volume useful.

Seattle, February 2022

THE CONTRIBUTORS

Ashritha D'Souza received her Master of Science in Information Management degree with a focus in data science from the University of Washington in 2020 and the Bachelor of Science in Computer Science and Engineering from Jawaharlal Nehru Technological University (JNTU) in 2010. Her professional experience includes completing a summer internship with SAP Concur's App Center team. Currently, Ashritha works as a technical product manager at Microsoft, providing product vision, creating a roadmap, and bringing a product to life.

Maeve Rogers Edstrom is the Director of User Experience at HeadLight, an infrastructure technology startup. She leads design and research for product development and aims to create informative user experiences that enhance productivity. Maeve received her Master of Science in Information Management from the University of Washington in 2019; and her Bachelor of Fine Arts from University of North Texas in 2007

Greyson Fields is a Product Manager at VMware where he is building out SaaS and subscription capabilities across VMware's product portfolio. He holds a Bachelor of Science in Informatics from the University of Washington. Previously, he was an intern at Smartsheet and a small construction company in the Seattle area.

Melanie Keane is a Business Intelligence Analyst at Boeing and Tableau Certified Professional with several years of experience creating interactive dashboards and transforming complex data into simple, clearly articulated insights that enable proactive decisions. She received a Master of Science in Information Management degree from the University of Washington and a Bachelor of Science in Strategic Communications degree from Texas Christian University

Peyton Lyons received her Bachelor of Science in Informatics and Bachelor of Arts in Spanish degrees with honors from the University of Washington in 2019. During her time at UW, she completed two summer internships at Intel on a business solutions team and worked at the Latino Community Fund as a data management fellow. After graduating, Peyton joined Liberty Mutual's rotational Analyst Development Program. Upon completion of the program, she joined the Product Design & Experience team where she works closely with the company's digital teams to enhance the product experience.

Raphael Kyle Caoile Manansala graduated with a Bachelor of Science in Informatics focusing on information assurance and cybersecurity and an English minor from the University of Washington in 2021. He was a former IT for the University of Washington College of Education before graduating. He is currently a cybersecurity consultant at Deloitte.

Gabriel McCoard received his undergraduate degree from the University of Wisconsin and holds a Juris Doctor from the University of Maryland School of Law. He has previously served as Legislative Counsel to the National Congress of the Republic of Palau and directed a not-for-profit legal services office in Chuuk State, Federated States of Micronesia.

Kha Nguyen completed his Bachelor of Science in Informatics at the University of Washington in 2021. He currently works as a Program Manager at

Microsoft, and his passions include building software, watching films, and engaging with music.

Alex Osuch is a consultant at Coalfire who specializes in PCI DSS assessments for cloud-hosted service providers. He works to help compliance requirements meet the nature of the cutting-edge application architecture deployed by his clients. He earned a Master of Science in Information Management degree from the University of Washington in 2020, focusing primarily on information security; and a Bachelor of Arts in Writing Seminars from Johns Hopkins University in 2009.

Kate Peterson graduated from the University of Washington in June 2020 with a Master of Science in Information Management and a Master of Arts in International Studies with a focus on Russia. Passionate about the intersection of technology and the human experience, Kate is an advocate for greater data privacy protections. She is currently employed at Accenture as a member of the data protection team.

Amanda Phillips is a data management specialist for the Pacific States Marine Fisheries Council. Partnered with the National Oceanic and Atmospheric Agency, she is currently researching the impact of fisheries management decisions and climate change on West Coast fishing communities. She received her Master of Science in Information Management with a focus on Data Science and Bachelor of Science in Aquatic and Fishery Sciences from the University of Washington.

Allessandra Quevedo will receive her Bachelor of Arts in Political Science from the University of Washington in 2021. Her professional experience includes working as an intern for the Boeing Company and for Expedia Group. She will work for Expedia Group as a Data Scientist, starting in 2022. Her interests outside of her line of work are cybersecurity and UX design.

Rochelle Robison received her Bachelor of Arts in English and Master of Arts in Education in Educational Technology (1992 and 1999, respectively) from Arizona State University. Her professional experience includes working in broadcast television and corporate learning and development. Currently Rochelle works as a senior learning consultant and facilitator at DocuSign. She is currently working towards a Master of Science in Information Management, with a specialization in Information Architecture and User Experience.

Roger St. Louis graduated in 2020 from The University of Washington with undergraduate degrees in Sociology and Informatics (concentration in Cybersecurity). He has over 15 years of specialized wide-range experience within the financial world - including investments, business, and financial technologies. He has also interned at Microsoft and Amazon working in IT network security and risk management projects on large-scale events.

Connor Tatman received his Bachelor of Arts in Economics degree with a minor in Informatics from the University of Washington in 2020. Currently, he works as a Human Resources Process Team Lead for Target, ensuring that all employee data is in compliance with local, state and federal law.

Ting-Yen Tsai received a Bachelor of Business Administration in Finance from National Taiwan University in 2021, and she was an exchange student at the University of Washington in the 2019-2020 academic year. Her professional experience includes completing an internship with Fidelity International, where she conducted data mining and market research in the APAC Product Development Team. Currently, Ting-Yen is pursuing a Master of Science in Financial Engineering at Columbia University.

Sophie Werner is a cybersecurity consultant in the Government Risk and Compliance sector for Edgile LLC. In 2021, she received her Bachelor of Science degree from the University of Washington in Informatics (Cybersecurity and Information Assurance) with a minor in International Studies.

Bingyan Wang received her bachelor's degree with a major in Education, Communities, and Organizations, and a minor in informatics from the University of Washington in 2021. This fall, she enters the MSEd program, "Teaching English to Speakers of Other Languages" at the University of Pennsylvania Graduate School of Education starting from fall 2021.

Vincent Xu is an Information Security Policy and Management Master's student at Carnegie Mellon University. He is also currently a privacy engineer at humanID, where he uses information assurance and cybersecurity skill sets to safeguard anonymity. He graduated from the University of Washington in 2021 with a Bachelor of Arts degree in Economics, with a minor in Informatics from the UW iSchool.

SECTION ONE

Information Infrastructure

PAPER	AUTHOR
COVID-19 Vaccine Supply Chain Risks	Vincent Xu
ESD – System Under Fire	Kha Nguyen
Essex Lorry Death: A Tragedy of Migrant Smuggling	Ting-Yen Tsai
IoT and SCADA Risk in Smart Grids	Alex Osuch
Water in Trouble	Clarissa Pendleton

COVID-19 Vaccine Supply Chain Risks

AUTHOR: Vincent Xu

PUBLISHED: January 2021

WRITTEN: December 2020

KEYWORDS: COVID-19; pandemics; supply chains; pharmaceuticals

ABSTRACT:
This paper discusses the global dissemination of COVID-19 vaccines, perhaps the biggest and most consequential product launch in modern history. In December 2020, Pfizer reduced its vaccine production plan by 50% due to a combination of challenges arising from brand new ultra-cold refrigeration equipment requirements, far-reaching nation-state malicious cyberattacks, and crucial weak links discovered in logistic processes. The challenge that the worldwide health sciences sector faces requires an agile coordination amongst law enforcement, threat intelligence, pharmaceutical firms, and logistics providers. A strategic plan that protects the viability of the COVID-19 supply chain plays a vital role in maintaining the global trust bestowed upon the healthcare system in the long run.

Introduction

As the number of coronavirus cases continues to surge in the United States, Pfizer, the leading COVID-19 vaccines manufacturer, announced the first week of December 2020 a shocking 50% cut in its planned vaccine production for the remainder of the year.[1] This shortage in vaccine supply suggested risks in not only the American pharmaceutical industry, but also risks within the worldwide health sciences sector. Moreover, the ongoing pandemic continues to stretch thin the resources of freight companies and logistics fulfillers, highlighting the global vaccine supply chain's fragility.[2] Currently, the limited capacity of vaccine logistics systems, the ever-escalating cyber threats and the complex vaccine supply chain procedures cast unprecedented challenges for the global COVID-19 immunization efforts.

The Supply Chain

The success stories related to COVID-19 vaccine development has brough global attention to issues within the vaccine supply chain. Due to the urgency in vaccine demands, distribution requires an unprecedented number of freight planes to fulfill the large bulk of air shipments.[3] The head of pharmaceutical division at Emirates airline estimated that one Boeing 777 freight plane can carry approximately one million doses of vaccine.[4] At this rate, it is estimated that providing half the world's population with two doses of COVID-19 vaccine would require around 8,000 cargo planes.[5] Orchestrating such massive fleet of airplanes entails extensive outsourcing, which requires careful management of freight subcontractors.[6] Harnessing the power of this large cargo plane fleet safely and effectively requires a unified, collaborative global strategy to achieve optimal allocation of aviation resources.

Another challenge that resides within the COVID-19 vaccine logistics system involves refrigeration. The new mRNA COVID-19 vaccines developed by Pfizer require an ultra-cold environment during transportation, with a minimum refrigeration temperature of at least negative 80 degrees Celsius (negative 176 degrees Fahrenheit).[7] The truth is that a large part of the world's population "simply doesn't have a supply chain that can operate at that temperature."[8] In fact, only 14 percent of air carriers can ship at negative 80 degrees Celsius or lower.[9] The highly likely event of a vaccine degradation can result in decreased health protection and may require a patient to be revaccinated.[10] Without well-established, ultra-cold refrigeration equipment systems, the current worldwide vaccine supply chain remains largely unprepared to take on the great challenge of COVID-19 vaccine dissemination.

COSO Risk Rating

The significant shortage in vaccine logistics equipment renders the vaccine supply chain highly vulnerable to system failures. The risks can be quantified by utilizing the COSO risk assessment framework and a risk assessment scale.[11] Below are this author's risk ratings for the vaccine supply chain by each risk measure (Impact, Likelihood, Vulnerability, and Speed of Onset/Velocity) on a scale of one to five, with five being the highest / most significant rating.

- Impact score = 5: Impact (or consequence) refers to the extent to which a risk event might affect the vaccine supply chain. A logistic system failure would likely lead to delayed vaccination for not only front-line healthcare practitioners, but likely an overall delay in vaccinating the population. As any delay at this point would likely result in fatalities from COVID-19 contraction, the impact score is assessed at 5 (extreme).

- Likelihood score = 5: Likelihood represents the possibility that a given risk event will occur. Since Pfizer has already delayed its vaccine dissemination plan,[12] the likelihood of such system failure appears to already be occurring, so the likelihood score is assessed at 5 (almost certain).
- Vulnerability score = 4: Vulnerability refers to the susceptibility to a risk event in terms of criteria related to preparedness, agility, and adaptability. Because Pfizer has also confirmed that "there are no other main logistics partners beyond" DHL, FedEx, and UPS in the U.S distribution plan, freight plane fleet and refrigeration equipment must be addressed daily.[13] Considering freight companies have only partially procured and implemented refrigeration equipment,[14] the vulnerability score is assessed at 4 (high).
- Speed of Onset score = 5: Speed of onset (or velocity) refers to the time it takes for a risk event to manifest itself. Since the first phase of vaccination will be executed at extreme urgency, the speed of onset score is assessed at 5 (very high).

- The total risk score, therefore, is a staggering 19/20 risk rating. This indicates a clear picture that the global vaccine supply chain is both deficient and fragile.

Cyber Threats

As pharmaceutical companies continue to develop COVID-19 vaccines at an accelerated velocity, there is also an increasing level of external cyber threats that are against organizations that are crucial to a properly functioning vaccine supply chain. Recently, IBM X-Force discovered a cybercriminal disguised as a business executive from Haier Biomedical, who sent spear-phishing emails out to material providers within the COVID-19 cold chain supplier network.[15] It is highly likely that the cybercriminal strategically chose Hair Biomedical as target due to its status as the world's only complete cold chain provider.[16] Since Haier Biomedical is a key provider to the global undertaking of COVID-19 vaccines dissemination, the adversary utilized Haier's far-reaching network to illicit critical credentials from the European Commission's Custom Union, World Health Organization, UNICEF, and the United Nations. Furthermore, the recently discovered COVID-19 phishing campaign spanned six countries as well as organizations within the energy, manufacturing, software, and information security solutions sectors.[17] Most importantly, one commonality between all targets of this attack is their close association with the Cold Chain Equipment Optimization Platform (CCEOP) program.[18] From a cybersecurity defense perspective, a breach within any part of this global alliance can expose vast coverage of computing environments worldwide.

While the identity of the adversary is unknown, the rare precision and specificity of targets point to nation-state malicious hackers at a high likelihood.[19] Through harvesting credentials, the malicious campaign directly threatened confidentiality, integrity and availability of top-secret processes, methods, and plans that pertain to the COVID-19 vaccine distribution.[20] At an age of cyber warfare, virtual external entities can damage the lifeline of the vaccine supply chain no less than those that are physical.

Theft

The process of vaccine distribution requires protection against one great looming threat: theft. Given the limited COVID-19 vaccine supply with the increasing vaccination demand, it is paramount that the global supply chain treats physical security of the vaccines with caution. At the process level, freight forwarders are the glue that connects all working parts of a massive vaccination effort together.[21] However, freight forwarders are also under tremendous risk of theft at their weak linkages. The U.S. has assigned federal marshals to accompany shipments of vaccines,[22] however risk from organized crimes persists. Interpol, an international police organization, issued a global orange notice,[23] warning of imminent threats from organized crime groups that may disrupt the vaccine supply chain and undermine the integrity of the vaccines. Regarded as "liquid gold," criminal organization, foreign governments, and individuals who want to get the vaccine before front-line healthcare workers are all increasingly targeting the COVID-19 vaccines.[24] As international travel gradually resumes while vaccination processes gradually progress, criminal networks are also likely to engage in distribution of unauthorized and falsified vaccines. Handling and storing COVID-19 vaccines under tight security constraints play a vital role in both protecting the public safety of communities and preserving the public trust within COVID-19 immunization initiatives.

Recommendations

Some would argue that the dissemination of COVID-19 vaccine is the biggest and most consequential product launch in modern history.[25] In fact, logistics leader DHL estimated that the scale of this global operation involves 15 million cooling boxes and 15,000 flights.[26] To ensure proper functioning of this massive program, the first recommendation is to revamp key logistics systems. Logistic forwarders are expected to increase their procurement of temperature-controlled containers to strengthen the worldwide cold chain. At the same time, airports must supplement appropriate support in container battery charging to lengthen refrigeration duration. Utilizing existing cold chain framework, vaccine manufacturers can collaborate with gene therapy and clinical trial sites to establish glacial distribution networks for the novel vaccines to ensure optimal distribution efficiency.[27]

Echoing national alerts issued by the Department of Homeland Security and the Cybersecurity and Infrastructure Security Agency,[28] the second recommendation encourages the global vaccination initiatives to remain vigilant to cyber threats. All involved organizations should create and test their Incident Response Plans, to ensure they can take smooth and swift action in the event of an attack. Exercising the Principle of Least Privilege, security officers at these organizations should apply a zero-trust approach in only granting access to data that is essential to the functioning of the vaccine supply chain. Most importantly, all organization should increase their educational trainings to employees to highlight email security best practices and foster a culture of vigilance.

On the process side, protecting COVID-19 vaccines requires a reduction in the number of stops in logistics. As much as possible, manufacturers should ship the vaccine directly from manufacturing sites to the vaccination locations.[29] Hospitals, vaccination sites, and pharmacies need to ramp up their security systems and the overall physical security posture. To counter organized crimes, logistics systems could use GPS software to plot fake shipments to confuse criminals and to ensure location and temperature of vials are visualized in real time.

The distribution of such valuable product at the height of the COVID-19 pandemic cast unprecedented challenges for the life sciences industry. As vaccine manufacturers initiate rollouts, the coordination between law enforcement, threat intelligence, pharmaceutical firms and logistics providers plays a vital role in safeguarding trust within the global healthcare system and the wellbeing of communities worldwide.

ESD—System Under Fire

AUTHOR: Kha Nguyen

PUBLISHED: September, 2021

WRITTEN: October, 2020

KEYWORDS: Employment Security Department, Fraud, ESD

ABSTRACT:
This paper discusses how the use of effective controls within an organization is critical for safeguarding the reputation of the company as well as the safety and assets of its customers. During the COVID-19 pandemic, the Washington State's Employment Security Department (ESD) experienced major failures of its systems and controls, leading to tens of thousands of fraudulent claims made worth hundreds of millions of dollars.

Controls

Corporations and government agencies need *controls.* More importantly, they need *effective* controls. Controls safeguard a company's assets and prevent theft of their most valuable resources.[1] For the Washington Employment Security Department (ESD), usage and refinement of the controls they use to protect themselves has never been more important. Essentially, ESD provides unemployment benefits to citizens in Washington State, in other words "temporary income when you lose your job through no fault of your own."[2]

In terms of risks that affect enterprises, *fraud* is a major one – this includes criminal activities such as theft and receiving benefits for which one should not legally have access to. Take a look specifically at ESD. Their assets are their cash, systems, and reputation. In 2020, thieves took advantage of the unemployment benefits system of Washington State, fraudulently taking money by filing unemployment claims with stolen personal information of other Washington residents. This likely occurred in part because of weaknesses in ESD's control environment. This paper breaks down the control failures in order to produce *alternatives* that could strengthen ESD's ability to manage risk.

Control Failure – System

The purpose of a system is to serve its duties while also protecting against bad actors that wish to use it in a way it was *not* intended. Attack and defense. Cat and mouse. Fraud in this space exists in two variations.

- First: imposters signing up for unemployment benefits under someone else's name and info.
- Second: people enrolling in or continuing to receive benefits *despite* not being eligible.

The defense used by ESD against these cases currently consists of "working with other states and federal government to cross match data to detect fraud."[3] Although public information on ESD systems and anti-fraud practices remains vague, a Senior Manager at Microsoft's Dynamics 365 Fraud

Protection Team working directly with ESD to strengthen their defense has been able to provide first-hand information. He describes ESD and other government websites as having "custom software solutions woven together across different custom solutions, products, and platforms."[4]

Now, what this entails—and what makes ESD's systems so vulnerable—is that these technology systems can only ever be as strong as its weakest component. If you have seven different services interfacing with each other in a system, all it takes is an attacker to identify a single weak point in this system to expose a vulnerability that can be exploited.

Unfortunately, ESD's website and supporting technological systems are *not* the only ones to face these problems. Many other government websites have suffered the same fate.[5] Alongside a disarray of custom tech woven together, these government tech systems also suffer a "poor or complete lack of proper tech audit controls in place." In other words, government systems are not nearly *updated* nor *stress-tested* enough.[6] This issue has been further made extremely evident through website launch disasters such as "healthcare.gov" which proved to be unfit for the high stress load they were presented with.[7]

In regard to ESD, their systems have not been working well to the point of satisfaction since ESD itself reported that from late April through early May 2020, "tens of thousands of individuals whose stolen information has been used to file fraudulent claims" which ends up translating into "hundreds of millions of dollars."[8] This system can be better.

Fixing the Control Failure – System

The first means of fixing these vulnerable systems within ESD is to seek help from those who have built powerful and protected systems for their own needs – the tech field. By vetting and hiring strong technology-based companies or agencies to assist with or even revamp ESD systems, it will have a better shot at protecting against fraud and attackers. Government agencies have utilized third-party consultants and engineering in the past but have failed to properly vet these entities to ensure proper practices in stability and data storage.

Furthermore, the bureaucracy and red tape surrounding government tech contracts has dissuaded many strong, talented development teams from participating in government projects.[9] Striking a balance between proper vetting of those taking on government tech contracts and having *too* much red tape will allow for the creation of more secure and durable systems.

In the short term, ESD can make relatively quick and effective progress by integrating existing anti-fraud systems provided by companies such as Microsoft and Sift into the current ESD system infrastructure. In the long term, they should have a trusted core team or third-party company rewrite the entire ESD technological system from scratch to ensure total quality and integrity. This in fact has been done before with a startup called Marketplace Lite, which was hired to completely rewrite Healthcare.gov in full. As reported by *The Atlantic,* they replaced "contractor-made apps with ones costing one-fiftieth of the price."[10] In fact, *The Atlantic* describes them as the "secret startup that saved the worst website in America."

Control Failure – External Events

Now, we explore another attacking mechanism that bad actors use to defraud ESD, and it involves an attack vector that some argue may even be more vulnerable than technology systems themselves – people. *Phishing* refers to any form of email, text, or fake website that thieves use to deceive people into providing their personal information to.[11]

System security against external events has become so important that *Coalfire* reported that in a survey done by the New York Stock Exchange, "66% of directors do not believe their companies are properly protected."[12] Especially in an entity such as ESD where access to personal information is such a quintessential part of unemployment benefits fraud, attackers will utilize the weaknesses of people themselves as part of their arsenal. ESD itself has reported on a "giant uptick in phishing websites" and has issued warnings on their official website.[13]

Phishing has clearly become a giant threat to organizations, with even "22% of organizations seeing phishing as their greatest security threat."[14] Unfortunately, ESD's current controls to protect against these external phishing attacks are not effective. In other words, they do not do enough. Firstly, ESD says that people discover their identities have been stolen either through a letter they do not expect from ESD in the mail or through their employer.

Since people end up not knowing how their identities were stolen, future attacks remain just as likely. These days, phishing tactics have become so tricky that it becomes difficult to know if you have been phished or not and which fake website you got tricked into putting your information into. In an effort to inform more people of these ongoing phishing attacks, ESD attempts to do so through the phishing announcements on their website. However, these warnings are barely visible to most everyday users of the ESD site, and even those who end up seeing them can still be deceived by tricky phishing attacks.

Fixing the Control Failure – External Events

While phishing for now cannot be completely *eradicated,* ESD can take actions to help *decrease* the quantity of these attacks. By requiring a two-factor authentication system in order to verify one's identity when logging into the ESD website or using its services, this can help reduce a substantial number of account hacks. This can take the shape of requiring the user to enter a code sent to their personal mobile phone, which an attacker would not have access to two-factor authentication can help thwart many phishing attempts and account hijackings but depending solely on it is *not* enough.[15]

Providing more accessible and widespread information to the public regarding phishing will encourage users to be more informed and mindful whenever inputting their personal information. An easy first-step is to present phishing warnings more obviously throughout ESD sites. A more long-term facing step would be to cooperate with big tech in charge of email services such as Microsoft Outlook and Google Gmail to be more vocal and involved in protecting users against phishing. On its own, ESD can improve its diligence in preventing phishing attacks by reporting to other government agencies all ongoing phishing attempts as ESD discovers or users report.

Not Simple but Necessary

Government often can be associated with slow moving processes and outdated technology. However, in an age where technology continues to move fast and bad actors become smarter, government agencies such as ESD must adapt to thrive and keep their assets safe. ESD owes it to its citizens to protect government assets while also guarding their peace of mind.

Essex Lorry Deaths: A Tragedy of Human Smuggling

AUTHOR: Ting-Yen Tsai

PUBLISHED: October 2020

WRITTEN: December 2019

KEYWORDS: Human Smuggling; Human Rights; Migration; Immigration; Global Migration

ABSTRACT:
This paper describes the tragic death of 39 Vietnamese people in Essex, England, who suffocated in the air-tight cargo container in an attempt to be smuggled over the border into the United Kington. The analysis focuses on the event's significance, the risks it poses, and potential recommendations for the UK government and law enforcement authorities.

Background

On October 23rd 2019, the bodies of 39 Vietnamese were found in the trailer of a refrigerated lorry (a large, flatbed truck used for carrying goods) in the town of Grays, located in Essex, England. These victims— aged between 15 and 44 —died from asphyxia and hyperthermia – a lack of oxygen and overheating – in the enclosed space. Since officials often check the refrigerated containers of truckers less frequently, the smugglers were transporting their "customers" in an air-tight container. In November

2019, the driver—Maurice Robinson—admitted to being part of the illegal people-smuggling ring. This incident is a terrible example of the risks associated with human smuggling, which along with trafficking of persons are two of the fastest growing areas of international criminal activity.

These deaths—referred to collectively as the Essex Lorry Deaths—were a consequence of human smuggling. The United Nation Protocol against the Smuggling of Migrants by Land, Sea and Air defines human smuggling as "the procurement, in order to obtain, directly or indirectly, a financial or other material benefit, of the illegal entry of a person into state party of which the person is not a national."[1] In an interview video made by Channel 4, the victims' family said that they paid the smugglers anywhere between 10,000£ and 30,000£ pounds,[2] the equivalent of approximately $13,000 to $39,000 U.S. dollars. This is a significant amount of money, especially considering that the GDP per capita in Vietnam in 2018 was approximately $2,564.[3]

Risk Analysis

There are two divisions under the UK Home Office that are responsible for immigration issues, which are Immigration Enforcement (IE) and Border Force (BF). The IE division has three main objectives, consisting of 1) preventing migrants from entering the UK illegally and overstaying; 2) dealing with threats associated with immigration offenses; and 3) encouraging and enforcing the expulsion of illegal migrants from the UK.[4] The BF division is responsible of securing borders—including searching baggage, vehicles and cargo for illicit goods or illegal immigrants—and its officers have the power to arrest and detain both at ports and inland.[5] Currently, the UK uses the Immigration Act 1971 to regulate assistance in unlawful immigration, but there is still room to improve its ability to identify potential victims and crimes.

In the Essex Lorry Deaths, the smugglers found an extreme way to avoid inspection by border officers and transport their "customers" to the UK. It can be safely assumed that the driver was not only involved in this single incident, but likely participated in other human smuggling incidents, because he had admitted conspiracy to assist unlawful immigration between May 1st 2018 to October 24th 2019. Also, the border security check may have been looser than it should have been. A Polish lorry driver using British port Fishguard in Pembrokeshire said that he had only been stopped twice by border control for a "proper" check in his 17-year career. He said the officers just look if the cargo seal on the back is broken, check documents, and let the truck through the checkpoint. As for Irish ferries, the check is done by asking the driver what is in the back.[6] Moreover, the length of the UK's coastline and the sheer volume of passengers and freight entering the UK every year make identifying shipments containing illegal migrants a significant challenge.[7]

The Essex Lorry Deaths also demonstrates the risks of human rights being violated. Although the victims paid money to the smugglers, the smugglers did not provide their "customers" a way to call for help in emergency. Furthermore, even if those "customers" managed to enter the UK successfully, it would still be almost impossible for them to get successfully integrated into society. They could apply for legal stay, however, their chances of getting permission to legally stay were quite slim. If they could not stay in the UK legally, they may have been exploited at work, struggle to find housing, fall victim to human trafficking, and suffer from a cycle of exploitation.[8] Thus there are enormous hazards to the victims lives not only during but also after the smuggling process, highlighting the increasing need to eradicate human smuggling.

Global Risk in Human Smuggling & Trafficking

Human smuggling does not only take place in the UK or Europe—it takes place all around the globe. There are thousands of unlawful migrants from Central America who are apprehended at the U.S.—Mexico border,[9] and there are North Koreans risking their lives and their family's fate to cross the Yalu River.[10] Those migrants may have different reasons to leave their country: economic condition, political pressure or chaotic war, but they are all in a quest of seeking for a better life. It is irritating that there are people exploiting these desperate people through providing illegal and unsafe transportations.

On June 20th, 2019, U.S. Secretary of State Michael Pompeo has released the 2019 Trafficking in Persons (TIP) Report. In this report, the government of the United Kingdom was listed as "Tier 1" since the UK government fully meets the minimum standard of human trafficking, and it continuously demonstrates the serious and sustained effort by identifying possible victims.[11] The national College of Policing is offering for all front-line officers to strengthen their abilities of victim identification. If there is a case in a country with strong response to human smuggling and trafficking, other countries classified as Tier 2 or Tier 3 may even have a higher risk.

Aside from human smuggling, human trafficking is another serious and related issue. Different from smuggling, the victims of human trafficking were more vulnerable and subject to coercive and abusive actions by traffickers, and the violation of human rights is more severe. Back in 2009, United Nations Office on Drugs and Crimes (UNODC) released "A Global Report on Trafficking in Persons"[12], which mentioned the seriousness of current situation – there are 91 countries (57% of the reporting countries) had at least one human trafficking prosecution, and 73 countries had at least one conviction. Also, the Global Slavery Index 2018 indicates that they were 40.3 million people living in modern slavery in 2016, including 24.9 million in forced labor and 15.4 million in forced marriage.[13]

Thus, human smuggling and trafficking must be viewed from a global perspective, and governments should seek for cross-country cooperation to break down the crime ring.

Current Effort

Compared to the humanitarian shock and grief brought by such a tragedy, there have not been many fundamental changes in UK laws in response to the Essex Lorry Deaths – or even after the Dover Incident, which took place in 2000 and claimed the lives of 58 Chinese people in an extremely similar way. Chinese state media criticized the UK government for failing to prevent a repeat of tragedy.[14]

The government's only effort that relates to human smuggling is the introduction of Modern Slavery Act 2015.

The act was introduced in March 2015, and it increased the maximum jail sentence for human smuggling up to life imprisonment from 14 years to demonstrate the force of the government to the smugglers.

There are more efforts related to human trafficking, and some of them are helpful for responding to crime of smuggling; however, they may not always be applicable in the cases of human smuggling. For instance, the National Referral Mechanism (NRM) is a framework for identifying victims of human trafficking and ensuring they receive the appropriate protection and support. As the Border Force (BF) division was able to identify more than 1,100 potential victims in 2018, compared to 500 in 2017, the adoption of NRM has likely helped authorities identify potential victims of human trafficking.[15] Nevertheless, since the people being smuggled enter into the initial agreement with the smugglers, they and their fellow companions will not use the reporting system to expose themselves, and once their actions are controlled by the smugglers, they lose their ability to contact others and protect themselves.

Recommendations

The primary recommendation to UK government for combating human smuggling is to break down the demand and supply in the "market," so there would be fewer human smuggling activities, and the number of incidents that are similar to Essex Lorry Deaths could be minimized in the future.

To decrease "demand," it is important to understand what factors make the people in developing countries to risk their lives. In Essex Lorry Deaths, the likely reason the individuals were attempting to leave Vietnam was their economic conditions, based on the background of the victims and additional information given by their family. Most victims came from the northern part of Vietnam, where is a relatively poorer region across the country, and they even had to borrow money from their families to pay the smugglers.

Therefore, the UK government should work with other governments and non-governmental organizations (NGOs), such as micro-finance organizations like Grameen Bank, and try hard to improve the economic condition in developing countries. As a member of G20 who has more power and resources, the UK government should take on the responsibility of providing assistance; as a potential destination for many illegal migrants, it can get benefits from making improvements in social security by reducing the number of illegal immigrants.

In other cases, political environment, violence, and labor exploitation could also be the pull factors that make people to risk their lives to leave their countries. They may also seek out smugglers due to a lack of legal migration routes or insufficient relevant information. For example, in North Korea, people will pay smugglers to increasing their odds to escape, since they do not have any other ways to get out of the tyranny. There is not much to be done except to negotiate with the North Korean government. However, in other countries in Southeast Asia, it is possible for NGOs to provide practical information or consultancy about migration for the locals. By knowing safe and legal migration routes, people would likely be less likely to seek help from smugglers, pay an extortionate price and travel unsafely.

On the "supply" side, the UK government can reduce the crime of smuggling by strengthening its law enforcement. First, it should improve the effectiveness of border check. The government should adopt random comprehensive checks, which demands the driver to open the back of their vehicles, in the interior of lorries and ferries, so that the border officers can ensure security while the efficiency of the ports is not hugely affected. Second, it should share information about human smuggling crimes not only with its neighboring countries, but also developing countries in Asia, Africa, and Eastern Europe. By sharing the database of human smuggling and trafficking crimes, the police forces in each country can deal with or even prevent smuggling and trafficking in a more efficient way. Third, a RACI matrix approach could be used to clarify and define the responsibilities of each division, so they can quickly deal with emergencies,[16] The matrix should include the following organizations: Home Office, Immigration Enforcement (IE), Border Force (BF), UK Visas and Immigration (UKVI), National Crime Agency (NCA) and local police.

Conclusion

The operational risk in law enforcement and the risk in violating human rights are both massive in the tragedy of Essex Lorry Deaths. To prevent similar event from recurring, the UK government should execute comprehensive check to all entering vehicles and ferries, and actively work with other police forces around the globe. Also, it should make effort on economic development in developing countries, and partner with other governments and NGOs to educate people about the legal routes to move to another country, and the consequences of illegal migration. By adopting these recommendations to mitigate risks, the vulnerabilities in law enforcement and human rights can be reduced.

IoT & SCADA Risk in Smart Grids

AUTHOR: Alex Osuch

PUBLISHED: March 2020

WRITTEN: April 2019

KEYWORDS: Cybersecurity; critical infrastructure; Internet of Things; energy infrastructure

ABSTRACT:

This paper discusses the emerging risk associated with the new systems of automation and networked devices becoming embedded in the critical energy sector's infrastructure. The nation's energy infrastructure is becoming increasingly connected and continues to converge, producing new kinds of vulnerabilities and areas of exposure, including in the realm cybersecurity. Cyber-physical systems produce cyber-physical risk. This discussion examines advanced metering, substation automation, and nation-state risks in the smart grid in order to sketch out a useful snapshot for cyber risk managers interested in critical infrastructure

---

Introduction

The tectonics of security are volatile and abrasive, and the organizations set atop them face pressure from every conceivable angle to increase efficiency. Fortunately, automation via interconnected remote sensors and controllers is helping enterprises to stay ahead. Unfortunately, and, in some ways, unremarkably, the pace of security has not kept up with efficiency-driven innovation. Internet of Things (IoT) systems, a broad category of interconnected sensors that work in conjunction with automation and analytics, present a unique and expanding kind of risk that requires new levels of effort to mitigate. For IT professionals in every industry, the expectation is that IoT devices will compose an exponentially increasing chunk of the connections to a given network, and as a result, conventional security strategies will be pulled towards these devices over human-based connections.[1] Of course, the stakes vary. A vendor that deploys IoT sensors in parking garages to automate customer usage and billing is primarily concerned with customer satisfaction, privacy controls, and compliance.[2] For power grids, as one facet of the national critical infrastructure, the stakes include the safety of our homes and the foundations of U.S. national security.

In 2015, an attack on the industrial control system (ICS) components in parts of the Ukrainian power grid cut power to over 225,000 customers for almost six hours, and, due to the exceptionally malicious nature of the attack, some of the grid's automated infrastructure was destroyed, in some cases taking the better part of year to replace.[3] That same year, Lloyds of London published a study that modeled the impact of a major cyberattack on the U.S. power grid, the most extreme case of which examined a four week outage resulting in a $1 trillion impact on the gross domestic product and more than four years needed to recover to pre-attack conditions.[4] The imaginative landscape of cyber risk will need to continually expand to accommodate this new reality. The elevation of information security in the IoT space requires not only traditional cyber protections of confidentiality, integrity, and accessibility, but also a clear sense of the (often cascading) physical dangers posed by compromised devices.[5] Many organizations are already engaged with these ideas, but the scope of the problem cannot be overstated.

Defining Smart Grids and Connected Systems

Power grids are typically divided into three main parts: generation, transmission, and distribution.[6] Generation describes the point (e.g. a power plant) from which electricity originates and from which power is sent to substations to be stepped up to a higher voltage. Transmission lines from these substations broadly distribute this bulk power to distribution substations, which in turn step down the voltage. Distribution lines connect the current to feeders that supply transformer grids, and from these local transformers, power arrives at a customer's meter and into their local wiring at a useable voltage. Transmission voltages can be anywhere from 14,000 to 1.5 million volts, while distribution voltages range from 2400 to 34,500 volts, and by the last mile of the system, the power has been stepped down to the typical 120/240 volts demanded by most customer appliances.[7] The design of these elements of the grid aims to maximize efficiency in meeting customer demand, both individually and in the aggregated sense, part of which is to ensure that the final voltage of power delivered is always within the 10 percent variability range tolerable to most appliances.[8] Although these systems have been around for many years, power grids are remain difficult to manage.

Smart grids are power grids that implement digital systems to solve these challenges and increase efficiency. All electrical equipment is subject to failure, and when assembled into a grid, a failure in one point can damage or disable other parts of the system. The dangerous currents behind this process are referred to as faults and can take a number of forms.[9] The term for controlling faults is electrical or system protection, which uses equipment such as relays, circuit breakers, fuses, and grounds to detect and isolate faults and failed transformers.[10] In essence, circuits within grids must be closely monitored for faults, quickly broken, and quickly restored. Since consumer demand between 2015 and 2050 is projected to triple, grids must scale up, and the corresponding increase in complexity makes them prime candidates for automation and real-time analytics for controlling faults.[11] Besides better fault control, well-managed smart grid systems can help ensure that demand is met as efficiently as possible in the face of supply and consumption fluctuations. The elements that would constitute a smart grid system are generationally diverse and operate at a number of levels, so it is worth going over what they consist of.

The Internet of Things (IoT) is the term most often associated with the "smart" in smart grids, but phrase can be employed alongside terms like cyber-physical systems (CPS), supervisory control and data acquisition (SCADA), industrial control systems (ICS), and a host of more specific elements such as intelligent electronic devices (IED). The distinctions are important within their various operational contexts, but from a risk-based security perspective, the rigorous categorization of these systems is less important than what they have in common as networked devices. These terms can and often are used interchangeably, to varying degrees, and the few distinctions discussed below are loosely relational rather than rigorously hierarchical. As an additional note, the umbrella term "connected" will often be used to refer to the above and generally any device that functions as part of a networked system.

IoT refers to connected sensors that gather and transmit data, usually for analytic or remote physical control purposes.[12] The sensors themselves wirelessly communicate with their nearest gateway (and each other) using a variety of protocols, but once their data reaches the edge, it is typically communicated via an IP-based protocol to a cloud platform.[13] IoT devices themselves can also function as their own gateway, connecting directly to the cloud, although power and processor constraints usually preclude this capability.[14] The distinction between IoT and the other systems under consideration is the emphasis on Internet-based data gathering and connectivity.[15] Their value is to make information remotely accessible and actionable without human intervention.

As a related term, Industrial IoT (or IIoT) refers to a subset of IoT that excludes consumer-purchased devices in order to focus on industrial use cases across any number of sectors.[16] This doesn't necessarily mean that the devices cannot be customer-facing, so to speak, but the responsibility and value associated with their implementation is primarily of benefit to an industrial process. An example of a power grid IIoT implementation would be smart meters at the point of home delivery, with which a normally human process (an employee physically reading a meter) can be automated, and which can also generate real-time data and controls to support crucial enterprise processes like demand response.[17] These systems will be discussed in more detail later. Since the scope of discussion here is limited to power grids in the context of critical infrastructure, the phrase IoT will serve in the same capacity as IIoT.

CPS, by contrast, are primarily concerned with governing a physical object performing a task using digital oversight. NIST defines CPS as systems that "integrate computation, communication, sensing, and actuation with physical systems to fulfill time-sensitive functions with varying degrees of interaction with the environment, including human interaction."[18] A related term is would be ICS, which would refer more specifically to CPS in a smart grid. The focus here is on the physical system, the interaction with the environment, and the time-sensitive nature of the function. Time sensitivity is especially important to the value and risk of CPS, something which will be discussed later, since the urgency of a given automated task can preclude trust-based security controls used to authenticate sources of information.[19] One example of a CPS device is a phasor measurement unit (PMU), a sensor that measures the phase angle in a current and digitally processes the measurement into time-stamped data to aid in state estimation (SE), a crucial process for keeping grids stable, all with less than one millisecond of latency.[20] The implication is that the further organizations scale up the use of these devices, the more they become exposed to risk arising from associated CPS vulnerabilities.

SCADA serves as the real-time control and operations structure for many sectors. These systems use information, often provided by CPS, to execute the day-to-day controls protecting power grids from faults and other threats. SCADA systems are architected much like IoT systems, in that data is collected at local gateways that transmit information to a master station via a wide area network.[21]

The station sends back automated control instructions and transmits useful information to the human operators of the system. One use case for SCADA in a smart grid is equipment monitoring, since heat degradation is a perennial concern. Devices like tap changers (which help transformers step down power to different voltages) can be paired with connected monitoring devices in order to extend equipment life and aid in the early detection of failures.[22] In another example, SCADA-administered devices in relays can also generate and sequence circuit information for post-incident reports, a process which informs future grid design and troubleshooting.[23] As an integral part of the smart grid, these systems are only expected to proliferate.

The Last Mile: Advanced Meter Infrastructure

This first section is will examine a customer-facing element of the smart grid: metering. The final mile of the power distribution system, also referred to as the utilization system or the low-voltage network, covers the space defined by neighborhood transformers, meters, and customer appliances.[24] Since consumption is the defining feature of the grid as a whole, major concerns at this level include managing power demand and assessing use for billing purposes. This section will focus on the ways in which cybersecurity for connected devices impacts these concerns, with a focus on the IoT-adjacent aspect of smart meters and advanced metering infrastructure (AMI).

Connected meters expand upon the capabilities of conventional electromechanical meters by delivering readings remotely. The two major types of connected meters currently in use in the U.S. are automated meter readers (AMRs) and those employed as part of AMI, typically referred to as smart meters.[25] AMRs can perform one-way communication of information via short-range radio to personnel equipped with wireless meter readers, eliminating the need for them to physically touch the meter or even to leave their vehicle, or, in many cases, the AMR can communicate directly to a central facility through a fixed-line network.[26] As part of AMI, smart meters expand on this remote functionality by employing two-way communication (usually via a wireless network protocol) to facilitate a number of monitoring and control capabilities, independent of any physical human intervention, and in that sense they could be considered the 'next generation' of connected meters.[27] As of 2017, almost 70 million of the 133 million meter-bearing households in the U.S. were using AMI.[28]

Smart meters are designed to support AMI in a number of ways. They are solid-state devices and thus have application-based computing capabilities that can be modified and expanded, with the main function being the conversion of analog electrical input into useable time-correlated data.[29] Example functions include consumption, voltage, load profile, and service interruption monitoring.[30] The meters report in intervals of anywhere between five minutes and one hour, depending on customer needs and network capacity, with most residential metering operating at one-hour intervals and industrial customers operating at 15-minute intervals.[31] Remote control functions for smart meters can include remote configuration and firmware upgrades, service cutoff for billing or load control purposes, and even two-way power flow management for customers making use of personal power generation systems (such as solar panels).[32]

The analytics and control facilities of AMI use smart meter data to fulfill a number of important distribution management tasks. Because of the vast scale of the power distribution system, even in a single metropolitan area, accurate real-time modeling of a power grid is critical for maintaining service and increasing efficiency.[33] AMI contributes to this broader issue by providing accurate demand data that can be used to model things like peak usage and which can be later used in research.[34] Similar benefits can be extended to outage management, as smart meters feed geo-located "last-gasp" and "power on" signals to control centers as power is lost or restored.[35] This enables coordinating of repair crews to target problem areas more quickly and spend less time assessing recovery efforts, as well as to quickly diagnose unique small-scale disruptions in the midst of large-scale events.[36] The last task to mention here is voltage monitoring, where AMI can be used in conjunction with distribution monitoring to determine whether voltage issues are related to infrastructure or the customer premises, something which is of special benefit to industrial customers with voltage-sensitive equipment in need of quick turnarounds on power issues.[37]

Because of these capabilities, smart meters and AMI can offer tremendous benefits to the business side of power delivery. Increases in efficiency due to a reduction in personnel and vehicle costs are a clear case of this. Centerpoint Energy, a power utility based in Houston, Texas, reported $61 million in operational savings over a three-year period after rolling out a full-scale AMI implementation, with an additional $4.5 million saved through the detection of faulty meters and theft.[38] ConEdison, the major power utility in New York, projects over $1.1 billion in savings over the 20 year period following their 2015 rollout of 4.7 million smart meters (both electric and gas).[39] Because AMI is expensive to deploy, it can be a difficult prospect for smaller utilities, and many rollouts (such as Centerpoint's) have the benefit of government grants to support their implementation.[40] Seattle City Light, for instance, had 75,000 smart meters deployed as of 2017 as part of a multi-year rollout, but by mid-2018 the rollout had been delayed and run 20 percent over its initial $86 million dollar cost.[41]

Another advantage of AMI is the customer-facing benefits, which are probably more significate (if less tangible) than the operational benefits, and certainly more interesting in terms of connected risk. The concept is to increase the amount of information supplied to customers regarding their usage. The enhanced usage data acquired by smart meters can be processed into user-friendly reports that help customers understand the nuances of their usage and their bills, especially when variable pricing structures (peak-time rates, for instance) are in effect.[42] Much like the benefit to outage recovery, the analytics and control aspects of AMI allow utilities to reduce response times to customer complaints, whether they arise from billing issues or from requests for changes in service, without customers having to schedule repairs with service personnel, make phone calls, or even necessarily be the first to detect a problem.[43]

The most promising aspect of AMI for proponents is the automated interfacing of the system, via cloud platforms and the smart meter, with a customer's smart home infrastructure. In this scenario, consumption can be automated at the connected appliance level in conjunction with (or, in some cases, directly by) an AMI platform that delivers grid and pricing data in real time, assisting in a processes called demand response and demand side management.[44] The smart meter is positioned as a wireless gateway for what is referred to as the customer's Home Area Network (HAN).[45] From there, any connected thermostats, water heaters, air conditions, charging electric vehicles, or other devices can be turned on or off in response to changes in rates, with the end result being that utilities can better maintain a balance between peak and off times more effectively than depending on customers to adjust their appliances manually.[46] Further features of HAN integration include the incorporation of household sensor systems that trigger on/off functions for entire rooms based on occupancy.[47] Beyond typical load balancing efforts, demand response controls can also assist in times of sustained systemic stress, such as summer heatwaves in places like California, in a real-time manner as a complement to conventional government-issued notices.[48]

AMI Security Issues

With so much customer-facing integration, data gathering, transmission, and critical service management, the AMI environment is home to serious security and privacy concerns. The important modeling, maintenance, and incident response features of AMI expose these critical functions of the grid to disruption and attack in unexpected ways.

Alarm over the ability of utilities to gather and analyze data about home energy use has been an element of AMI since it was first introduced, largely because of the extensive inferences that can be made about individuals from usage data. Variations in energy consumption can indicate number of family members, whether someone is unemployed, when someone is on vacation, what types of appliances are in the house and how they are being used, and so on.[49] While utilities generally limit their use of smart meter data to enhance their business functions, having that data passed on to third parties, even accidentally via their AMI vendors, could have a disastrous impact on the well-being of customers.

An accepted notion within the privacy world is that seemingly innocuous data can become highly sensitive data, a concept that would apply to AMI as much as anything else.[50] This leaves aside the even clearer set of issues that arise from demand response control access to household appliances. From the perspective of obfuscation, the anonymous user of a smart meter would seek to have either a continuously flat rate of consumption or a consumption profile that never varies, which could conceivably achieved by a complex automated system of batteries drawing and discharging power as needed, but, of course, this bears little relationship to how actual customers behave.[51]

While there have been no highly visible AMI data breaches to negatively sway public opinion, some customers are nevertheless weary of being profiled within their own homes. Examples of aversion to AMI range from individuals refusing to consent to meter upgrades to community campaigns and attention from large privacy advocacy groups. The issue has also begun to wind its way through the courts. In 2018, the 7th Circuit Court of Appeals found that the data collected by the City of Naperville through its 2011 smart meter program (which did not offer customers a chance to opt-out) was sufficiently detailed to constitute a search under the 4th Amendment.[52] The amicus for the case was filed by Privacy International and the Electronic Frontier Foundation, and while the court ultimately decided that sufficient government interest rendered the search reasonable, they qualified their ruling by stating that if any other body beside the utility had access to the data (e.g. law enforcement, without a warrant) or even if the interval for data collection were shorter than 15 minutes, they might have ruled otherwise.[53]

In 2017, Duke Energy had to back down from its system of opt-out tariffs for refusing smart meters, one way in which utilities attempt to incentivize weary customers to sign on.[54] More recently, Duke was fined $10 million by The North American Electric Reliability Corporation (NERC) for 127 violations of their critical infrastructure security standard, a result of poorly implemented controls and problems (including wayward laptops) that "were rooted in 'cultural issues' at the group of companies" operating within Duke.[55] While NERC's cybersecurity framework under which Duke was fined is primarily concerned with bulk electric systems (BEC), meaning organizations responsible for the upstream generation, transmission, and distribution parts of the grid, the controls that constitute the framework are fundamental network security principles that would no less apply to last mile metering systems.[56]

Privacy concerns in this context are clearly warranted, since it is still unclear whether or not utilities are informationally mature enough to handle AMI and to be entrusted with so much sensitive data. Seattle City Light is an example of one utility that has been intentional in this respect, incorporating itself in Seattle's city-wide privacy initiative and winning praise from organizations like Washington's ACLU.[57] In their customer-facing material on AMI, City Light explains the set of identifiers transmitted by the smart meter ("only the meter number and the amount of energy used will be relayed through the wireless network"), the level of security used while the data is in transit ("similar to security used with online banking and ATM machines… national encryption standards…"), and the entities who are able to access the data (" you and authorized City Light personnel").[58] Interestingly, the more-detailed Privacy Impact Statement (PIA) released by City of Seattle explains the way in which City Light's AMI vendor, Landis+Gyr, is contractually limited to providing the data through its SaaS platform, whereas the customer-facing material completely omits the existence of the vendor.[59] This belies the complex, difficult-to-secure, and difficult-to-explain networking stack of IoT devices like smart meters. Landis+Gyr does use good controls that address security in this environment, such as FIPS 140-2 compliant encryption and independent audits.[60]

The wireless component of AMI (and of IoT and CPS in general) is a prime area of security concern, particularly in terms of communication between smart meters and the customer's HAN, and especially when home IoT devices are connected to demand side management systems. The standard protocol used to connect a HAN to smart meters is Zigbee, a low-energy IEEE 802.15.4-based wireless protocol that is usually deployed in a mesh topology, which gives it a resilience important for demand response.[61] Other smart grid protocols have been proposed. 6LoWPAN, for instance, is an IEEE 802.15.4-based IP protocol that provides support for IPv6, which allows networking of low resource devices through the Internet in a more secure way than past IP-based protocols.[62] If systems at different levels of the smart grid were standardized using a protocol like 6LoWPAN, then modeling and control would become accessible at a massively interoperable scale, but an advantage of keeping devices off the internet is that they are more difficult to find remotely through using tools like Shodan.[63] Depending on the application and the vendor, there are at least five other commonly used wireless protocols that IoT devices can use, which is partially what makes IoT so difficult to manage from a security standpoint. The issue can be compounded by the fact that once smart meters are rolled out in particular distribution system, which, as mentioned earlier, is an expensive prospect, the devices are intended to last decades before being replaced, and vendors do not always engage in regular security or infrastructure updates.[64]

One example of a consumer-side vulnerability in Zigbee is the default security setup in new devices, which can include the use of pre-installed default vendor keys or the non-activation of encryption and data authentication altogether.[65] Use of demand side management in this context could allow the compromise of a smart home, presenting a particular threat to residents that have devices like IoT door locks.[66] Generally speaking, it is uncommon for typical users to reconfigure the default settings in their devices, if they are even aware of the security functions in the first place. Given that many property managers, for instance, would welcome the demand side features of AMI and are also increasingly deploying smart locks in their apartment buildings, the potential for attackers to compromise multiple targets could become a concern.[67] As an example, an academically demonstrated attack called Chain Reaction compromised Philips Hue lightbulbs by penetrating their Zigbee networking structure.[68] The designers studied the bulbs' power usage to determine the shared secret key used to encrypt the firmware , and then exploited a vulnerability in the communication authentication process between bulbs to continuously spread malware to new bulbs and disable any future over-the-air firmware updates.[69] The study demonstrated an automated method for employing the attack by flying a malware-laden drone into proximity of a set of bulbs.[70]

If an attacker were able to gain control of an unsecured smart home device and use a trusted connection to gather information about the smart meter, they could conceivably discover vulnerabilities in the device or even (in the case of directly connected devices) attempt to compromise the meter.[71] Smart meters are also vulnerable to physical compromise due to the presence of unsecured diagnostic serial ports, representing another opportunity for side-channel techniques to discover the device's secret cryptographic key.[72]

Whether or not the smart meter itself is used as a point of attack, the ability to compromise AMI gateways and even control facilities would allow an attacker to cut customers off the grid or spoof modeling and visibility data.[73] The result could be the covert jeopardizing of accurate load balancing, with the even more severe possibility for the open use of rapid on-off switching across many smart meters (disruption of grid or DoG attack) that could result in equipment damage, failure, and blackouts.[74] It is little wonder that the Department of Energy made security monitoring an integral part of the grant-assisted AMI rollouts they oversaw from 2011-2015.[75] Compromises of this kind could leave communities without power for the better part of day, or worse.

There is another kind of IoT risk that is not a product of AMI as such, but which plays an important role in the stability of local distributions systems, and that arises from mass compromise of devices that are then leveraged for malicious tasks, otherwise known as botnets. A botnet is a collection of malware-infected devices that are governed by one or more command and control (C&C) servers over the internet, or, in some cases, arranged in a peer-to-peer topology where each device can act as a C&C.[76] Bad actors who run botnets write or acquire malware and design automated ways in which they can scan for vulnerable devices, compromise them, and use the newly compromised devices to find new targets.[77] Botnet owners can employ these devices themselves, but more often they lease portions of the botnet to others for malicious use.[78] The larger the botnet becomes, the easier it is to lease to more customers and offer services at a larger scale. Botnets can be employed for all sorts of tasks, including cryptocurrency mining, ransomware attacks, spam campaigns, and, most often, distributed denial of service (DDoS) attacks; botnet malware is designed to carry out tasks and attacks unnoticed, so users typically remain unaware that their device has been compromised.[79] Poorly secured consumer IoT devices have become a favorite target for growing botnets, and with total spending on IoT projected to reach $1.2 trillion in 2022 (led by the consumer sector), bot proliferation is expected to increase.[80]

The Mirai botnet, being perhaps the most well-known, provides a good example of how IoT devices can get rolled into these types of networks. Mirai was built by scanning for and exploiting a known vulnerability in many IoT devices, namely, the fact that many manufacturers leave port 23 (for Telnet) open and unsecured to the Internet.[81] Once identified by Mirai, a Telnet connection was established using a credential-stuffing attack comprised of 62 factory default username & password pairs.[82] From there, the Mirai malware was downloaded from a C&C server, installed, and obfuscated, although it is interesting to note that the malware was not stored in persistent memory, and as such could be removed by simply rebooting the device.[83] For most IoT consumers, though, power cycling a device is usually only performed when performance is noticeably impaired. 15,194 attacks were issued from Mirai over the five months it was most active, demonstrating that while hundreds of high profile targets suffered the full extent of the botnet's firepower, botnet-as-a-service users had the capability and desire to target any size organization.[84] The effect of these attacks were widespread, prompting the Electricity Information Sharing and Analysis Center (E-ISAC) to issue a white paper outlining measures to take to secure or remove Internet-facing devices to defend against botnets and botnet harvesting.[85]

Like all electronics, IoT devices running malware tend to draw energy and heat up while carrying out malicious tasks. In household cases, this can produce an increase in energy usage. In an examination of IP cameras, DVRs, and routers (among the most common devices infected by Mirai), a study by Fong et al. observed increases in power consumption as much as 16 percent above average while carrying out Mirai tasks.[86] However, given that the IoT devices tested were low-powered consumer electronics, the study concluded that the financial impact on customers' power bills were negligible. Another study that examined connected heaters and air conditioners arrived at more startling conclusions. A class of attacks using high-wattage devices referred to as manipulation of demand via IoT (MadIoT) was shown to be effective for causing frequency instability and cascading line failure in distribution systems, if executed at proper scale.[87] The premise of the attack is that demand is systemically increased in an opportunistic way, e.g. during peak hours or other times of potential stress or imbalance. In one simulation, increasing or decreasing demand using air conditioners sufficiently disrupted frequency in the grid to trigger generator relays to disconnect it, hence causing a blackout, and only required the attacker to control and simultaneously power 18,000 air conditioners on or off.[88] In a large metropolitan area in the height of summer, especially five or ten years from now when smart homes devices are more prevalent, such an attack does not seem far-fetched. In another simulation, an attacker with control of 210,000 air conditioners would be able to trigger cascading line failures that would result in a blackout for 86 percent of the entire Polish power grid.[89] The Mirai botnet was thought to have controlled over 600,000 devices worldwide at its height, and a more focused actor or team of actors could patiently acquire the capability for this type of large-scale attack; the study noted that the number of air conditioners correlated to 1.5 percent of the total households in Poland.[90]

The Substation

This second section discusses some examples of connected systems within substations. It is at the substation level where the CPS and SCADA elements of the smart grid monitor and control power that travels via transmission lines. Because substations connect critical elements of the power grid, whether in preparing power for bulk energy transmission lines or for stepping down voltages for sub-distribution lines to feed into customer meters, their smooth operation is a top priority, and so they make for tempting targets of attack.

The central type of equipment for substation operations are transformers.[91] Current transformers and potential transformers, for instance, are responsible for managing the magnitude of current and voltage.[92] Because they convert these elements of power flowing through the station from a higher magnitude to a lower magnitude in order for substation equipment to more easily process it, their failure would result in disruption across the entire station.[93] Larger transformers are expensive pieces of equipment, usually in the millions of dollars, which are beholden to the unique service requirements of any given substation and are difficult to replace if they fail. They are often made overseas and thus require special transportation equipment because of their size; on average, a new transformer implementation requires two years from planning and startup.[94]

One example of a SCADA component for a transformer would be a sensor that measures successful execution of tap changes, during which a transformer shifts its voltage conversion ratio, a critical function for adaptively addressing changes in demand.[95] Another system would be intelligent bus failover, which quickly responds to the failure of a transformer—that could transfer load to another transformer, overloading it was well—by shedding load to other parts of the grid, such as outgoing feeders, and then redistributing the excess load to return operations to normal.[96] As is probably clear, failure or compromise of these automated systems could lead to extensive downtime or equipment damage.

Two other components of substations that are critical for grid protection are protective relays and circuit breakers. Smart grid relays are programmable solid-state modules that monitor current and voltage conditions and issue commands (usually to circuit breakers) in order to isolate dangerous power flow e.g. from a lightning strike or an incoming fault from elsewhere in the grid.[97] An example SCADA system that supports relays would be adaptive relaying, which can automatically adjust relay settings in the event of an overload in such a way as to avoid tripping circuit breakers altogether, thus reducing downtime.[98] Circuit breakers, as implied above, are used to open or close a circuit in order to isolate an problematic current.[99] An example of a SCADA system that supports circuit breakers would be equipment condition monitoring, which compares real-time information about performance with benchmark profiles to deliver early alerts if maintenance or replacement of a breaker is required.[100] Besides increasing efficiency, one can imagine the value of preventing a circuit breaker failure in a crisis event.

State estimation (SE) is another good example of an important tool for controlling substations that relies on functioning SCADA. A state estimator generates a real-time model of substation conditions and provides this information to human operators.[101] This has many control applications, not only for components like the protective relays described above, but for higher-level analysis and research as well. A similar need for modeling was mentioned earlier in assessing last mile distribution demand, and so in that sense SE can be a broad and even scalable concept. SE makes use of legacy SCADA sensors and newer phasor measurement units (PMUs) simultaneously to measure voltage, current, and phase angles within the substation and transmit time-correlated data.[102]

The integration of legacy systems with newer smart grid components, an issue across the entirety of the power grid, can have a mixed impact on SE because of the variable capabilities in sensors, networking infrastructure, and data processing capabilities in a given substation.[103] Legacy SCADA devices like remote terminal units (RTUs), hardwired gateways that have connected sensors to control platforms for decades, have been gradually phased out for devices like PMUs, which typically connect directly to control platforms via wireless WAN.[104] One can imagine how prohibitive it would be to fully swap one generation from the other, however, given budget and uptime demands. Another limitation on SE, this time human, is the design of SE-driven incident response given the variety of incident contingencies beyond the real-time decision-making capabilities of human operators, something which is usually accounted for by performing pain-staking simulation analysis.[105] Both despite and because of the increases in efficiency delivered by SCADA SE, the stability and standardization of the smart grid can be an area of concern.

The non-standardization of the SCADA that supports SE can leave substations open to attacks like false data injections (FDIAs).[106] Variability in legacy system measurement accuracy already requires SE systems to incorporate counter-measures that can correct or toss out anomalous readings.[107] This bad data detection (BDD) function screens for data outside of certain thresholds related to equipment tolerances and ambient signal noise.[108] FIDAs are structured such that attackers who have compromised sensors or gateways can send false data to control facilities without triggering BDD detection algorithms, thus poisoning SE and related processes while remaining undetected.[109] FDIAs require a sophisticated understanding of SE systems within the target substation, since a targeted attack on certain types of state data must take into account standard BDD tolerances, as well as avoid manipulating important classes of state data that are protected by additional (and often expensive) countermeasures; newer SCADA systems are also more resilient to this type attack.[110] The attacker would presumably need a long-term plan and plenty of resources, on the order of an advanced persistent threat, in order to execute an FDIA. Such an actor could benefit from the resulting undetected degradation in SE over the long term if it were coordinated with other kinds of attacks.

This kind of highly targeted long-term degradation of SCADA systems was the main accomplishment of Stuxnet, perhaps the most well-known (and one of the earliest) examples of a sophisticated ICS attack. Early analysis of the worm showed that it contained an inordinate number of exploits that individually could have facilitated large cybercrime attacks, which indicated that the creators of the worm were probably state-sponsored and motivated to accomplish their task for non-monetary reasons.[111] The worm's target, a type of Siemens controller that oversaw nuclear centrifuges at a suspected Iranian weapons facility, was successfully compromised in ways that disabled and damaged the equipment over a long period of time, disrupting operational timelines and leading to a severe drop in morale amongst personnel.[112] It was unique from an ethical standpoint in that it intentionally avoided human harm or compromise of any system that did not fit the exact specifications of the Iranian facility, part of what researchers noted when the worm was eventually discovered after having spread to other Siemens systems across the globe.[113]

One imagines that if the worm had been just a bit more thoughtfully designed and had avoided propagating widely, Iranian scientists and the world at large would still have no idea what happened. The novel complexity of Stuxnet and its rampant spread late into its deployment eventually drew attention, but for most SCADA systems and attack strategies, forensics can be very difficult. Besides the mix of new and legacy equipment, the necessity of system uptime means that traditional digital forensic workflows aren't possible, and logging for most devices is limited in both taxonomy and persistence; most SCADA systems are designed for constant operation under restricted conditions.[114] In a newer generation PMU, for instance, the TCP/IP networking and time-correlation features that allows richer data gathering also introduce an attack vector where GPS data can be jammed or spoofed without triggering an alert in the unit, disrupting the modeling and control processes that rely on it.[115] In an examination of a Schweitzer Engineering Laboratories PMU, a study found that logs kept by the device could be overwritten as soon as 4 events later, and that the limited log taxonomy did not include connection events other than the device to the control server i.e. no GPS information.[116] While future products will likely become more sophisticated in their logging and secure networking capabilities, the challenges of persistent legacy infrastructure (the PMU mentioned above costs roughly $7,000) will remain.

The last substation vulnerability to discuss, which is partly a function geographical isolation, is the non-standardized remote networking access infrastructure that leaves ICS devices exposed on the Internet. There are many reasons to have Internet-connected ICS devices, of course, because of useful features like vendor remote desktop access, but the methods for exploiting these devices are becoming more wide spread every day. A well-known tool for finding these exposed devices is the banner-indexing site Shodan.io.[117] Shodan randomly scans IPs across the Internet, collects their banner metadata about which software and services they are running, and indexes the information into a searchable database.[118] Using Shodan to find SCADA controllers with unsecured web interfaces is relatively easy: ask it to list devices with active communication ports related to ICS processes (e.g. port 502 for Modbus) within a certain area, and try to connect to the web services of the IP list that's returned; it is not hard to use Shodan to gain access to a login page for a controller's software, which, if the manufacturer's default credentials have not been changed, only requires one to search for the device manual PDF on Google and plug in the factory username and password to gain access.[119] It is also possible to use publicly available power infrastructure charts to identify the location of substations, use a tool like MaxMind to generate a list of all IPs associated with that region, and then perform a Shodan-like scan to identify ICS devices within that IP list.[120] A study released in 2014 surveyed ICS and SCADA systems discoverable through Shodan and found nearly 590,000 devices, with over 100,000 from a single manufacturer.[121]

Devices discovered in this way, especially SCADA human machine interfaces used by operators, can deliver important grid information and control access to attackers. Trend Micro found numerous exposed power plant interfaces that showed real-time operations information, allowed important commands ("Stop," "Reset") to be issued, and delivered webcam footage of critical facility elements.[122] Because of their geographical isolation, this kind of visual reconnaissance could be the precursor to a physical infiltration of a substation from which any number of devices or open network ports could be compromised.[123] It could also be used to identify targets for other techniques like DDoS attacks.[124]

For smaller organizations, choosing lower-cost off-the-shelf solutions only adds to the patchwork problem from which these vulnerabilities arise; it can be easy to purchase a system, not secure it properly, and then fail to regularly audit some or all of it.[125] For substation devices that are not directly accessible from the Internet, traffic to and from a control center can still be insecure. The demanding speed and availability requirements for SCADA monitoring and control tend to preclude most conventional encryption schemes, since processing cycles for encryption/decryption, message authentication, and other secure networking tasks have to be added to the already resource-limited infrastructure.[126]

The Nation State

The most commonly discussed context for cybersecurity in the power grid is geopolitics. Much has been written about the ability for nation-state actors to remotely compromise an enemy's critical infrastructure during a conflict. Very recently, for instance, the Venezuelan President Nicolas Maduro accused the U.S. of executing a cybersecurity attack on the Venezuelan power grid after the failure of the Guri Dam hydroelectric plant; the outages plunged the country into crisis, resulting in a brief failure of their entire telecommunication infrastructure and severe stress on hospitals and the elderly.[127] After many days without power, other critical infrastructure like waters pumps failed, forcing people to seek out mountain springs, and social unrest in cities lead to extensive looting.[128] Ironically, while the cause of the blackouts was most likely the Guri's electromechanical failure cascading throughout their notoriously antiquated grid, everything about the timing, extent, and political context of the crisis suggests a textbook critical infrastructure cyber-attack.[129] Venezuela's non-cyberattack is an instructive example of what a real remote strike on a power grid could look like.

A more concrete example of a cyberattack on a national critical infrastructure is the series of attacks deployed by Russia against the Ukraine, such as the CRASHOVERRIDE malware. Identified by Dragos as part of a trend in the ICS-targeting malware designed and deployed by teams connected to the Russian hacking group Sandworm, CRASHOVERRIDE did less damage in 2016 than Russia's 2015 attack on the Ukrainian power grid mentioned in this paper's introduction, but the implications of its design are more alarming.[130] Dragos found that the malware had a modular structure, centered around a platform of sophisticated IT exploits, which allowed for the delivery of payloads designed for specific ICS facility manipulation; depending on the type of critical infrastructure being targeted, the main malware team could contract with a sector-specific team to swap out a module for substation RTUs, for instance, with one controlling storages tanks at a chemical plant.[131] CRASHOVERRIDE was specifically designed to manipulate substation relays into either continuously forcing breakers to remain open or to rapidly open and close them, both of which would lead to the deactivation of the substation.[132] In another report, Dragos identified the group behind the malware as just one of five active hacking groups targeting ICS infrastructure across the globe.[133]

CRASHOVERRIDE did not go unnoticed within the U.S. security community. The National Cybersecurity and Communications Integration Center (NCCIC) released a whitepaper soon after the Dragos report rating the malware a medium priority risk because of its modularity.[134] NERC and E-ISAC also issued reports on the malware, discussing its capabilities and modularity as urgent issues and noting that the malware had been operating within the Ukrainian system for more than six months.[135] The NCCIC also released a broader report, in coordination with the Department of Homeland Security and the FBI, on the extent of Russian cyber targeting of U.S. critical infrastructure, highlighting that U.S. ICS & SCADA systems had already been compromised and studied by Russian actors across a number of sectors.[136]

There is an uneven level of preparedness for these kinds of attacks within U.S. critical infrastructure. The Government Accountability Office (GAO) surveyed organizations overseeing 16 sectors about their implementation of NIST's critical infrastructure cybersecurity framework, and they found that several sectors had not attempted to implement the framework at all, that others had struggled to do so due to lack of resources, knowledge, existing regulatory constraints, and that none of the organizations were measuring the actual extent to which their sectors were implementing controls.[137] As it turns out, the energy sector was one of the most proactive in adopting and propagating the framework, and at the top, the Department of Energy has detailed multiyear cybersecurity strategies for both itself and the energy sector as a whole.[138] The challenges that lie ahead for government agencies overseeing the critical infrastructure sectors will be to stay nimble in the face of rapid technological change. 5G LTE, for instance, will introduce even more opportunities for IoT and SCADA systems to expand their functionality, but the geopolitical context is such that the U.S., Canada, and parts of the European Union have considered banning China (specifically Huawei) from deploying their much-needed hardware to support the rollout.[139]

Conclusion

The connected devices proliferating across the world, whether they fit under the category of IoT or SCADA or otherwise, have been referred to as "the largest attack surface on earth."[140] Although we expect round-the-clock availability of the power grid, the increasingly complex systems helping it scale to meet demand are becoming a risk;

a 2018 study commissioned by Fortinet, for instance, revealed that "56 percent of organizations using SCADA/ICS reported a breach in the past year, and only 11 percent indicate they have never been breached."[141] The vulnerabilities of these systems can threaten the stability of our private lives and our social fabric. The strongest recommendation this paper can make is for a critical infrastructure cybersecurity framework that is applicable and enforceable at every level of the power grid, from metering to nuclear power plants, and for a radical approach to implementing this framework that goes beyond financial incentives. The exact details behind this idea remain to be potentially explored in future work. The fragmentation of the organizations overseeing critical infrastructure is reflected in the fragmented deployment of connected devices and the automated control platforms they serve; in all probability, the issue will persist, as Coburn et al. put it, as a collective action problem.[142]

Water in Trouble

AUTHOR: Clarissa Pendleton

PUBLISHED: November 2020

WRITTEN: March 2020

KEYWORDS: Water and Wastewater Systems Sector; EPA; critical infrastructure

ABSTRACT:
The Water and Wastewater Systems Sector is critical to life and operation of the nation but has operational flaws that could have severe consequences. This paper explores the risks and vulnerabilities of the sector by analyzing its current state and examining the private and public sector from an operational risk lens

---

Water is life. It is necessary for the survival of humans, plants, and ecosystems all over the world. But in some cases, water can kill. Every day, more than 700 children die from unsafe water or insufficient sanitation.[1] It is clear that for countries water and the infrastructure surrounding it is important for its people and its land, which is why the United States labeled it as one of sixteen critical infrastructure sectors.[2] This paper will provide a current state of water and wastewater systems in the United States, discuss the risks, controls, and failures the public and private sectors face, contemplate the effectiveness of said controls, and finally will provide recommendations on the path forward.

The Water and Wastewater Sector is highly complex, vast, and critical to life in the United States. The sector affects all critical infrastructure sectors, as water is necessary for human survival, and humans operate the sectors. Even when the human component is not taken into consideration, all sectors are either dependent on drinking water or wastewater somehow. The 2015 Water and Wastewater Systems Sector-Specific Plan outlined these dependencies—many sectors rely on water for equipment cooling such as the communications and critical manufacturing sectors, while other sectors like food and agriculture and healthcare and public health use water for cleaning and sanitation purposes.[3] It appears that the sectors that rely the most on water systems are the Food and Agriculture Sector, the Healthcare and Public Health Sector, and the Emergency Services Sector. The Food and Agriculture Sector directly depends on water for most, if not all operations, including food processing, restaurant operation, irrigation, water reuse, fertilizer, and animal drinking, feeding, and cleaning.[3] For healthcare, water is needed for laboratory services, sanitation, and nursing home, hospital and clinic operations.[3] In a state of emergency, water is necessary for the Emergency Sector to function—it is necessary for decontamination services, emergency water supplies, and firefighting or hazardous material spill cleanup.[3] To supply the nation's homes, businesses, farms, and cities with water for daily operations, water systems must extend across the country. The sector currently consists of over 150,000 different water systems with millions of pipes covering thousands of miles.[4] Many of these underground pipes are reaching or have exceeded their usefulness, as many were laid in the mid-20th century and last about 75-100 years.[4] The age of the infrastructure causes nearly six billion gallons of treated drinking water to be lost due to leaking pipes, with an estimated 240,000 water main breaks occurring every year.[4] According to the American Society of Civil Engineers, "the amount of drinking water lost every day could support 15 million households".[4] These pipes are maintained by public agencies and, at times, private organizations. As of 2016, 33 of 52 states and territories had more public than private water systems, and 50 of 52 had a larger portion of their population served by public over private systems.[5] While public systems outnumber private systems, they do serve over 36 million people in the United States.[5] These two systems differ in many ways—public water systems are managed by local or state governments, while private are for-profit organizations. Additionally, a governing board sets the rates for customers belonging to public systems, while rates are monitored by a state's public commission, but not necessarily subject to the regulating board for private systems.[5] The public sector is funded largely through revenue generated by ratepayers and some federal support, mainly through the U.S. EPA Drinking Water State Revolving Fund.[6] However, the private sector is an organization and is self-funded. Public agencies and private companies belonging to the water and wastewater sector share some similarities but also have different goals. Because of this, they are vulnerable to some of the same risks, but also have specific risks to their respective sector.

In the public sector, the U.S. Environmental Protection Agency (EPA) is the government agency responsible for the Water and Wastewater Systems Sector, and currently faces many risks. The U.S.'s aging water and wastewater infrastructure is the most critical risk, and the EPA's budget further exacerbates the issue. As stated above, much of the infrastructure is aged and is due for replacement or upgrade soon. According to the EPA's 6th Drinking Water Infrastructure Needs Survey and Assessment conducted in 2018, $472.6 billion dollars is needed to maintain and improve the sector's water infrastructure over the next 20 years "to ensure the public health, security, and economic well-being of our cities, towns, and communities".[7] The American Water Works Association estimates that number even higher at 1 trillion over the next 25 years.[8] While the U.S. EPA Drinking Water State Revolving Fund offers financial support to local governments through low interest loans for water infrastructure projects, its budget is unable to meet all investment needs or fund every project.[4] This lack of funding for the EPA to help local governments maintain and replace the aging water infrastructure has the potential to lead to leaks, main breaks, blocked or broken pipes, and extended periods of time without running water. Thus, impacting many businesses, healthcare facilities, and possibly, emergency services. Additionally, the age of the infrastructure has the potential to cause public health emergencies.

In this year, 2020, the average age of the 1.6 million miles of water and sewer pipes stretched across the United States will be 45 years old.[9] Disintegrated and corroded pipes have already caused emergencies, such as unsafe levels of lead in Flint, Michigan's water supply and the two outbreaks of Legionnaires' disease, a form of pneumonia, also in Flint.[9] The lead issue is equally as important as the disease occurrences because prolonged exposure to lead and copper can result in brain damage, kidney failure, and delay the production of red blood cells.[10] In response to these findings, the EPA introduced the Lead and Copper Rule in 1991, which defined the maximum contaminant levels for lead and copper in drinking water and requires utilities to use corrosion control measures to prevent heavy mental contamination in drinking water.[10] While some short-term revisions have been made to the rule, long-term revisions continue to take place.[10] The aging water infrastructure poses a threat to the health of the citizens of the United States, and is a risk to the EPA—events like Flint prove there is a control failure in its regulation of the Water and Wastewater Systems Sector.

Because of the state of the water systems infrastructure, the EPA also faces natural disaster and cyber risks. Emergency preparedness is necessary and has been proven to be lacking with incidents like hurricanes Harvey, Irma, and Maria. The EPA responded with America's Water Infrastructure Act of 2018, in particular, Section 2013 of the Act addresses community water system risk and resilience by requiring water utilities to complete and update risk and resilience assessments every five years, as well as complete and update an emergency response plan every five years.[7] According to the Act, the risk assessment should include,

> "the resilience of the pipes and constructed conveyances, physical barriers, source water, water collection and intake, pretreatment, treatment, storage and distribution facilities, electronic, computer, or other automated systems (including the security of such systems) which are utilized by the system".[11]

The EPA chose to include the physical infrastructure required for the sector to function, as well as electronic, computer, and other automated systems. These additions are important because creating a cyber-resilient sector is necessary in the world we live in today. According to the Verizon 2019 Data Breach Investigations Report, 16% of breaches that occurred in 2019 were in the public sector.[12] A cyber event in this sector has the potential to cause harm to people, property, operations, and potential regulatory liability.

While the EPA's goal is to ensure the Water and Wastewater Systems Sector is operating and carrying out sector-specific activities, the objectives of private companies in the sector are mainly to produce revenue. Here, the EPA's lack of funding is a point of opportunity for private companies—they can market their services to cities without the budget to create or maintain homegrown solutions. Aqua and Suez are two large private water utility companies who have done this and currently have stakes in the U.S.—Aqua serves more than 3 million residents in Pennsylvania, Ohio, North Carolina, Illinois, Texas, New Jersey, Indiana and Virginia[13] and Suez serves nearly 6.7 million people in 19 states.[14] These organizations have in-common process risks, including a lack of testing. Both companies have had occurrences in which a chemical added to the drinking water supply led to undrinkable water. In Rockland, New York, Suez added a copper sulfate to combat an algae bloom in the city's water source, which resulted in water that "tastes like dirt", according to several residents, and a protest at the Suez corporate office in Rockland.[15] In the case of Aqua, the company was sued by Illinois for causing lead to contaminate a suburb of Chicago's drinking water—Aqua switched the suburb's water source from groundwater wells to the Kankakee River in 2017, and also added a chemical that removed a protective layer in residential plumbing, causing the lead contamination.[16] Both of these incidents lead to bad press and are reputational risks for each company—cities may lead toward a self-investment strategy or different private water companies not plagued with bad media coverage.

Atlanta is a case in which the city decided to terminate its business with a private water company, United Water, a subsidiary of Suez, and moved to public management.[17] This move was made because the cost savings from using United Water was half of what the city expected.[17] Additionally, service was not up to par, with many water main breaks and occasional "boil only" alerts caused by brown water in taps.[17] From the Atlanta example, one can also determine that these companies face the risk of loss from flawed assessment models. United Water's operating costs soared, leading to heavy losses for the company.[17] They blamed the city of Atlanta when it stated how the city's pipes, fire hydrants, and water treatment plants were in worse condition than the city let on, and lost at least $10 million annually while operating the water system.[17] However, United Water should have done their due diligence in assessing the city of Atlanta before a contract was signed. The United Water and Atlanta case also serve as an example to another process risk—improper documentation. James Lam explained in *Enterprise Risk Management*,

"Improper or insufficient documentation may result in miscommunication between the parties to a contract, creating additional, unnecessary risks if there is a dispute".[18]

Atlanta expected to gain more in savings but did not explicitly state that expectation in the contract between the two parties. In another instance, Hoboken, New Jersey filed a suit against Suez in 2018 in response to 17 main breaks that occurred within a 64-day period—the mayor partially blamed the city's contract with Suez that was signed in 1994 that required little investment into the Hoboken water infrastructure.[19] A spokesman for Suez responded, "Our contract calls for us to run the system. It does not call for us to make investments into the system".[19] These situations call into question the effectiveness of government regulation and sector-specific controls.

From the risks and real-life events discussed, there is clearly a problem with the management of the Water and Wastewater Sector in the United States. Major legislation that manages the sector are the Lead and Copper Rule, America's Water Infrastructure Act, both discussed above, the Clean Water Act (CWA), and the Safe Drinking Water Act (SDWA). The CWA was enacted in 1948 and significantly expanded in 1972—it established the basic structure for regulating water pollutants and quality standards for surface waters.[20] Under the Act, the EPA has implemented pollution control programs that include setting wastewater standards for the sector.[20] The SDWA was passed in 1974 to protect the Unites States' public drinking water supply.[21] It was amended to further establish protections for rivers, lakes, reservoirs, springs, and ground water wells.[21] Even with regulations in place, as many as 63 million people, nearly a fifth of the U.S., were exposed to potentially unsafe water more than once during the past decade.[22] This was found in a News21 investigation completed in 2017—they analyzed 680,000 water quality and monitoring violations from the Environmental Protection Agency from a 10-year period starting January 1, 2007.[22] It is difficult to understand whether that number may or may not be considered "normal" from a global perspective, but when the U.S. is compared to other developed nations it still seems to lag behind. The 2018 Environmental Performance Index (EPI) ranked 180 countries on their respective environmental performance.[23] Of the 10 categories investigated, two included water and sanitation and water resources. Overall, the U.S. ranked 27th, and last, at 22nd, in the region of Europe and North America.[28] As a developed nation, the United States is falling behind other countries, and may lag further behind with new amendments to the CWA. In January 2020, the EPA announced that many of the U.S.'s streams and wetlands would no longer be protected under the CWA.[24] Wetlands play a key role in filtering surface water and protecting against floods, but the rule change would allow the destruction or filling of wetlands for development projects.[25] Additionally, landowners and property developers would be allowed to dump chemicals and other pollutants could be discharged into these unprotected bodies of water, and eventually pollute larger water bodies that they drain into.[25] Research has suggested that more than 6 million miles of streams, half the total in the U.S., and more than 42 million acres of wetlands, again, half in the country, will no longer be protected because of the rule change.[24] This leaves many water sources at risk for potential situations like Rockland, where their water source has an algae bloom, and a chemical was added to the water to make the water safe to drink. Government regulations have proven not to be effectively managing the Water and

Wastewater Systems Sector and are currently making changes to make it more vulnerable. There are changes the sector needs make in order to take steps toward higher levels of resiliency.

Given the current state and risks of the Water and Wastewater Systems Sector, there are several strategies the EPA and private companies can employ to mitigate their vulnerabilities. The most obvious recommendation is to allocate more funding to the sector. This would improve the overall infrastructure, and help both the private and public sectors by reducing the number of water contamination cases, improve the amount of drinkable water lost every day from main breaks and leaks, help private companies by not needing in depth assessment models, and improve reputation on both sides. While one may argue more funding to the public sector is not in the interest of private sectors, an argument could be for more funding when considering cities may not have the industry experience to carry out large water infrastructure projects, and will seek private companies to manage them. Water contamination reduction is not the only benefit for the public sector—the return on investment in water and sewer infrastructure has greater returns than most other types of public infrastructure.[7] It has been estimated that a $1 investment in the water and sewer infrastructure increases private output, or gross domestic product (GDP), in the long term by $6.35.[7] Moreover, according to the U.S. Department of Commerce's Bureau of Economic Analysis, on a yearly basis, for each additional dollar of revenue in the water and sewer industry, the increase in revenue that occurs in all industries is $2.62.[7] These figures prove that investment in water systems not only improves water quality and reduces water loss across the country, but also increases revenue. In addition to the funding, an improved documentation process is needed to further improve the resiliency of both private and public sectors. There should be no assumptions for either party, and contracts should be properly understood and agreed upon before signing. This will help both parties understand expectations, making their collaboration more amicable. Furthermore, this will improve reputation for both sides, as governments will not appear incompetent and private companies, like Suez and Aqua, will be less vilified in the media. James Lam stated, "Best practice companies include business risk and reputational risk in their operational risk definition", and this policy complies with what de defines as best practice.[18] Finally, in order to address poor policy controls, the EPA needs to stop repealing environmental rules related to water systems, and employ long-term revisions to the LCR established by the National Drinking Water Advisory Council Lead and Copper Rule Working Group. Some of their recommendations include: the LCR should follow the principle that there is no safe level of lead and enforce replacement of lead service lines, the LCR should separate requirements for copper from those for lead, states should include the cost of this replacement in the criteria for allocating Drinking Water State Revolving Funds, the EPA should create a manual that helps water agencies understand how they can make use of the latest technology in corrosion control treatment, the EPA should provide free consumer-requested lead testing, and finally, the EPA, the Centers for Disease Control and Prevention, the Department of Health and Human Services, and the Department of Housing and Urban Development should conduct training on lead poisoning for local health agencies, medical professionals, and local and state lead poisoning prevention agencies.[10] By improving policy and prohibiting repeals, the EPA can enforce better standards on governments and private companies in the Water and Wastewater Systems Sector and improve its overall resiliency.

The U.S.'s current state of water and wastewater systems was discussed, the risks and controls the public and private sectors face were analyzed, the effectiveness of the controls were scrutinized, and recommendations were made on how to improve the sector's resiliency. With current rollbacks of water protection laws and the age of the water infrastructure, the Water and Wastewater Sector is at risk. While much of the U.S. has clean drinking, some communities do not have that luxury, and many more may face the same issue if the proper risk mitigation is not carried out.

SECTION TWO

Information Integrity and Privacy

PAPER	AUTHOR
A Need for Increased Support of Cybersecurity Education	Peyton Lyons
Cybersecurity in the Pharmaceutical Industry	Allessandra Quevedo
Following Up on the Internet Bill of Rights	Maeve Rogers Edstrom
From Fintech Darling to Bankruptcy: Control Failures of Wirecard	Vincent Xu
Wash Your Hands and Update Your Software	Roger St. Louis

A Need for Increased Support of Cybersecurity Education

AUTHOR: Peyton Lyons

PUBLISHED: May 2020

WRITTEN: March 2019

KEYWORDS: Cybersecurity; Education; STEM; Workforce; Diversity

ABSTRACT:

This paper discusses the current state of cybersecurity education programs in the U.S. and the need for increased support from the government to meet the demands of the growing industry. This paper goes on to examine China and Israel to discuss how other countries are approaching cybersecurity education and how programs in the U.S. compare. With increasing demands for cybersecurity professionals, the U.S. needs to invest more in STEM education and offer hands-on learning opportunities that support developing the necessary skills to be successful in the cybersecurity industry.

Cybersecurity as an industry is growing every year in the U.S., and governments report increased concerns that cyberspace will become the next primary setting of warfare.[1] The current cybersecurity workforce in the U.S. cannot satisfy the increasing demand for qualified cybersecurity professionals. Due to the continued growth expected in the cybersecurity industry, this shortfall is expected to worsen in the coming years. To close this gap, increased focus must be placed on improving the education pipeline, or the U.S. will be at risk of falling behind international standards. Cybersecurity education must improve in order for the U.S. to maintain high standards, because as Sandra Jontz describes, "The primary challenge facing the cyber workforce today is the lack of personnel coupled with the lack of experience of those who are employed to fight the fight."[2] Cybersecurity education can begin in elementary school, but without a specific curriculum and support from private and public industries, the U.S. will increasingly become unable to produce enough cybersecurity professionals who can keep up with global threats. Improving and expanding cybersecurity education is critical to enhancing and improving the cybersecurity industry.

The U.S. has systems in place that promote the advancement of cybersecurity education. One key initiative within the U.S. government is the National Initiative for Cybersecurity Education (NICE), which is led by the National Institute of Standards and Technology (NIST) within the U.S. Department of Commerce. To understand some of what is already in place in the U.S. for cybersecurity education, it is important to discuss NICE and its goals. NICE is a collaboration between government, academia, and the private sector that focuses on education, training, and workforce development within cybersecurity.[3] The vision of the program is "a digital economy enabled by a knowledgeable and skilled cybersecurity workforce" and

NICE works to fulfill this vision through supporting the challenges of the cyber industry by creating standards and best practices.[4] NICE provides an important framework for how to support and promote cybersecurity education.

NICE has a robust strategic plan which supports its vision and mission. This plan includes three goals, the first of which is "Accelerate Learning and Skills Development." NICE promotes the use of apprenticeships and programs that create an immediate workforce. The initiative also calls for raising awareness about workforce needs to develop training that specifically addresses these gaps. NICE's second goal is to "Nurture a Diverse Learning Community," which includes starting with elementary-aged students to inspire awareness of cybersecurity careers, continuing this exploration in middle school, and then enabling career preparedness for high school students. In addition to creating a strong educational baseline, this goal also incorporates the need to increase the number of women, minorities, veterans, persons with disabilities, and other underrepresented populations in the cybersecurity workforce. The third goal is to "Guide Career Development and Workforce Planning" by creating state and regional consortia to identify local workforce needs and address these via cybersecurity pathways. This goal also includes assisting human resource professionals and managers in the recruitment, hiring, development, and retention of cybersecurity professionals. Overall, NICE focuses on end-to-end solutions for promoting cybersecurity education and careers, and is an important tool for the U.S. in improving the industry as a whole. NICE is a good place to start when analyzing the current state of cybersecurity education because it addresses gaps in the system and provides solutions to address these issues. This paper builds on the mission and goals of NICE in order to focus on specific areas of growth for the U.S.

Science, technology, engineering, and math (STEM) education plays a key role in the development of cybersecurity education, as the skills are interrelated. The White House addresses a strategic plan for STEM education in a report "Charting a Course for Success: America's Strategy for STEM Education" and explains, "The Federal Government has a key role to play in furthering STEM education by working in partnership with stakeholders at all levels and seeking to remove barriers to participation in STEM careers, especially for women and other underrepresented groups."[5] The support of STEM education by the government is a key way forward for developing the skills students need to become professionals in all STEM related fields, but especially cybersecurity related careers. In order to become cybersecurity experts, students likely need to begin developing their skills well before college.[6] While there has already been a large focus on STEM education, the U.S. needs to strengthen the academic pathway for elementary, middle, and secondary school students that specifically addresses the interrelated, but unique skills required of cybersecurity professionals.[7]

In the U.S. there are already some programs that focus on the education of young students, including GenCyber, which the National Security Agency co-sponsors for students and teachers in order to improve cybersecurity teaching in kindergarten through high school.[8] GenCyber is a camp that focuses on increasing interest and diversity in cybersecurity careers, as well as improving cybersecurity teaching methods in K-12 curricula.[9] In "Charting a Course for Success," the authors explain that elementary and secondary school is the best time to learn basic STEM concepts, because they are essential prerequisites for increasing one's technical skills and advancing to college and graduate-level studies. This is just one example of the growing recognition that cybersecurity concepts must be introduced to even young students to address the growing need for professionals in the field.

Some high schools have also begun to create programs and pathways for cybersecurity education, and Melissa Delaney explains: "Districts don't need to build such programs from scratch. They can adopt curriculum from a variety of government and business resources. For instance, the School District of Palm Beach County's cybersecurity CTE program is based on a pathway offered by the Florida Department of Education."[10] High schools that do not already have cybersecurity curriculum in place can look to those that have found success in their programs. One way the U.S. is looking to improve cybersecurity curriculum in high schools according to NICE's "National K-12 Cybersecurity Education Implementation Plan" is by increasing coordination "among teacher preparation, professional development, support, and recognition efforts within existing and proposed cybersecurity educator programs." Increasing collaboration and coordination will be vital for supporting teachers in high schools to promote cybersecurity curriculum and provide ways for students to develop skills. Partnering with local businesses and colleges is a way for students to more easily transition from high school into jobs or higher education, because these partnerships will allow for students to learn skills that are transferable to the specific needs of their region. High schools are an important place for students to develop their technical skills, and some school districts have taken note of the demand for cybersecurity talent.

Many students' first exposure to cybersecurity is in college, especially as high schools are still working to develop strong STEM programs. That said, many students do not ever get exposure to cybersecurity curriculum, as Sarah K. White describes: "out of the top 10 computer science programs in the U.S., not a single program requires a cybersecurity course to graduate."[11] The curriculum in universities in the U.S. is not including cybersecurity and in "Cybersecurity Education in Universities," Fred B. Schneider further highlights this gap: "Curriculum development suffers without input from the full spectrum of faculty members—the absence of leading technical thinkers means that topics needed to prepare students for adopting new trends and directions are unlikely to be incorporated into a curriculum."[12] Universities need to incorporate cybersecurity programs into the required curriculum for students in order to develop professionals that can contribute directly to the field, and guidance from expert faculty members can help better prepare students. Masters programs need to evolve as well by "updating the contents of their courses as well as changing the structure of programs to incorporate more specific security courses into the set of core courses and to offer more elective courses." There is a need for both undergraduate and graduate programs to evolve to include specific skills that cybersecurity professionals need when entering the workforce and addressing to the demands of the field. Currently, U.S. universities are not doing enough to develop cybersecurity programs that support students pursuing these careers. Ideally, every university would require computer science majors to complete comprehensive cybersecurity training so that security is front-of-mind for people when delivering products to market.

While some important programs exist to support students in developing the skills needed for cybersecurity careers, work still needs to be done to address the security demands of the country. The U.S. should look to other countries to understand how to create continuously improving education systems, and what to avoid. China is one country that has faced issues in the development of its cybersecurity education - it may have a shortfall of around 1.4 million cybersecurity professionals by 2020, one of the largest cybersecurity skills deficits of any country in the world.[13] China's failure to develop its cybersecurity workforce may largely be related to its education policy, which Austin describes to be very heavily in favor of the technical aspects of cybersecurity, while not appreciating it as a socio-technical phenomenon. In addition, universities in China with undergraduate cybersecurity majors were producing not much more than one doctoral program graduate per year, which provides a weak foundation for expanding educational opportunities. China did not do enough to focus on the needs of workforce and is now having to backtrack to make changes to the programs to match the needs of the industry. Recognizing this gap, China now plans to build four to six world-class cybersecurity schools by 2027 in order to strengthen the country as a strong Internet power.[14] For these programs, "the guideline stresses that the evaluation of cyber security talents will be based on their expertise and creativity. Academic degrees, papers and records of service are no longer the only standards."[15] China still has a lot of work to do to address the failures of its previous education systems, but there is something to be learned from this shift to focusing on practical training and innovation.

Israel's cybersecurity education system is one of the most innovative in the world and the small country has become a cyber super-power. Gil Press explains that Israel is "collaborating with super-powers, Israel is assisting smaller nations (e.g., Singapore), creating 300+ cybersecurity startups, exporting last year [2016] $6.5 billion in cybersecurity products, convincing more than 30 multinationals to open local R&D centers, and attracting foreign investors."[16] This success did not happen overnight. As Estrin explains in "In Israel, teaching kids cyber skills is a national mission," in Israel, students in kindergarten learn computer skills and robotics, fourth graders learn computer programming, and cybersecurity education starts in middle school. Press explains that there are six university research centers dedicated to cybersecurity and Israel was the first country that offered PhDs in cybersecurity as an independent discipline, not a computer science subject. This country has ingrained cybersecurity into its education system, but an important aspect of this is described by Alix Pressley in "Israel becomes 'breeding ground' for cybersecurity tech talent": "the government has taken a leading role in developing a cybersecurity strategy and supporting the sector. This has created an ecosystem for collaboration between the government, businesses and universities that is well-equipped to both respond and proactively prepare for cyberthreats."[17] Government-sponsored programs have helped the cybersecurity industry grow rapidly and successfully and the deep technological focus paired with specialized training that focuses on teaching even the youngest students has created a stable cybersecurity ecosystem that can cope with the rapid innovation and unique challenges of the industry.

While we have seen some of the efforts the U.S. has already made to improve cybersecurity education, there is still much to be done to ensure that the U.S. can face future threats with a strong and diverse workforce. Both private and public sectors need to do more to invest in cybersecurity education. In "Charting a Course for Success," this necessary investment includes "bringing together schools, colleges and universities, libraries, museums, and other community resources to build STEM ecosystems that broaden and enrich each learner's educational and career journey." All sectors need to work together to strengthen relationships and develop new connections to support all communities. Students need support in all areas of their lives, both in and outside of the classroom, so it is imperative that schools incorporate cybersecurity education, but also that there are opportunities in other contexts for students to develop. As the system is currently, there is not enough support from all sectors and the cybersecurity industry will not be able to meet its own needs. Private and public entities need to invest more deeply to develop the highly trained people that are needed in the cybersecurity industry.

To support these pathways to cybersecurity careers, academic pathways need to be clarified and strengthened. The U.S. should take note of Israel's incorporation of cybersecurity at all levels of education. In addition to simply providing more exposure to cybersecurity topics earlier in their education, students should be provided the opportunity for real-world application beyond the classroom in internships, apprenticeships, and research experiences. Dark et al. explain that "A viable path forward could be to increase interaction and collaboration between the cybersecurity and education communities."[18] The collaboration of these communities would mean educators are exposed more clearly to the needs of the industry and could be better supported in creating curriculum that provides a more direct path for students into cyber careers. To facilitate a successful transition from the classroom to security roles, educators "should expand and more deeply integrate their hands-on learning opportunities."[19] By combining hands-on experiences with stronger curriculum that is informed directly by cybersecurity experts, the education system in the U.S. would better support students' transitions from their role as students to their role as cybersecurity experts.

In addition to providing hands-on learning experiences for students, there is a growing need for a diversified education that focuses not only on academic and technological methods, but an understanding of the business and social context of cybersecurity. John Morello argues that "Equal weight should be given in cyber education to developing communication and presentation skills to enable security practitioners to credibly work with nontechnical decision makers, using their vocabulary and from their perspective."[20] Students need the skills to communicate their technological skills in a way that is understandable by others in order to reinforce the importance of their work. Cybersecurity professionals must be able to work in teams to address problems and advance the industry. Students will not be able to fully contribute to the industry by drilling technological skills alone. Manson and Pike discuss the importance of a diversified education as they say, "there must be support for students to work independently and in teams along with a competition landscape to test and reinforce skills." The "soft skills", like teamwork and presentation skills, are vital to the success of the cybersecurity industry, and the education system must include opportunities to develop these strengths as well. Adam Stone explains that "Cyber isn't just a technology challenge, it's also a business challenge, and people need to understand how our security decisions can have broader implications in a business context."[21] There is a large need for strong technological skills in the cybersecurity industry, but without the business context and the ability to apply technological skills in a team setting, students will not succeed in making the transition to a professional career. The education system needs to include learning opportunities that provide a setting for developing a diversified set of skills.

The cybersecurity education system needs more support, robust curriculum, and opportunities for a diversified education. In "Advancing Cybersecurity Education," Melissa Dark adds to this list: "Like so many other science, technology, engineering, and mathematics fields, we desperately need to experiment with programs and initiatives to increase diversity."[22] In all STEM fields, there is a need for diversity, and cybersecurity is another example of an industry that does not incorporate a diverse workforce. Susan Morrow explains this situation in "Minorities in Cybersecurity: The Importance of a Diverse Security Workforce," by citing statistics: "in 2016, the workforce for this post [Information Security Analyst] was made up of 74% white employees, 11.9% black employees, and 7.9% Asian employees."[23] Morrow goes on to explain that cybersecurity requires a multidisciplinary approach to problems and "having a team made up of diverse individuals can only work to improve the outcome of that team." Incorporating diverse voices in the workforce is an important aspect, but educating young people is the first step in developing strong, diverse teams. Education systems must develop curriculum that supports the unique needs of all students, not only the students who have historically already had access to high levels of educational support. There needs to be strong investment in the education of underserved and underrepresented students by providing high-quality STEM education and programs that support the continued success of these students. The cybersecurity industry needs to incorporate diverse perspectives to be successful, and this starts by specifically improving the education systems for historically marginalized groups.

The U.S. has important work to do to create an education system that supports the growing cybersecurity ecosystem. While the government and the industry have taken some steps to develop the systems needed to support this demand, the need for highly trained professionals is constantly growing. This essay has discussed some of these existing support for cybersecurity education in the US, like NICE, and has examined both China and Israel's education systems. This examination showed areas for improvement in the U.S. system and ways to move forward as a country as the need for highly skilled cybersecurity professionals grows. To continuously improve the education system, the U.S. needs to invest more in STEM education, with a specific focus on cybersecurity programs that provide students with hands-on learning opportunities and diversified non-technical skills. There is also a need for the education system to focus on creating programs that celebrate diversity and leverage all perspectives. The U.S. is a superpower in cyber, but there are growing threats that the country must be ready take on. Without more investment in cybersecurity education, the U.S. will fall behind.

Cybersecurity in the Pharmaceutical Industry

AUTHOR: Allessandra Quevedo

PUBLISHED: August 2020

WRITTEN: December 2019

KEYWORDS: Cybersecurity; Pharmaceuticals; Proprietary Information; Biotechnology; Intellectual Property

ABSTRACT:
This paper discusses the heightened levels of risk exposure spanning across the entire technological infrastructure connected to the pharmaceutical industry, from research and manufacturing, and from distribution and hospitals. Companies in the pharmaceutical industry contain increasingly growing (and massive) bodies of sensitive data, including proprietary information related to products as well as consumer healthcare information. Therefore, it is imperative that companies adapt systems and processes to making sure their proprietary and sensitive data remains secure and accessible from emerging cybersecurity threats.

Today's pharmaceutical industry is one of the largest industries in demand. This billion-dollar industry has rapidly shifted into one of the richest markets that propel the U.S. economy. The pharmaceutical industry is comprised of two main sects. One side handles the manufacturing, development, and marketing of drugs; while what is more commonly known as 'Big Pharma,' is the side of the industry that pushes 'high priced' drugs and medications to consumers.[1] Some of the major pharmaceutical companies in the U.S. (by revenue) include Johnson & Johnson ($363 billion), Novartis ($205 billion), Pfizer ($212 billion), Merck ($218 billion).[2]

Each product (vaccines, drugs, treatments, and research) is patented and held exclusively to a single company. A patent for each drug typically lasts for 20 years, while the development of a new drug can take an average of 10 years. [3] Thus, the patents and regulations of new medicines mean a competitive market for consumer attention. As millions of dollars are poured into the advertising for these new drugs,[4] millions of dollars are also spent towards the research and production of them. This means that each drug that is patented becomes strictly owned by one company. These billion-dollar companies make up a large portion of the pharmaceutical industry, and in turn, are exposed to enormous amounts of risk. As the digitalization of the world increases, companies in industries like Big Pharma and Biotechnology heavily rely on their proprietary information being withheld from the rest of the world and major competitors.[5] Big Pharma companies are constantly at risk of losing information regarding their customers, Intellectual Property (IP), and patents from other Big Pharma competitors or from foreign entities abroad.[6] Most of the data each company holds is stored online or on to an online database.

To prelude the analysis on recent cybersecurity breaches within the pharmaceutical industry, it is also imperative that a background of cybersecurity is established. In the light of new technologies in today's age, it is no surprise that talk of cybersecurity attacks and data breaches encompass much of the news today. Hackers and cybercriminals are individuals who have "developed methods to exploit security holes in various computer systems."[7] Hackers find weaknesses within computer systems to gain access to private information and software on those computer systems.

Once private data and information is accessed, hackers can choose to sell that information in places such as the dark web or secret markets. The dark web 'looks like a marketplace or another e-commerce site.[8] It is used to sell anything illegal, and hides the identity of sellers and buyers on that platform.[9] The information can be sold to individuals attempting to steal patented information from select companies, individuals, or government institutions.[10] For example, in the pharmaceutical industry, hackers might try to steal patented medicines and sell that information to individuals looking to remake the drug for cheap and re-sell it, or it could be sold to foreign competitors around the world. Those who repeatedly perform attacks on major companies, individuals, or even government agencies are be labeled as 'cybercriminals.'

While for much of the internet's history, hackers and cybercriminals have targeted the banking/finance sector (phishing and email scams have sought out unassuming individuals for personal information); many of today's hackers and cybercriminals are also specializing in attacks towards specialized industries.[11] Once companies have been hit with a cybersecurity breach, the IP rights to their products have been taken away, and the reputational loss in the industry is what can affect their financial gains in the long run.[12] The research and effort put into these pharmaceutical companies are sold off by hackers.

According to IBM Security and Ponemon Institute's most recent 'Cost of Data Breach Study', the average cost of a single data breach incident rose to $3.92 million in 2019, an increase from $3.86 million in 2018.[13] In the healthcare industry alone, the highest cost of a single data breach in healthcare was totaled to be $6.45 million dollars.[14] Cybersecurity Ventures, a cybersecurity company, published an article predicting that "the total cost of cybersecurity breaches will equate to $6 trillion annually by 2021. This is nearly double from the $3 trillion cost in 2015."[15] They also said that "it represented the greatest transfer of wealth in economic history." While data breaches are becoming more frequent, another aspect of them that makes them unpredictable, is that it can take businesses an average of 196 days to detect that a breach had occurred.[16] Most often, companies don't detect breaches until after information has been accessed. And as hackers continue to attack these companies, hackers are developing ways to further conceal their attacks, meaning even longer detection times in the future.

In June 2017, one of the top Big Pharma companies, Merck ($218 billion), was hit with a ransomware attack that affected the company's offices around the globe. The attack used a computer virus known as 'NotPetya.'[17] The ransomware attack affected many of Merck's Ukrainian offices, where it appeared that the attack was concentrated in. The attack had then also spread to some the company's offices in the United States. That morning, Merck's employees had arrived to find a message on their computers.[18] The message demanded (on each computer) to pay funds (in Bitcoin) to retrieve the encryption key.[19] The computers also appeared as if their hard drives had been completely wiped. Employees were encouraged to disconnect mobile devices from the Wi-Fi network and go home from their offices while investigation began. Merck was just one of the entities affected by attack. Companies around Ukraine, the United States, and Australia were also reportedly hit by this ransomware. These companies/organizations ranged from hospitals to government institutions.

As a result of the attack, it was reported that Merck had lost over $300 million in the third quarter of 2017 alone.[20] As for Merck's insurers, it was initially reported that the attack could have cost them up to $275 million to combat the damage that had been done.[21] NotPetya is a computer virus that spreads quickly across computer networks, which then encrypts the data on the computer's hard drives; rendering them unable to run or use. The attacks on these computers were a high threat to the company, because without computers, the company could not operate. Additionally, replacing the hard drives of all the infected computers (all done individually) was a time-consuming and labor-intensive process.[22]

The attack not only affected Merck's quarterly earnings. The attack caused a shutdown in the production of the human papilloma virus (HPV) vaccine Gardasil 9, from the U.S. Centers for Disease Control and Prevention. It impacted the manufacturing, research, and sales for nearly a week's time. This delay alone meant the company was at a standstill. Emails were frozen and production had halted. Merck was then unable to meet the production quota nor deliver the drugs on time.[23] This event exemplifies why taking precautionary cybersecurity measures matters. The effects of a single week without production cost the company over hundreds of millions of dollars and ultimately, it affected consumers around the country. The ransomware is an example of how these types of attacks have the potential to damage entire ecosystems that an organization heavily relies on.

While it is not completely known the exact computer that was first infected, previous ransomware cases show that there are two main ways ransomware enters a system; outdated software or through a phishing attack.[24] In Merck's case, NotPetya "used an exploit in the Windows 7 operating system."[25] When companies do not update their systems, hackers try to find weak points within that operating system; which can be used as an entry point for an attack. A Senior Security Engineer at TSI concludes that, "Merck's problem was that they had systems, partners, contractors, and subcontractors that were not secure and patched in the ways that they should have been."[26] He goes on to explain that "Pharmaceutical businesses in particular, need to understand that all of these systems are connected. If any link in the chain is broken, the entire chain becomes compromised."[27] Because these companies have so much information, it becomes difficult to organize and keep track of the multiple systems in use within a single organization's infrastructure. Integrating and properly securing all the systems that are encompassed within a single organization, are the only way to minimize the likelihood of a data/security breach.

Merck's data breach can arguably be pinpointed to a 'cultural flaw.' That being, they simply overlooked what needed to be done in terms of IT. For example, companies that have operated for decades—are known for having legacy systems (old, outdated technology or computer application systems).[28] Having outdated software means that they often are not fully supported to withstand evolving cyberthreats and cyber risks. And without the immediate internal push for the newest software or update, it leaves many companies operating with legacy systems in danger. This issue also relates to the rest of the pharmaceutical industry, as many organizations still believe that their systems are protected from cyber security threats or underestimate the amount of money, they need to invest into their IT systems.[29]

Information Technology is arguably transitioning into the foundation of many companies and industries today. Much of the data and the operating systems of organizations (especially those that span across the globe) rely on, are dependent on the way technology runs collectively. It is important for pharmaceutical companies to recognize that because they have become the number one target for cybercriminals, the necessary steps to minimize damages must be taken. Maintaining a strong cybersecurity integration within pharmaceutical companies needs to be a core aspect within their infrastructures. Some of the cybersecurity practices seen in today's pharmaceutical companies include maintaining software (updates, anti-virus applications, anti-malware, firewalls, etc.), two factor authentications, and avoiding phishing emails.[30]

However, it is important for pharmaceutical companies to recognize that their industry has become one of the most targeted industries for cyberattacks.[31] In the case of Merck's cybersecurity breach, the computers were using outdated software—and many of the company's computers with this exact vulnerability were affected. It is extremely important that all parts within the company's network of devices are protected against the many threats that are posed against it. It is recommended that they maintain an up-to date IT system. While it is also important to recognize that there is a risk relying on third party vendors (in Merck's case, Microsoft), minimizing the potential damage that can be done because of events like this require proactivity within the company.

The Merck incident was not the only recent data breach to occur in the pharmaceutical industry. Other major pharmaceutical companies such as Johnson & Johnson,[32] Roche, and Bayer (affected by hackers tied to the Chinese government) were also affected by hackers.[33] Having such large companies all attacked in some way, is proof that individuals in the pharmaceutical industry need to think of cyberattacks as a matter of "when" they get attacked, rather than assuming they are protected. For the Merck incident, the goal of the ransomware was not to steal information per se (the effects of the ransomware were to shut down hardware and as a result, halt production), but for other data breaches such as the Johnson & Johnson breach, consumer information was specifically targeted and retrieved by the hackers.[34]

Typically, cybersecurity has been practiced with an 'incident-response' approach.[35] This means that many companies often learn from one another after a breach has occurred from someone else. It also means that once an incident occurs, it will then be immediately treated after the event. Only after companies see that others like them have been breached, will they begin to pay more attention to their own systems.[36] But as technology systems are constantly changing, companies must not wait until another entity gets attacked to effectively protect themselves. Companies, especially those in the pharmaceutical industry, need to go beyond maintaining software or their devices.

The '2019 Future of Cyber Survey' published by Deloitte, reveals that another challenge with managing pharmaceutical companies is that their company's networks span across many facilities and databases. According to the survey, "The transformation gap can arise as organizations adopt modern infrastructure concepts, while still operating their legacy environment." [37] While companies recognize that change and unification across their company's ecosystem needs to occur, there needs to be specific plans in which companies try to attain those goals.

Thus, in order to manage such a large and complex network of Internet of Things (IoT) devices, manufacturing facilities, and hybrid data-storage centers, another recommendation for pharmaceutical companies is to invest in the technology of 'AI-driven threat assessments.' The Deloitte survey published that "the surveyed C-level executives most commonly selected AI-driven threat assessments (20 percent), security automation (20 percent), and scaled cyber solutions (18 percent) as the top ranked defense concepts that their companies are prioritizing for future investment."[38] It is no question that companies in the pharmaceutical industry should also follow suit in the research and investment needed to keep their information secured. Implementing an AI system would allow the company to be routinely assessing points of entry for hackers and it would allow companies to constantly prepare for data breaches.

Maintaining cybersecurity within manufacturing facilities is also as equally important in maintaining a cohesive and secure network of devices. Taking care of the manufacturing aspect of these companies is also important because it is the level in which much of the company's data is being accessed and used. Security between IoT devices and networks of machines and lab computers are important to manage. [39] Even more so—the connection between facilities and office computers. To access this data, companies rely on successful cloud storage and secure deployment.[20] It is also important to understand that manufacturing facilities rely on industrial control systems (ICS), which manage the GMP-based drug production process.[40] Most modern manufacturing systems contain automated systems that talk to each other. Thus, it is also important that the maintenance and monitoring of all devices that are integrated in the security practices of the organization. It also is significant because the use of each additional device poses a new risk/threat to the entire system.

Overall, it is important for pharmaceutical companies to practice a holistic approach to cybersecurity. Every device within these systems needs to be protected and compliant with existing government regulations and protocols. Devices within each network also need to be constantly monitored—as previous breaches are evidence that any 'chain in the link' can be attacked, which then can spread to other parts of the company. Understanding how to operate offensively towards cyberattacks, not just defensively, is also what is recommended to help protect these companies from a major breach and to help them establish a routine response to one. Whether it may be an IT network service provider constantly testing the company's network security for weak points or an automated AI-driven system to test the company's weak points, or simply a better understanding how the company can maintain production in the case that some offices or computers get shut down during a breach, cybersecurity should be of utmost importance to these entities.

The future of the pharmaceutical industry lies in one that embraces technology and establishes relationships with companies that develop such technological capabilities to hold their entity safe and secure. Companies must use that to strengthen their internal processes and capabilities. The future of pharma is very much rooted in the adaption and digitalization of the healthcare industry, and the regulation of these systems to function as a cohesive unit. Moving forward, companies—especially those in the pharmaceutical industry which contain massive amounts of consumer information—need to careful about monitoring the weaknesses in their entire IT system. Information is important both in the company's headquarters and in the company's manufacturing facilities. The future of pharma is bright; however, it needs to be willing to fully adapt its systems and processes to the changing world of

Information Technology. Research and resources need to be dedicated to making sure that fields of such proprietary and uniquely developed information remain intact and insured against external forces.

Following Up on the Internet Bill of Rights

AUTHOR: Maeve Rogers Edstrom

PUBLISHED: December 2019

WRITTEN: March 2019

KEYWORDS: Privacy; data collection and security; autonomy; net neutrality.

ABSTRACT:
This paper examines the feasibility of implementing the Internet Bill of Rights proposed by Congressman Ro Khanna in 2018. The policy topics of data collection and security, net neutrality and data autonomy are evaluated through past precedence, a return on investment analysis and a survey of the current political landscape.

> "Our Founding Fathers drafted the Bill of Rights to safeguard our freedoms in the physical world. Today, as Americans are living more of their lives online, the digital age demands that we have new rights to protect our freedoms in the cyber world."
>
> — Ro Khanna, 2018

Introduction

In recent years, there have been several data breaches that put millions of Americans' personal data in jeopardy, including from companies such as Target, Facebook, Google, and Equifax. Despite this, the U.S. government has not passed any federal legislation to prevent future data breaches by adding requirements for companies to have additional protections or protocol. Many who witnessed the hearings of Mark Zuckerberg after the Cambridge Analytical scandal noted that many in Congress were unaware of how social media operated, not only as a business model but as an online tool.[1]

Among those who were frustrated by the hearing committee's lack of knowledge on the subject was congressman Ro Khanna, of California's 17th District which covers geographies in Silicon Valley. He realized that a lack of knowledge in Congress equaled an inability to fully understand the problems of security, privacy and ownership at stake; this ultimately signaled a lack of expertise to regulate it through proper legislation. With a thumbs up from Nancy Pelosi, Khanna set out to create a task force that would set the tone for future legislation.[2]

Breaking Down the Internet Bill of Rights

Khanna met with representatives from Facebook, Amazon, Microsoft and other tech firms, as well as a few former Obama Administration members and representatives from organizations that focus on information technology. He also brought in Tim Burners-Lee, inventor of the Internet,[3] to advise on the project. Together this task force formed a set of ten principles that would become the Internet Bill of Rights (IBOR). These were introduced to the public in October 2018.[4]

The 10 Principles

The full Internet Bill of Rights is detailed below. Citizens should have the right:

1. To have access to and knowledge of all collection and uses of personal data by companies;
2. To opt-in consent to the collection of personal data by any party and to the sharing of personal data with a third party;
3. Where context appropriate and with a fair process, to obtain, correct, or delete personal data controlled by any company and to have those requests honored by third parties;
4. To have personal data secured and to be notified in a timely manner when a security breach or unauthorized access of personal data is discovered;
5. To move all personal data from one network to the next;
6. To access and use the internet without internet service providers blocking, throttling, engaging in paid prioritization, or otherwise unfairly favoring content, applications, services, or devices.

7. To internet service without the collection of data that is unnecessary for providing the requested service absent opt-in consent;
8. To have access to multiple viable, affordable internet platforms, services, and providers with clear and transparent pricing;
9. Not to be unfairly discriminated against or exploited based on your personal data; and
10. To have an entity that collects your personal data have reasonable business practices and accountability to protect your privacy.

The Three Primary Issues

The Internet Bill of Rights offers a spectrum of principles that primarily fall into three policy areas: data collection and security, data autonomy and net neutrality. It stipulates that citizens have the right to know what data is being collected and how it's being used. Regulations would ensure that data breaches are reported and resolved in a timely manner. Citizens would have the right to control their data in several ways: opting into what is shared, having the ability to download and move personal data from one location to another and be able to delete personal data, within reason. Additionally, Internet service providers would be barred from discriminatory service and restricted from the collection and sale of customer data.

While broad in scope, these principles all aim to enable citizens with rights that should have been in their hands to begin with. Currently our digital footprint is monopolized by tech companies, Internet service providers (ISPs), data brokers and marketers. With the repeal of net neutrality, we risk losing access to information that was once right at our fingertips. Technology companies have let our personal data be bought, taken and abused. While the range of consequences on the public has varied in severity, the root of the problem lies in a lack of regulation. Our digital footprints are likely larger than we believe and the problem of not knowing how wide our swath stretches across the Internet is troubling. Without regulation, we risk putting our rights and security into the hands of corporations.

Implementation

If the Internet Bill of Rights were to be implemented in its entirety, what factors must we consider for making it happen? First, an examination of historical context and existing legislation to determine precedent. This is necessary to provide current lawmakers a framework for designing the regulations and forming policy. Second, an evaluation of the potential return on investment for all parties involved—government, tech firms, Internet service providers, data brokers and the general public—this can help determine what's at stake and whether it's worth the effort. Finally, an evaluation of the current political landscape is helpful for determining the likelihood of bills being created, passed and signed into law.

Historical Context and Other Precedents

Why do we need to protect our data privacy and why now? The Fourth Amendment of the Constitution protects against search and seizure of persons and effects; however, the protection of personal information has not been included in the current interpretation. Katz vs United States (1967) dictated the Fourth Amendment protects people rather than places, especially when there is a "reasonable expectation of privacy."[5] Expanding that protection to protecting the privacy of peoples' online presence would help give ownership of data back to the people. Title II of the Communications Act of 1934 prohibited ISPs from blocking content or offering certain sites faster service—yet, without net neutrality, ISPs are free to engage in a pay-to-play model.[6] According to the Federal Communication Commission (FCC), six percent of U.S. households have access to just one broadband provider and are subject to the pricing of that monopoly in 2019.[7]

Although many companies have privacy policies that disclose how their organization collects and uses patron data, most lack a transparent explanation. This creates a problem of users agreeing unknowingly to having their data collected, shared and manipulated. With the adoption of the European Union's *General Data Protection Regulation* (GDPR) in 2018, many U.S. companies opted to use more transparency in how they collect data of all users, but there is room to improve. Additionally, we are seeing states like California and Washington develop legislation that will protect data privacy.[8] However, these protections only affect the residents of those states. Adopting a federal policy would give every person in the United States the ability to protect their data. The European Union has proven that a high-level privacy policy can be enacted, and the benefits of transparency have extended beyond citizens of the EU. A similar policy would not only help protect Americans, but a using an approach such as this could help further influence privacy protections across the world.

Another precedent is how our country regulates health and financial data. There are very strict regulations that protect citizens from fraud and offer privacy and ownership. These regulations have been in place for many years and it's not too far a stretch to envision regulations that protect other types of personal data.

It is also worth noting that the Obama Administration was in favor of data governance regulation and net neutrality. In 2012 the administration proposed ambitious policy on data security, transparency and accountability.[9] However, when Snowden released information about the NSA and surveillance under the Obama Administration, the public reaction eclipsed further efforts towards new policy for data regulations.[10]

The precedents outlined above show that there is a need for data regulation and net neutrality. Current events have taught us not to question if, but when the next data breach will be, and the combination of known and unknown impacts pose a necessity to act sooner rather than later.

The ROI of IBOR

The key players who would be affected by policies outlined in the Internet Bill of Rights are the general public, Internet service providers, tech firms and other online businesses, data brokers and the government. Understanding the costs and benefits of imposing regulations for net neutrality, data autonomy and data collection and security for each party is helpful in evaluating the net return on investment for implementation. Doubtless, the general public would benefit the most from these regulations but understanding how it would affect those regulated can determine the likelihood of how willing those affected would be to cooperate with the government to develop effective policy.

KEY PLAYERS FOR IMPLEMENTING THE INTERNET BILL OF RIGHTS

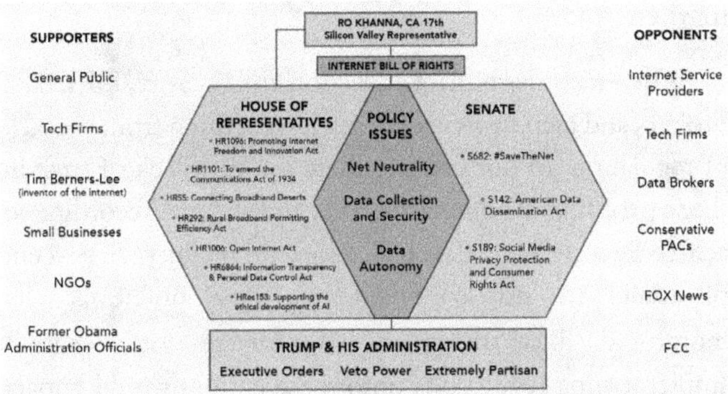

Of the three policy issues, net neutrality has the highest net positive return on investment (ROI). Without net neutrality, ISPs are free to charge customers more for faster service and can profit from data brokers and corporations who are willing to secure deals to ensure better service and access. A pay-to-play model hurts small businesses and consumers and enacting these "paywalls"[1] would contribute to furthering the digital divide in the United States.[11] Implementing net neutrality would enable equal access to the Internet. Many tech firms are supportive of net neutrality because they value an

[1] Farley discussed paywalls as a term to represent how charging for access to information creates knowledge barriers against people who cannot or choose not to pay for it.

open Internet system. ISPs and data brokers stand to lose the most, however, they would only be losing additional profits. Overall, implementing net neutrality would allow for more competition in the market.

When it comes to data collection and security, ISPs, data brokers and tech firms are currently benefiting from the lack of regulation. In our country there is a high lack of trust in those profiting off our clicks, likes and shares. According to a 2015 Pew study on data collection and security, 76 percent of adults are not confident that their online activity monitored by advertisers is private or secure.[12] Implementing regulations onto these entities would impact the business models of these organizations, but the tradeoff for tech firms and ISPs would be renewed customer trust.

Data autonomy would allow users to take full control of how their data is collected and used. This policy would be more complex in nature, because systems would need to be put in place to give users the ability to opt in and out of data collection practices and be able to download and move their data from one network to another. However, enactment of GDPR and the upcoming California law has already pushed tech firms towards setting up a framework to support a regulated system. ISPs would need to update their systems to comply and data brokers would have limited, if any access to data, based on selections by the user.

Overall, the general public stands to benefit the most from all three of these policies. They would gain more knowledge and control over how their data is used, have access to Internet services without fear of discrimination and experience renewed personal privacy and security. Additionally, the government would also benefit from implementing these policies both in the form of fines or taxes and expressed in the means of approval ratings for restoring and securing civic rights. While tech firms support net neutrality, they are less keen to implement data regulations that would affect their business model and revenues. Khanna's inclusion of tech representatives in the creation of IBOR suggest he was fully aware of that reluctance and getting them involved early would help garner support in the long term. Tim Cook of Apple is one leader in tech who has begun speaking publicly to the need for regulation and if more join in, it will help in crafting policy that serves both businesses and consumers.[13] Data brokers and ISPs would likely suffer the most from regulation in the form of lost profits and increased overhead costs, but is that really such a bad thing?

What's Happening in Congress

With the 2018 election, Democrats became the House majority leader and Republicans still control the Senate. The Trump Administration tends to oppose anything backed by Democrats. However, that does not mean legislation reflective of the principles in IBOR cannot be passed. If there is enough bipartisan support, we may see elements of IBOR come to fruition in the next couple years. This section will introduce the two committees in Congress that will be tasked with proposing relevant legislation, examine some of the bills currently being circulated in Congress and will share some viewpoints of representatives in Congress and the Trump Administration.

Any proposed policy for IBOR will need to be sponsored by members from either the House Committee on Energy and Commerce or the Senate Committee on Science, Commerce and Transportation. Both committees have subcommittees devoted to ICT, or Internet, Communications and Technology. The House committee has 31 members of the Democratic party and 28 Republican members.[14] The committee in the Senate has 14 Republican senators and 12 Democratic senators. Both committees have slim majorities, which means there will need to be enough bipartisan support to bring a bill to the congressional floor for debate.

Congress is currently circulating ten bills related to net neutrality, data autonomy and data usage.[15] Three of the four bills calling for data collection and security also have provisions for data autonomy. If citizens have the right to know how their data is being used, they might as well have some level control over it as well. Two of the seven bills related to Net Neutrality call for broadband expansion and four of the seven bills were introduced by Republican congressmen. Only one of the four data regulation bills were proposed by a Republican. While ambitious in nature, the likelihood of data regulation bills becoming law in the current 116th Congress seems low now. But it's only the third month into this session of Congress, so there is time and opportunity for building public awareness and there's always a chance that a current event could swing attention back to these issues.

It is important to note that democratic Senator Amy Klobuchar introduced one of the four data-focused bills, *S. 189: Social Media Privacy Protection and Consumer Rights Act of*

2019 in mid-January. She is currently running in the Democratic primaries for the next presidential election, so she has an opportunity to bring this issue to the campaign trail. It remains to be seen if this bill becomes a priority for her or not.

A recent bill introduced on March 6, 2019 is *S. 682: A bill to restore the Federal Communications Commission's Open Internet Order and its Net Neutrality Protections.* Democrats held a press conference to announce the introduction of the bill, with a promise to #SaveTheNet.[16] Their actions suggest they feel this issue will have strong public support. Considering that half of the current bills related to Net Neutrality have Republican sponsors, it likely will have a better chance of implementation than the bills related to data collection and security and data autonomy.

However, this will likely not be an easy bill to pass; it may get bogged down in the Senate Subcommittee on Communications, Technology, Innovation, and the Internet, of which Ted Cruz is a member.[17] In 2014 he infamously declared "Net Neutrality is Obamacare for the Internet," a partisan-fueled blow that would still resonate with some supporters today.[18] In 2017, he reiterated his position, arguing that classifying the Internet as a utility hampered economic growth.[19] Cruz and several other Republicans are also monetary beneficiaries of ISPs, having accepted reportedly over $1.7m in campaign contributions as of 2017.[20] Additionally, since the Republican-backed repeal of net neutrality by the FCC has only been in effect for a year, it may be hard to convince the President to sign a bill to reinstate an Obama-era policy. However, the Trump Administration has shown support for broadband expansion. In early 2018, the president signed *Executive Order 13821: Streamlining and Expediting Requests To Locate Broadband Facilities in Rural America.*[21] There is some favor for bridging the digital divide, but that doesn't mean that he will also favor regulating ISPs to meet the goals of the executive order.

Additionally, in September 2017, the NTIA released an online town hall outlining policy ideas for data collection and security.[22] It has some overlap with IBOR but is less prescriptive in outlining citizen rights. While it's positive to see that the Trump Administration is aware of data security needs, it's unclear whether this is an issue they will follow through on.

Conclusion

Of the three policy issues outlined in the Internet Bill of Rights, net neutrality is the issue that is likely to make the most ground over the next couple years. While protecting our data privacy and gaining autonomy over data collection practices is highly necessary as our world becomes more digital and globalized, our current political landscape will likely need to shift towards a Democratic majority to make that happen. However, all three issues can be used to inspire voters in the next election cycle and any small victories that can be made in the meantime will take us one step closer to implementing IBOR. As Moore stated, "...the right to control access to oneself along with use and control rights to personal information and places is an essential part of human flourishing."[23] In order to flourish, we must recognize what's at stake and reclaim our Internet rights.

From FinTech Darling to Bankruptcy

AUTHOR: Vincent Xu

PUBLISHED: August 2021

WRITTEN: December 2020

KEYWORDS: Wirecard, accounting fraud, fintech, revenue validity, third party risk, third-party acquirers, payment networks, revenue validity, reputation risk, regulatory ignorance

ABSTRACT:
This paper discusses the recent bankruptcy of Wirecard, which has been called as one of the worst financial disasters in Europe since the financial crisis. A combination of opaque business practices, ignorant culture of non-compliance and lack of business partner control all contributed to the eventual revelation that $2 billion was missing from the company's accounts. The downfall of the German fintech darling sparked conversation about the trend of false optimism in the up-and-coming fintech industry "disruptors." As the success of the fintech industry relies heavily upon the trust that is given by society, fintech companies must close the gaps in regulatory policies and compliance practices.

Prior to events in 2020, the online payment processing company Wirecard AG was considered one of the leading businesses in the German financial technology (Fintech) industry. Established in 1999, the company has been providing software and systems that connect consumers, retailers, and global financial systems.[1] Due to the high hopes that investors had in the firm, Wirecard once sat on the Germany's premier stock-market index DAX with blue-chip status—indicating it was an established, stable, and well-recognized company.[2] However, the recent Wirecard scandal is described as "one of the worst disasters in Europe after the financial crisis."[3] In summary, the company's external auditors were unable to account for approximately $2.1 billion that was supposed to exist in Wirecard's accounts. The missing money caused not only the company's insolvency, but also caused a tremendous disturbance across the fintech industry.[4] In retrospect, Wirecard's lack of due diligence in confirming revenue validity, the culture of regulatory ignorance, and the insufficient governance of business partners all contributed to control failures that eventually led to its bankruptcy.

Opaque Business Practices

Large parts of the Wirecard downfall resulted from the firm's opaque business practices. In October of 2019, the *Financial Times* published an article, accusing Wirecard's of suspect accounting practices after an investigation and reviewing internal documents.[5] In reviewing spreadsheets, the *Financial Times* investigators found that Al Alam in Dubai, Senjo Group in Singapore and PayEasy Solutions

Inc. in the Philippines contributed more than half of Wirecard's revenue and, in some years, 95% of earnings.[6] However, these business partners, or "third-party acquirers" in fintech jargon, lacked essential validations from payment networks such as Visa and Mastercard.[7] Wirecard's main business, credit card payment processing, requires close connections with payment networks in order to help clients accept credit card transactions. Thus, the missing connection from payment networks cast serious doubts to the Wirecard's business validity.

Furthermore, the unusually large amount of external revenues suggested significant inherent risks in Wirecard's business model. Wirecard utilized a highly spread-out business model to explain the $2 billion hole in its balance sheet as "in escrow accounts."[8] It is worth noting that Wirecard's board of directors did not address compliance risks prior to the *Financial Times* investigation. Under tremendous external pressure, Wirecard hired public accounting firm KPMG in October of 2019 to conduct an independent audit.[9] According to the KPMG report, the audit investigated quarterly statements of the escrow accounts but found no details of payments in or out of them.[10] Therefore, with insufficient materials to work with, KMPG reflected this deficiency in its report and was not able to confirm the validity of Wirecard's revenue.

In June of 2020, only days after the audit report was published, Wirecard finally admitted that the "$2.1 billion account balance do not exist."[11] The investors and shareholders finally gained a clearer picture of the illegal practices at Wirecard, which included deceiving auditors by providing false balance confirmations.[12] With fraudulent intents all the way from its CEO Markus Braun to its senior management, Wirecard's internal processes had been corrupted, which called areas beyond business processes into questions.

Regulatory Ignorance

Another public accounting firm, Ernst & Young (EY), served as Wirecard's main auditor for many years. EY responded to the revelation saying that there are "clear indications that this was an elaborate and sophisticated fraud involving multiple parties around the world in different institutions."[13] However, Wirecard's fraudulent conducts was not stopped over the years, despite concerns raised about its accounting practices and internal controls. For example, an internal presentation highlighted potentially fraudulent activity in 2018.[14] The presentation—titled "Project Tiger Summary"—outline potentially fraudulent behavior and potential violations of local laws related to money laundering and falsified accounts. Edo Kurniawan—who ordered the suspected transactions—was responsible for the payments group's accounting in the Asia-Pacific region. Two years after the internal presentation, Kurniawan remained employed in the same position at the Wirecard head office in Singapore.

The false public impressions that Wirecard had an impeccable reputation bolstered the firm's ability to not only ignore reputation risk, but also to attempt to undermine the reporting credibility of *Financial Times*.[15] The culture at Wirecard has directly led to its employees feeling discouraged, and believing that no actions would be taken against the management's criminal activities.[16] Multiple aspects of the company's management employees' performance suggested that considerations of risk were either missing or a low priority on the board's agenda. Perplexed and disgruntled, the whistleblower acted in part because of the inaction to address fraudulent behaviors by management of a company presenting itself as a blue-chip firm.

Failures in Third Party Risk Control

Over the past decade, Wirecard has been gradually expanding its geographical reach by working with hundreds of partner processing companies. In fact, about half of Wirecard's transactions are from countries that lack local payment licenses.[17] Yet, the management of Wirecard lacked diversity and competencies to lead a multinational operation. With the firm's rapid business expansion in the Asia-Pacific region, the Wirecard executives took advantage of this flourishing market by forging longstanding and large commercial debts owed to the firm to inflate its balance sheet.[18]

The registered office of two Wirecard partners — Centurion Online Payment International and PayEasy Solutions — shared space with a bus and coach rental business that operates across the Philippines named Froehlich Tours.[19] According to public filings, PayEasy and Centurion are owned by no other than Christopher Bauer, former Wirecard Asia Pacific executive.[20] When asked about the documented role of PayEasy representative in relations with Wirecard, Christopher Bauer denied having a managerial role in PayEasy.

Beyond the Philippines, Wirecard along with its acquiescent advisory board have constructed hollow "third-party acquirers" around the globe and artificially inflated its balance sheets for years.[21] The network of management board members corroborated to deceive regulatory bodies across multiple nations, rendering the Wirecard scandal an enterprise accounting fraud on a global scale.

Fintech Industry Flaws and Recommendations for the Future

Wirecard's fraudulent accounting practices had clear warning signs that raised numerous red flags for the regulators and investors early on. However, false optimism in the fintech "disruptor" has blurred judgements of key stakeholders and caused responsible parties to ignore Wirecard's opaque operations, suspicious business partners and its ignorant culture. Management of fintech firms must realize that their endeavor is subject to risks beyond technology alone. The Wirecard disaster clearly indicated that operational, compliance and reputational risks must also be properly managed throughout any enterprise.

The Wirecard scandal also signifies increasing necessity for the fintech industry to formalize their risk management procedures. As competitions between small fintech firms and large banking institutions intensify, the gaps in regulatory policies and compliance practices found in fintech companies call for immediate actions. Fostering and maintaining trust from customers, merchants and regulatory institutions is critical to the success of the financial technology industry.

Wash Your Hands and Update Your Software

AUTHOR: Roger St. Louis

PUBLISHED: April 2020

WRITTEN: March 2020

KEYWORDS: Pandemic; COVID-19; cybersecurity

ABSTRACT:
This paper discusses how cybercriminals are exploiting the new opportunities and exposures stemming from the coronavirus pandemic to increasingly acquire personal information and profit from the misery of others. As the coronavirus pandemic in 2020 has created new vulnerabilities, there is a need to strengthen cybersecurity approaches in three specifically categories: Blockchain, the Internet of Things (IoT), and the Human Component.

Introduction

> *"Exclusive: The natural way to stop the spread of the Coronavirus UPDATE: KEEP YOUR FAMILY SAFE!"*
> *"Worried about the new virus? Safe Mask's 5-layer activated carbon filter is able to stop 94% of viruses, bacteria,*

chemicals, pollution, dust, pollen, and smoke!"

These are only a couple of emails from the slew of similar messages currently being received in inboxes across the United States and the world. The above two were in my own inbox. These are unprecedented times. The COVID-19, the novel coronavirus, has disrupted our world in many ways. Lives are being lost, businesses are shutting down—some temporarily and other permanently—panic shopping continues, and many people sit at home quarantined, waiting on an uncertain future.

"As strategic continuity planners, it is still possible to buy time on the pandemic challenge while the existing imperfect plans are refined. This can either be done now, using data that have become available in the last year, or on the fly when a pandemic strikes."[1]

This quote is from Professor Annie Seale, writing in March 2008. That was over **12 years ago** to the month and could easily have been published in March 2020. It is somewhat uncanny how predictable our current state has been to those like Annie and others such as Bill Gates in recent years.[2] Pandemics cause vulnerabilities—and the exposure to harm is not only to our physical wellbeing. Pandemics increase our exposure to harm the form of cybersecurity risks. Specifically, the current coronavirus outbreak is unfortunately also leading to increased invasions of privacy, and "security experts say that hacking attempts are becoming more frequent in general, and one of the fastest-growing tactics is to use the coronavirus crisis as a ruse."[3]

By now, cybercriminals (or any of the cybercriminal categories: i.e. cyberterrorists, hacktivists, state-sponsored actors) are exploiting the new opportunities and exposures stemming from the coronavirus pandemic to increasingly acquire personal information and profit from the misery of others. While the context of the coronavirus pandemic in 2020 is used for this paper, however, the strategic insights and analysis related to strengthening cybersecurity and reducing data vulnerability apply to much wider circumstances. This paper explores the vulnerabilities and need for strengthen cybersecurity approaches across three categories: Blockchain, the Internet of Things (IoT), and the Human Component.

Blockchain

Blockchain refers to a relatively new technology, which allows information to be chained in blocks, which are linked to others in the chain through an encrypted hash (or key). Despite the conceptual security of blockchain technology, it is still vulnerable to flaws in coding, people failing to implement security standards, and changes in the field such as quantum computers breaking cryptographic algorithms.[4] Analysis shows that within the context of blockchain technology, "even if strong encryption is employed on personal data, the result is almost surely pseudonymous, not anonymous."[5] With this in mind, individuals and organizations alike must consider these vulnerabilities and continue to prepare against cyberattacks even if new technologies such as blockchain are promising. The truth still remains that, "our name or phone number, say — but also any data that, perhaps when combined with other data, can potentially at some point and by some means be used to identify us."[6] During a period of increased confusion, such as in a pandemic, it would be easy to over-depend on thinking blockchain technology is keeping information safe, even though it does not guarantee that valuable information is fully protected.

On the positive side, blockchain has revolutionized technology and cybersecurity in various ways. The structure of having new updated information submitted, as opposed to altering prior data, helps keep this information impartial. Although, "hashing is at the heart of many of the most important properties of blockchains, providing much of the 'magic' of decentralization. This question of whether hashed personal data should be considered personal data is hotly debated at present."[7] Due to this uncertainty, we are still left with a relevant vulnerability. The benefit of this technology is its "power" in the numbers – those requiring consensus, however more and more technology is being created to find ways to gain majority of the system to plan an attack. Current situations with the health crisis yield chances for cybercriminals who hope that the world is more focused on their wellbeing than cybersecurity. This too often can be the case and cybercriminals utilize such moment to strike.

The Internet of Things

The second area that requires a robust cybersecurity structure—particularly in healthcare—relates to the rising number of internet-connected devices, which collectively are referred to as the "Internet of Things." (IoT). There are extensive security risks that these devices pose. Additional risks arise as a multitude of IoT devices are being combined with applications of Artificial Intelligence (AI) and machine learning. A subset of machine learning, the combination of IoT and AI is often seen in a "deep learning" network, which "is the reigning monarch of AI...[powering] Alexa's speech recognition, Waymo's self-driving cars, and Google's on the-the-fly translation."[8] Companies across the globe and industries are investing heavily in AI and IoT, including ride-share services like Uber and the technology company Baidu.

To be clear, this new combination of technologies has the potential to help society in profound ways. Plainly speaking, "deep learning is self-education for machines; [you feed it a] huge amount of data, and eventually it begins to discern patterns or by itself."[9] Certainly, as a whole, the technology is incredible, but it is also early in its evolution and imprecise. For example, some computer scientists at Vicarious—an AI firm in San Francisco—did some testing to offer up "an interesting reality check. They took in AI...and trained it [to play a game] it [did] great. But then they slightly tweaked [some minor aspects]."[10] To clarify, "a human player would be able to quickly adapt to these changes; the neural net couldn't. The seemingly super smart AI could play only the exact style [game it learned and mastered]. It couldn't handle something new."[11]

The COVID-19 pandemic has resulted in more individuals being at home and using various devices they may previous used little or in limited ways. So now, more devices are being used and being used in new ways, increasing the risk that these IoT devices will be compromised, as the increase in data generated makes it difficult to separate out between "good" and "bad" data. As the authors of *Dirty Data, Bad Predictions* write, "data can be subject to multiple forms of manipulation at once, which makes it extremely difficult, if not impossible, for systems trained on this data to detect and separate 'good' data from 'bad' data, especially when the data production process itself is suspect."[12] This leaves IoT devices increasingly vulnerability, as cybercriminals look to invade IoT systems and retrieve personal data stored on individual devices.

Additionally, if the integrity of data is not protected, it increases the risk of individuals and society making decisions based on flawed information. "Data is seen as an important tool for policy making and governance because in its absence there is often too much reliance on subjective factors. The last twenty years have seen a widespread adoption of data-driven practices, policies, and technologies in the public sector."[13] The research also reveals that "this increasing reliance on data to assess and make decisions about complicated social, economic, and political issues presents serious risks to fairness, equity, and justice, if greater scrutiny is not given to the practices underlying the creation, auditing and maintenance of data."[14] Significantly, "research demonstrates the risks and consequences associated with overreliance on unaccountable and potentially biased data to address sensitive issues like public safety." This drives home the need to have a holistic approach to cybersecurity for IoT networks. So what responsibilities do individuals have for IoT cybersecurity practices during a pandemic?

The Human Components

This leads to the third category, arguably the most important when implementing improved cybersecurity practices during our current pandemic situation: "The Classic Human Component" or simply the human component. The term "classic" is added to denote that humans have always been the crucial part in successful cybersecurity. Technology and tools can make things easier and help solve problems, but they do not replace the "people" part of the equation of transforming data into useful information. While new technologies and IoT devices—such as Alexa, Echo, and Siri, to name a few—are marketed to make our lives "easier" and more convenient, they rely upon the human components to work in conjunction. They are simply tools, tools that can be used incorrectly and may cause harm instead of providing value. In the case of cybersecurity, "it's just as much about the human component of protection of personal data and information as it is having state-of-the-art technology to protect this data."[15]

One of the core problems during the current pandemic is that "personnel are not trained to identify and treat infectious diseases like this, and so containment did not take place."[16] Despite the existence of data that could have been used to foretell the current crisis, the current situation reveals that key individuals did not have the preparation or training that would have allowed them to trigger proactive, earlier responses. People must have the relevant knowledge and expertise in order to leverage data and technology effectively.

The same goes for cybersecurity, when people who are uneducated about fundamental practices are more exposed to new technologies and tools. This is particularly true during the current pandemic, as major employers as asking employees to work remotely (many for the first time), and schools are closing their physical operations and switching to online learning environments. This abrupt and radical shift has resulted in an unprecedented number of people are working from home, and increasing the likelihood of them becoming victims of cyberattacks. For examples, "individuals could provide personal details in response to a phishing attempt that promises information about a company's remote-work plan."[17] In other words, cybercriminals are attempting to exploit individuals under legitimate-seeming premises. These culprits are sending corrupt and counterfeit emails in hopes of getting individuals to open messages, which then unleash malware.[18] While some may be more obvious scams than others, many misleading messages are strikingly indistinguishable from the real thing. To illustrate, some cybercriminals are masquerading as World Health Organization officials:

'Dear Sir,
Kindly go through the attached document on safety measures, online training as a tool, regarding the spread of coronavirus.

...

Dr. Tredos Adhanom Ghebreyesus
Specialist wuhan-virus-advisory"[19]

This was posted as one of the many *The Wall Street Journal* reported people are receiving currently. The huge influx of people working from home, and/or being home without work, has exponentially increased the number of opportunities for cybercriminals. In particular, "the dearth of information about the [pandemic], along with plenty of conflicting claims, provides an opening for criminals."[20]

It is overwhelmingly clear that cybercriminals are using "current events to trick their victims…into acting against [their] better judgment."[21] An important consideration is what the long-term ramifications might be. Indeed, "experts say the attacks are increasing in frequency, and it's clear from hackers' behavior that they see the moment as potentially profitable."[22] Equally important is the fact that we must establish preventative measure that be implemented now to help mitigate the potential damage. Eva Velasquez—president and CEO of Identity Theft Resource Center— insists that "the impact of all these hacks will hit hardest down the road." She continues, "most of the time, people who fall victim to scams don't realize they've handed their personal information over to criminals until after the data has been abused. And the consequences could reverberate for a long time."[23]

Recommendations for Individuals

So, since this has assuredly been called to attention, what can be done? Well, the subsequent suggestions are highly potent ways to combat cybercriminals during a pandemic (or any time).

The first, and possibly easiest, action to avoid this fraudulent activity is – DO NOT open emails and/or attachments unless there is certainty of the sender. This may seem like common sense, yet this remains one of the most prevailing ways data is compromised. The National Cyber Security Alliance urges internet users to use caution when visiting websites or downloading apps related to COVID-19. You should always be wary of unsolicited emails that ask for your personal information.[24]

Second, and equally important, as the title of this paper indicates – stay clean. To put it another way, staying on top of the health of your physical body and technology devices is crucial. The COVID pandemic can largely be contended with by washing hand often. Technologies can also avoid a "virus" by having up-to-date software and patches. Prevention is often communicated as the top protective measure against biological and technological contamination. Every software company usually continues to come out with the most current version of their software. In this case, they certify this software will optimally formatted to combat cybercriminals. The time required to update, no matter the length, will significantly be less than the pursuit to recover lost personal data. Ultimately, it is always worth the effort.

Third, take pandemics (and other issues) seriously. When the news came out about COVID-19 some, from those in authority to unsuspecting citizens of the world, were blindsided by the stark deadly reality of the crisis. The same can be applied to technology during a pandemic. As previously mention, regardless of blockchain's advanced, diversified security structure, or having well encrypted IoT – it is important to plan for a severe cybercriminal infiltration. Some compelling evidence is made apparent from a cybersecurity firm called Proofpoint Inc., who monitors cybercriminal activity. The company has dedicated a specific analyst to follow the current situation, and reports seeing daily email campaigns during the current COVID-19 pandemic.[25] Of note, the company says, is that "natural disasters [usually] are very localized; events like the Olympics come and go and…something like the Olympics doesn't get the clicks that a health scare would."[26] This is, in part, due to the uncertainty of the timeframe. The Olympics have a start and stop date. So, if cybercriminals are relying individuals to be distracted, with the example of the Olympics, they potentially have a "limited window of opportunity" though of course they can strike at any time.

And finally, individuals should backup and then backup the *backup* of key personal information and records, to mitigate the pain of having personal information stolen or compromised. In the unfortunate case of data being held for ransom, for example, a cybercriminal would have minimal leverage to extort payment from an individual who regularly backs up their key data separately. It is important to remember cybercriminals want to extort people's fear of losing data to make them comply with their demands. This is especially true during a pandemic when most of the world is exhibiting heighten emotions of worry and uncertainty. Other cybercriminals are just malicious and utilize the hacking opportunity for "fun" against people. In either case, having a backup allows you to securely deny any demand without the chance of losing invaluable personal data.

Conclusion

There are a few final ways to help deal with the increased risks and cybersecurity vulnerabilities that have emerged in parallel with the coronavirus pandemic.

Following proper public health procedures and staying up to date on factual news is key. This includes keeping up to date on emerging schemes and attempts by cybercriminals. It is key to avoid toxic mis-information, by practicing due-diligence in verifying information is coming from reputable and known sources. Furthermore, once protocols (physically and technology security advice) are announced, it is imperative that people adhere to them. Experiencing a global pandemic is truly a mentally, physically, and emotionally disruptive and confusing time. People are genuinely, and understandably, filled with worry, shaken up, and stir crazy. Still, making sure to comply with accurate information helps to increase safety in all aspects. On the positive side, there can be some calm amidst the storm. There is solace in being prepared as much as possible. This involves making sure to consider care for ourselves as individuals, others around us, and our data – during a pandemic.

While pandemics cause vulnerabilities, especially within cybersecurity, disruption can also be the source of innovation and new opportunities. Out of this can emerge "an explosion of safer, more useful devices – Healthcare robots that navigate a cluttered, front detection systems that don't trip on false positives, medical breakthroughs powered by machines that ponder cause and effect in disease,"[27] and we surely could use positive outcomes. Maya Angelou gives a wonderfully stated piece of advice, very applicable amid our current circumstances, to "be present in all things and thankful for all things."[28]

SECTION THREE

Information and Society

Paper	**Author**
A Consequentialist Argument For A Centralized Genetic Databank	Amanda Phillips
AI and Policing – Bias, Failures, and A Path Forward	Peyton Lyons
An Analysis of the Indian Adoption Project and Current Migrant Family Separation Policies	Amanda Phillips
B Corporations: Purpose-Driven Business for the Good of All	Rochelle Robison
Instagram & Mental Health – Profits or Positivity?	Connor Tatman
Tech Development Policy in a Global Paradox: Digital Divides in a Shrinking Village	Gabriel McCoard
The Dubious Merits of Meritocracy	Melanie Keane

A Consequentialist Argument for a Centralized Genetic Databank

AUTHOR: Amanda Phillips

PUBLISHED: March 2021

WRITTEN: December 2018

KEYWORDS: Genetics; Personal Information; HIPAA; DNA Testing; Ethics

ABSTRACT: This paper discusses the argument for a centralized genetic database through the lens of consequentialism. The author examines the possible positive and negative consequences of establishing such a genetic repository, including threats to privacy and the risk of increasing systematic bias. The author concludes with the results of the evaluation of how a centralized genetic database might both provide benefits to people as well as how it might cause harm.

Introduction

Consequentialism presents an ethical framework to evaluate the successes and failures in amassing and using genetic data in the United States. Currently, the United States government, individual companies, and open-source platforms collect and store genetic data. As genome sequencing cost decreases, the amount of genomic data produced is rapidly increasing leading to robust genetic databanks that are unlike any that come before it. Population-wide genetic databanks could provide cures for diseases, criminal justice reform and even a greater understanding of humanity. However, genome data-management is primarily self-governed, leading to a litany of ethical concerns.

In determining whether the U.S. should impose more stringent policies on the management and usage of genetic data, utilizing the principles of consequentialism can aid in decision-making processes.[1] Consequentialism as an ethical framework evaluates the moral rightness of an act depending on the consequences of that act; a moral act would be one that provides the maximum good to the greatest number of people while providing the least amount of harm.[2] Consequentialism can be contrasted with deontological frameworks that rely on the morality of actions, rather than the results.[3] Genetic databanks may be considered moral under a deontological framework, in which intent is considered, however, in this circumstance the consequences truly illustrate ethical quandaries in utilizing personal genetic data for societal good.

Determining if the positive effects of genetic databanks outweigh the personal risk or if current ethical violations warrant new policies is essential for the future of genome research. Ultimately, consequentialism can provide insight into whether the United States should adopt and enforce a single, centralized, government-regulated genetic databank of volunteered genetic data. Three types of genetic databanks—government, private and open-source—have demonstrated significant positive societal impact. However, all three have revealed significant ethical failures including violation of personal privacy, lack of consent and unaddressed biases. Under consequentialism, a centralized genetic databank would provide the greatest social public good while minimizing the negative consequences of self-governed genetic databanks.[4]

Genetic Databanks in the United States

Consumers utilize genetic testing for a variety of purposes, including determining risk for disease, ancestry, kinship, and lifestyle choices.[5] The popularity of genetic testing has skyrocketed in the past decade: in 2013, half a million consumers had participated in genetic testing, by 2018 genetic test usage exceeded 17 million consumers.[6] By 2021, 100 million or one-third of the U.S. population is expected to have used a genetic test for DNA analysis.[7]

Genetic testing is initiated when a consumer orders a particular type of genetic test, sends the specimen to a laboratory or company where it is tested for single-nucleotide polymorphic anomalies and the resulting genetic profile is returned to the consumer.[8] There are two primary types of genetic testing: 1) healthcare-provided tests, which require a prescription, and 2) direct-to-consumer (DTC) tests provided by private companies. Healthcare initiated tests are used to determine the susceptibility of certain risk-factors whereas DTC-tests primarily address genealogy and a few medical risk metrics. DTC-tests function outside the healthcare realm, despite providing medical information, and are therefore not subject to the same

Health Insurance Portability and Accountability Act (HIPAA) laws as healthcare-provided tests.[9]

As genome sequencing moved into the mainstream from being primarily a medical research tool with the Human Genome Project (HGP) in 1996 to a test providing personal information, the personal utility of genetic information shifted.[10] Morphing from a health metric to an invaluable element of one's personhood, genetic data is viewed as medical information, representative of ancestry and kinship and an essential element of one's personal identity. Consumers find value in simply possessing one's genetic data.[11] In addition to personal utility by receiving a genetic profile, there is societal utility from the population-wide genetic databank produced, stored and shared by genetic testing companies.[12] Additional personal information is also stored within genetic databanks in addition to the genetic profile returned to the consumer.

One use-case of genetic databanks is forensic genealogy. Forensic genealogy is genealogical research, analysis, and reporting based on identity and kinship in a legal context.[13] Similar to traditional genealogy, forensic genealogy establishes bloodlines, researches family ancestry and using DNA to prove kinship, with a standard of proof acceptable in court.[14] The United States has maintained a genetic databank since 1989 for the use in criminal cases known as the Combined DNA Index System (CODIS). The information collected by CODIS is determined by individual states, though generally includes the anonymized genetic data of convicted offenders, missing persons and forensic samples collected at crime scenes.[15]

In the past, law enforcement only had access to genetic data in the CODIS database, comprised of individuals consenting to share their DNA in the case of missing victims, or knowingly compelled in the case of convicted offenders.[16] The landscape of DNA forensic genealogy has changed dramatically as DTC-genetic tests have become more common and law enforcement has begun using open-source and proprietary genetic databanks to identify suspects in criminal cases.[17] GEDmatch, an open-source platform where individuals can upload the raw data they receive from DTC-genetic tests, was primarily used by genealogists seeking to unite adoptees with their birth families. However, in the past two years, law enforcement has used GEDmatch to identify criminals in several cold cases.[18].

Many DTC-tests allow users to opt-in to medical research, where de-identified individual-level genetic data is shared with third parties, including commercial entities and pharmaceutical companies. 23andMe is a DTC-genetic testing company that provides kinship and ancestry information, offering a significant discount to consumers willing to share their genetic data for research purposes.[19] It is one of the largest DTC-genetic testing companies and has a 1.1 billion valuation.[20] Its high valuation is not for the service it provides, but rather the worth of the databank with the genomes of five million individuals. 23andMe's databank is much more robust than what is returned to consumers, including lifestyle, phenotypic data, and data collected on third-party sites.[21]

Positive Impacts of Genetic Databanks

In 1996, the development of the Human Genome Project (HGP) set the stage for how the United States views genetic databanks. HGP encouraged free and unrestricted access of anonymized genetic data to the scientific community allowing for creative science and maximal societal impact. Genetic databanks were categorized as a "global public good" and claimed an "ethical imperative to promote access and exchange of information."[22] This fundamental belief of the democratization of genetic data for public good shaped the positive sharing and utilization of genetic databanks.

One of the most frequent public good examples of genetic databanks is medical research. 23andMe collaborated with biotechnology company Genentech to establish pattern-matching and identify the genetic causes of Parkinson's. Unlike other diseases, there is no known single genetic signal for Parkinson's Disease and in 2017, 23andMe identified 17 new genetic variants associated with the disease.[23] 23andMe performed full-genome sequencing for a sample of individuals with Parkinson's Disease to create a robust databank to address this medical concern. Genentech has exclusive access to the Parkinson's databank for two years, after which it becomes available to the entire scientific community.[24] 23andMe has also used its databank to identify possible genetic markers for depression, working with pharmaceutical companies to pursue drug discovery for various mental health issues.[25]

Identifying and convicting violent criminals can also be considered a public good. In April 2018, investigators identified serial murderer and rapist Joseph James DeAngelo, known as the Golden State Killer, utilizing GEDmatch.[26] His case had seen few developments since his original crimes committed from 1979-1986, but he was identified investigators obtained a genetic that matched to relatives who had uploaded their genomic profiles to GEDmatch. Since DeAngelo's conviction, 27 additional suspects in cold murder and rape cases were identified in 2018.[27] At the end of 2018, 100 genetic profiles from crime scene evidence have been added to GEDmatch to further solve cold cases.[28]

While solving cold cases is an example of open-source databases used for societal good, the differences between CODIS and GEDmatch represent an even larger effect. As CODIS is primarily built from convicted offenders, it represents biases inherent in the criminal justice system. African Americans are 12.1% of the population in the U.S. yet comprise 40% of CODIS.[29] Offenders unlikely to have close relatives in CODIS are much more likely to escape detection with traditional forensic genealogy. GEDmatch, however, as a voluntary database comprised of people likely to complete DTC-genetic tests is skewed towards educated, middle-income, white Americans: a demographic underrepresented in CODIS.[30] By changing the common genetic populations within the genetic databank, law enforcement was able to address racial bias in the criminal justice system.

Risks of Genetic Databanks

VIOLATION OF PERSONAL PRIVACY & CONSENT

In the past decade, genetic testing moved from hospitals to home-testing kits, and concerns about personal data privacy and data-usage have grown. While CODIS represents a problematic databank in terms of racial bias, there are stringent privacy policies in place and enforced by government standards concerning how genetic information is collected and stored. Policies include a restricted database that only includes one or two alleles on loci that do not contain physically identifying information to ensure anonymized data and restrictions on familial searching.[31] In many states, CODIS requires permission from a judge to search the database.[32]

GEDmatch databank represents privacy concerns for suspects whose genetic material was found at crime scenes, individuals voluntarily uploading their DNA profiles, and the relatives of both parties. There are no policy limitations in uploading the entirety of a suspect's autosomal DNA to GEDmatch, as this DNA evidence is considered abandoned and thus not protected under the Fourth Amendment.[33] Similarly, genealogy data voluntarily submitted to public databases are considered outside of the jurisdiction of the Fourth Amendment. Of course, a familial genetic search does not only impact those who have surrendered personal genetic information but everyone whom that person is related to.

Many users choose to upload a genetic profile provided by a DTC-genetic testing company as well as a GEDCOM file, which identifies potential relatives within the database.[34] Individuals of European descent have a 90% chance of finding at least a third-cousin on a public genetic database.[35,36] Even if an individual considers themselves a private person and opts to not share their DNA with a private company, they could likely be identified through an open-source database due to the genetic data uploaded by other, related users.[37] The question of consent for relatives who volunteer shared personal data is an area that has simply not been addressed with policy in genetic databanks. Furthermore, individuals uploading their personal information may have a false expectation of anonymity. Supplying a name to GEDmatch is voluntary, however, given only a birthdate and name, a study analyzing GEDmatch was able to match a woman with her anonymized DNA.[38]

23andMe has also seen significant privacy and consent concerns with the ways in which data is shared with third-party users. While much of the information the 23andMe stores in its genetic databank is medical information, because DNA samples were voluntarily provided by the consumer, the information stored in 23andMe's databank are not subject to HIPAA and the data protection it provides.[39] Consumers are told that their information will be deidentified and aggregated to ensure anonymity, but a study of a similar genetic databank was able to reidentify the personal genome of 12% of consumers based on surname and age.[40]

23andMe utilizes the rhetoric of scientific democratization to encourage research participants to share additional data but fails to disclose the manners in which that data will be used. Rather than an open-source resource for medical researchers, the voluntary surrender of consumer's genetic data served to formulate a proprietary databank. Despite assertions of the overwhelming benefits to the scientific community, 23andMe sold the exclusive rights to their genetic databank for four years to GlaxoSmithKline, the ninth-largest pharmaceutical company in the world.[41] Consumers that garner personal utility of genetic tests based on their ability to contribute to medical research may still do so by directly contributing to open-source platforms utilizing the genetic profiles received by 23andMe. However, few consumers are motivated to take this additional step, as the communication provided by 23andMe implies that they have already done so; not that they have contributed to a proprietary databank.

Bias in Genetic Databanks

Privacy and consent concerns provide a significant risk to individuals, whereas bias present in genetic databanks have substantial societal impacts. In a positive sense, the inherent biases in the GEDmatch databank corrected biases in the CODIS databank, however, the majority of bias in genetic databanks does not serve as a societal benefit. Rather, genetic databanks other than CODIS are sold as "bias-free" but reflect the population of users likely to take a DTC-genetic test, rather than the United States population. The risk of utilizing biased data without addressing the biases can include false convictions using forensic genealogy, uphold the underrepresentation of minorities in medical research and a loss of personal utility by providing false results to consumers.

While using CODIS and GEDmatch in tandem can reduce racial bias, it does not alleviate the significant bias when used independently. CODIS racial bias serves to uphold racial inequality within the justice system and there have been several false or partial matches in the past that led to suspecting the wrong individuals.[42] Most people consider DNA to be genetically unique identifiers, but the manner in which is it is stored in CODIS and GEDmatch can result in false positives.[43]

Racial inequality in medical research is a significant issue. While black and Latinos comprise 30% of the United States population, they represented only 6% of federally funded clinical trials.[44] 23andMe genetic databank claims to represent a greater diversity of users compared to traditional medical research.[45] However, in 2016, 23andMe only had 45,000 African Americans in its research genetic databank. This represented 2.6% of the 23andMe database, compared the 12.1% of the United States population.[46] For other populations of color, the statistics are equally dismal; while users of European descent are often able to be identified to country, non-Europeans are only identified to broad regions.[47] While 23andMe discloses that its results are less accurate for users of non-European descent, and users of non-European descent are the most impactful towards 23andMe's goals to create a proprietary population-wide genetic databank, there is no reflecting price model to encourage more diverse consumers.[48] Furthermore, the methods of disclosure around the lack of accuracy in non-Europeans pale in comparison to the risk presented by providing personal genomic data without significant discussion of its reliability. Inaccurate test results can lead to family discord, ethnic tensions, and an impact on selfhood.

As 23andMe begins providing medical data in addition to ancestral data, the impact of bias on reporting medical risk provides even greater deleterious consequences. A study on a genetic test for an inherited heart disorder found that black Americans were more likely to be mistakenly told that they are at risk.[49] This effect was directly related to a white-biased genetic databank used to analyze genetic markers. While 23andMe may not intentionally be introducing racial bias, they fail to disclose the extent of their bias to both to their consumers and third-party entities accessing 23andMe's genetic databank.

Conclusion

Whether genetic databanks are run by private companies, like 23andMe, by the government like CODIS or open-source like GEDmatch, they represent both positive and negative consequences under a consequentialist framework.

In a perfect world, genetic databanks under consequentialism would be unequivocally ethical, providing positive consequences for the maximum number of people. Thus far we have seen on an individual scale a means to discover more about one's past and increase understanding of selfhood by knowing one's genome. It has allowed individuals to understand more about personal medical risk and make decisions to mitigate harm. On a societal level, positive outcomes include cures for disease, convicting violent criminals and reforming the justice system. Genetic databanks are toted as utilizing anonymized data, protecting consumer's privacy and contributing to an open-source, democratic system of data collection, available to maximize public good.

Unfortunately, the reality is that the organizations responsible for genetic databanks have repeatedly experienced ethical failures, which negate the personal and cultural benefits presented by the collection and use of genetic databanks. Forensic genealogy comes at the price of violating the user's privacy and impacting both user's and users' relatives' rights under the Fourth Amendment. Medical research has been conducted in such a way that user consent is disregarded and rather than contributing to an open-source database to maximally contribute to society, users donate their genetic data to a proprietary database used for profit. The fragmented nature of self-regulated genetic databanks ultimately ensures that the positive outcomes possible by analyzing genetic databanks are unable to be reached, due to amplified bias.

While the effects of a government-mandated and held genetic databank certainly have its own risks, it may still be preferable to continuing to allow private and open-source companies to self-regulate. The interconnectedness of DNA means the genetic information of nearly all persons of European-descent is currently held in a genetic databank; the privacy and benefits valued under the current system are a fallacy.[50] The pushback against a centralized data system is usually based on a fear of surrendering personal privacy, but the breach of privacy has already occurred and currently faces minimal policy and oversight. Limiting an individual's ability to share personal genomic data infringes on their personal rights: it would be impossible to regulate genetic data by creating policies around what individuals can share. Thus, regulating how genetic databanks store and utilize genomic information is a way to address privacy and consent.

A centralized database would allow the maximum reduction of bias by including the greatest number of samples and the closest approximation of the U.S. population. Creating a standardized genetic database would allow for increased oversite and policy, remove the profit from private companies and provide increased privacy for an individual's confidential data. Under consequentialism, a centralized database would provide the maximum positive good for the maximum number of people, while decreasing the overall risk.

AI and Policing: Bias, Failures, and A Path Forward

AUTHOR: Peyton Lyons

PUBLISHED: January 2020

WRITTEN: March 2019

KEYWORDS: Artificial Intelligence; Policing; Bias; Institutionalized Bias

ABSTRACT:

This paper discusses the intersection of artificial intelligence and policing by examining facial recognition surveillance and predictive policing technology. These technologies have a large impact on individuals and communities and run the risk of being impacted by institutionalized and internalized bias. There are many examples of the failures of artificial intelligence technology, especially due to issues with biases in the data used to inform these systems. The way forward requires regulation, incorporating diverse perspectives, and including the public and community leaders in conversations about artificial intelligence as a policing tool.

Technologies that use artificial intelligence (AI) and machine learning are prevalent in our everyday lives: in smart home devices, music and movie recommendations, social media feeds are curated by AI. AI has the potential to continue its positive impact on the world, but there is the reality that companies and organizations are also using AI in ways the general public may not realize. Despite many examples of its positive and life changing impacts, AI systems accurately diagnosing skin cancer and serving as a second opinion for the detection of breast cancer[1] for example, AI also has the potential to harm and has caused harm to individuals and communities. These impacts cannot be ignored. This essay will take a critical view on the use of AI by police forces and will discuss the harmful impacts of the existing biases and inaccuracies in these systems. This essay will then discuss recommendations for ways to move forward with AI and policing to provide potential solutions for reducing the harms associated with this intersection.

To understand the impact and importance of the intersections of AI and policing in the United States, it is important to first define algorithmic bias and some of the ways these methodologies specifically affect marginalized and at-risk groups. AI was preceded by less advanced surveillance equipment, like wiretapping, but as the ACLU describes, "throughout history, military and surveillance equipment has been used to intimidate and oppress certain communities and groups more than others, including those that are defined by a common race, ethnicity, religion, national origin, income level, sexual orientation, or political perspective."[2] There is a history of oppression related to surveillance technology which has now extended to modern technology, including AI. As technology advances, there are still glaring issues with the way these systems affect certain communities, which is largely due to the existing racial and gender bias that affects the United States. In "Risky Bias in AI," Mary-Anne Williams discusses that this bias presents itself in AI and machine learning primarily in three ways: through data, training, and algorithms.[3] Williams goes on to explain that data used to train models is often biased and is "a result of the human bias embedded in the assumptions or historical aspects of selection and preparation of the data sets." Algorithms are not inherently biased, but when AI intersects with human bias via training data sets, we see errors arise. Steve Lohr describes this phenomenon by explaining that AI software is "only as smart as the data used to train it," and, for example, if the data used to train a facial recognition system includes many more white men than black women, the system will be worse at identifying black women.[4] Lohr references a widely used facial-recognition data set that was estimated to be 75 percent male and over 80 percent white, demonstrating the way these datasets misrepresent the population in the United States and the problematic nature of this type of misrepresentation. From these statistics and explanations, we can begin to understand the way biased data directly affects AI technologies.

One example of the potential failures of using AI comes from an internal hiring tool that Amazon created with the goal of improving and expediting the hiring process. The company quickly realized the tool was largely favoring male candidates, which, as Jeffrey Dastin explains, is unsurprising if you know that the models were trained from resumes submitted to Amazon over a 10-year period and that these resumes reflected the male-dominated nature of the technology industry.[5] Although Amazon corrected the problematic nature of this tool by stopping its use, the company failed to recognize the reality that data is not neutral, and as Joy Buolamwini describes, "machines learn from historic hiring practices, [and] they can reinforce past inequalities instead of overcoming them."[6] Amazon's attempts to use AI to accelerate a process is one example of the ways in which AI can further perpetuate biased systems.

Amazon provides another example of the sweeping impact AI can have on society, and especially marginalized groups with Rekognition, a facial recognition system that the company marketed for government surveillance. Similar to Amazon's hiring tool, Rekognition did not work as expected. Jacob Snow explains that the ACLU conducted a test of the tool by building a face database with 25,000 publicly available arrest photos.[7] This test resulted in the software incorrectly identifying 28 members of Congress as people who had been arrested for a crime. The inaccuracy of this system demonstrates some of the potential issues that arise from the use of AI in policing or criminal legal systems. In a letter to Jeff Bezos titled "Re: Audit of Amazon Rekognition Uncovers Gender and Skin-Type Disparities," Joy Buolamwini explains "Even if the Amazon Rekognition services and products you [Amazon] are selling to police departments were completely flawless, the potential for abuse on historically marginalized communities would not be reduced."[8] Data that perpetuates bias is problematic, but what is more dangerous is the risk that these discrepancies could be used to harm people. Matt Cagle and Nicole Ozer from the ACLU reinforce this viewpoint, explaining that the Rekognition system would disproportionately affect minority communities and could allow for the identification and tracking of any individual.[9] In addition, with this tool, police could identify people attending protests, ICE could monitor immigrants, and cities would have the ability to routinely track residents. In discussing this example of AI, Buolamwini, Cagle, and Ozer explain clearly the possibilities for facial recognition technology specifically to adversely affect society, causing further harm to marginalized communities. The use of a system like Amazon's Rekognition by governments and police could lead to powerful surveillance systems and harm which could be difficult to undo.

These two examples of the failures of Amazon's AI technology help to set the groundwork for the main topic of this essay - an analysis of the dangers of the use of AI by police forces for facial recognition and predictive policing, which will be followed by recommendations for addressing these challenges. Amazon's systems prove that no system is immune to bias, so when these biases and inaccuracies begin to show up in policing and the criminal legal system there is a real risk of severely impacting lives. In "Amazon's Symptoms of FML" Buolamwini explains that police can misidentify innocent people as criminals and subject individuals to unwarranted police scrutiny, which could be extremely dangerous for people of color, especially considering that, based on a report from the Center for Policing Equity, police are far more likely to use force when interacting with black Americans than whites and other groups, even when taking into account racial disparities in crime.[10] In a report by Alvaro Bedoya, Jonathan Frankle, and Clare Garvie from the Georgetown Law Center on Privacy and Technology called "The Perpetual Line-Up," the authors acknowledge that facial recognition technology has been used to catch violent criminals and fugitives, but also report their findings about the misuse and risks of these systems.[11] Bedoya et al. explain that state and local police departments use facial recognition systems, but that it is unclear what lasting impact these tools could have on privacy and civil liberties and it is unclear how these systems will specifically affect racial and ethnic minorities. The authors also bring up the history of FBI and police surveillance of civil rights protests and that facial recognition runs the risk of stifling free speech. Of the 52 police agencies surveyed in "The Perpetual Line-Up," only one prohibits the use of facial recognition for the tracking of "individuals engaging in political, religious, or other protected free speech." While facial recognition does have the potential to help police more easily capture criminals, there is a real risk that these systems will also perpetuate the racial biases due to inaccuracies and datasets that misrepresent the true demographic of the public. As we have seen with the challenges of Amazon's Rekognition system and the ambiguities and risks presented in "The Perpetual Line-Up," the dangers of facial recognition negatively impacting individuals or, on a larger scale, civil liberties outweigh the benefits.

In addition to facial recognition, police forces have adopted predictive policing systems, which, as Kate Crawford, Rashida Richardson, and Jason Schultz discuss in "Dirty Data, Bad Predictions," are systems that analyze data to predict where a crime may occur during a given window of time, or who may be involved in a crime as a victim or perpetrator.[12] Crawford et al. bring up the concept of "dirty data," which they describe as a category of data that is "derived from or influenced by corrupt, biased and unlawful practices, including data that has been intentionally manipulated or 'juked,' as well as data that is distorted by individual and societal biases." This concept of "dirty data" is impactful when discussing predictive policing, because feeding a system with data that contains bias quickly results in the system making more biased decisions. What's more, Crawford et al. explain that the vendors of predictive policing systems are rarely fully transparent about what specific data is used to deploy the technology or how the vendor addresses potential accuracy, bias, or misconduct. Police forces use these systems to make decisions about how to interact with communities, but do not always take into consideration the negative aspects of relying on a system that does not clearly explain how it makes decisions. In "The Threat of AI to POC, Immigrants, and War Zone Civilians," Alex Chen argues that predictive policing systems are not perfect, but "police will assume it is, and use this technology to perpetuate the racism that already exists with the criminal justice system."[13] While this statement likely does not capture the feelings of all police officers, it is an important point to keep in mind. AI may seem like the perfect method to finding solutions and making predictions, but users cannot blindly trust these systems without a deeper understanding of how the solutions and predictions are generated and from what data the systems base decisions.

In looking more closely at the data used to inform these predictive policing systems, a pattern begins to develop demonstrating some of the dangers of these systems. Crawford et al. explain that the primary data source that informs predictive policing systems is historical police data and that, if this data is generated by unlawful or biased practices and policies, it can skew the way decisions are made throughout the criminal legal system. This means that if predictive policing systems use "dirty data," the ramifications go beyond the interaction between a suspect and a police officer, potentially extending through the full judicial system. There is also evidence that the data collected by police forces likely does not reflect the true crime level that occurs in a community. Logan Koepke and David Robinson explain that crime reports are more reflective of a record of the response by law enforcement to what happens in a community.[14] Koepke and Robinson explain that this is because citizens make decisions about what crimes to report to police and police make decisions about what is reported as a crime. These decisions are largely based on the relationships police have with communities and vice versa. Koepke and Robinson also note that "both crime and crime clearance rates can be manipulated dramatically by any police agency with a will to do so." This is to say that the data used to inform predictive policing systems better reflects policing tactics in a police force or in a specific community than a response to true criminal behavior. The large issue with predictive policing systems is the inevitable feedback loop. Relying on records of community reported or police identified crimes to train AI systems leads to more enforcement in communities that are already heavily policed as Nikita Malik describes.[15] Kirsten Lloyd explains the dangers of this type of feedback loop and the ability of bias to scale in "Bias Amplification in AI Systems."[16] Lloyd argues that if the bias in AI systems remains unchecked, serious negative consequences will impact populations at scale and resulting backlash could very well obstruct progress of AI technology. From historical patterns in policing data to evidence of the way predictive policing systems use this data to inform decisions, we see how bias can perpetuate using these systems.

Thus far, this essay has reflected a critical viewpoint on the use of AI by police forces through facial recognition and predictive policing. So, what can be done to address the existing biases in systems used for policing? An overall reform of the criminal legal system is needed, as evidenced by facts from the ACLU: for example, "the federal prison population has increased by around 790 percent since 1980" and "a black person is 3.73 times more likely to be arrested for marijuana possession than a white person is, despite approximately equal rates of use."[17] That said, a discussion of this sort of systemic change is not within the scope of this essay, as it extends widely beyond AI, and will require significant work from many entities to achieve. Ideally, systemic changes would happen quickly in the United States and would eliminate or reduce bias across the criminal legal system and other domains, but this is an overwhelming feat and an unrealistic way of managing bias in AI systems. The next section of this essay will discuss how, instead of taking on all of these issues, smaller changes can be made to improve the use of AI systems by police forces. These changes include creating regulations and laws for AI used in policing, encouraging police forces to take a more critical view of AI vendors, and including community leaders and advocates in conversations about these policing systems. Making domain specific changes will ripple out to impact the system as a whole and begin incrementally affecting change to the criminal legal system.

The regulation of AI is needed in the federal government, and private companies need to create internal policies that confront biases in AI systems. The authors of

"The Perpetual Line-Up" go as far as to say that the use of facial recognition to track people on the basis of their political or religious beliefs or their race or ethnicity should be banned outright. While this perspective may be on the far end of the spectrum, it is not entirely unreasonable when considering that lives and public freedom are at stake if AI is not properly monitored. Bedoya et al. go on to say that the use of facial recognition should be subject to public reporting and internal audits. Microsoft President Brad Smith echos this perspective in a blog post titled "Facial recognition technology: The need for public regulation and corporate responsibility," in which he argues that an effective way to manage government use of technology is for the government to proactively manage the use itself.[18] Smith also notes that it is necessary for the technology sector to prioritize reducing the risk of bias in facial recognition technology. There need to be policies implemented within private companies as well as public regulation from the government in order to approach bias in AI from different angles. More specifically, as discussed in the "AI Now Report 2018" by Kate Crawford et al., governments need to expand sector-specific agencies to monitor, oversee, and audit AI technologies by domain.[19] The need for more specific attention to applications within given domains will help ensure that the technology is implemented most appropriately for its use case. There is a case for the outright ban of facial recognition technology in certain domains, but there should be consideration for potential benefits of AI in certain use cases. The government must put more regulation in place and include regular internal audits of technology in order to identify and correct biases in AI systems.

Intervention from the government is needed to create policies and laws that apply to all police forces, but police departments must also take initiative to better understand the impact of the AI they are using to make decisions about the way they are policing. One way police departments can improve this understanding is by being more critical of vendors of predictive policing systems. In "Stuck in a Pattern", Koepke and Robinson explain that vendors often claim that their technology is proprietary and will not disclose their methods to police departments. Police departments need to push for improvements by vendors, because as Crawford et al. discuss in "Dirty Data, Bad Predictions" there are no mechanisms for identifying "dirty data" problems with predictive policing systems in real time. Crawford et al. argue in the "AI Now Report 2018" that AI companies should waive trade secrecy and other legal claims when working with the public sector in order to allow for full auditing and a deeper understanding of the technology. This would help police departments better address any problematic results that arise from predictive policing systems. In "Artificial Intelligence and Policing: First Questions," Elizabeth Joh presents a variety of questions police departments must ask vendors about the expected relationship between these two entities.[20] Joh outlines questions police departments should consider when working to sign a contract with a predictive policing vendor including "Will the training data be available to the police and the public?" and Will the algorithm using the training data be similarly available to the police and the public?" and "Does the contract between police agency and vendor confer ownership rights over the data and the analysis to the city, county, or state?" These are just a few of the questions

Joh presents, but they capture the need for police departments to dig deeper into the technology and the data that feeds predictive policing systems. Crawford et al. in "Dirty Data, Bad Predictions" explain that there is little incentive for police departments to self-monitor for biased data and to identify these problems for a vendor. That said, Crawford et al. go on to say that creating a mechanism for assessing harms from using historical police data and developing strong public transparency and accountability measures are more effective ways to mitigate biased data concerns. As the system exists currently, police departments are not encouraged to address "dirty data" concerns, but because of the resulting biases and dangers of predictive policing systems, departments need to take a greater role in mitigating these harms. The policies and laws discussed earlier would help to address these issues and create improved systems for police departments to engage with vendors and work to better understand how the AI systems are using data to make decisions.

Regulations from the federal government and internally in police departments are important and necessary. As discussed, social change is needed as well, but this is a large undertaking. Some ways to begin the process of improving these AI systems is to look more closely at the way these systems are created and by whom. Increasing the diversity of perspective and knowledge of the people creating these tools can begin to impact AI systems on a larger scale. In the TED talk "How I'm fighting bias in algorithms" Joy Buolamwini explains, "It really starts with people. So who codes matters. Are we creating full-spectrum teams with diverse individuals who can check each other's blind spots? On the technical side, how we code matters. Are we factoring in fairness as we're developing systems?"[21] As Buolamwini explains, increasing diversity in the teams that create facial recognition and predictive policing systems is needed and will improve the quality of the products as well. Creating more diverse teams gives additional perspective and allows individuals to use their lived experiences and perspectives to inform the creation and development of technology. Buolamwini goes on to say that if we make social change a priority instead of an afterthought, we have the opportunity to create greater equality with AI. When the people on teams are more diverse and the voices of diverse people are incorporated into the development of these systems, it is likely that we can begin to see the inclusive datasets that are needed to reduce bias in AI. Similarly to Buolamwini's argument about creating diverse teams, Lloyd explains in "Bias Amplification" that "The first line of defense against creating AI systems that inflict unfair treatment is to give more attention to how datasets are constructed before operationalizing them, which means that attention to bias cannot be an afterthought." It is imperative that diversity and bias are not afterthoughts when developing AI, because we have seen examples of the negative impacts of AI systems on individuals and communities that result from not taking these issues into account early and seriously. It is also important to consider that bias already exists in historical police data sets and that it is already impacting the decisions police forces make. Police forces need to begin to seek ways to mitigate existing biases, but this is very challenging because policing is tied to the systemic and internalized biases in the United States, as represented by the ACLU's statistics. Police forces can begin to make progress by taking these existing biases into account and allowing diverse teams to begin thinking about ways to mitigate the impacts of biased AI systems. There is a long road ahead to increase diversity both in AI development teams and the groups that use the systems, but beginning to take on these issues is a positive step toward decreasing the negative impacts of these systems. Including a broad range of perspectives improves technology as a whole and is a way to reduce the potential for biased systems.

In addition to creating diverse teams, police forces and government agencies need to engage with the public and community leaders as they work to develop regulations for AI used in policing. In the "AI Now Report 2018," Crawford et al. explain that, "More funding and support are needed for litigation, labor organizing, and community participation on AI accountability issues. The people most at risk of harm from AI systems are often those least able to contest the outcomes." Creating community dialogues and encouraging public input on policing systems is a way to incorporate the voices of marginalized communities and those who are most at risk of harm from AI policing systems like facial recognition and predictive policing. Residents should feel empowered to include their voices and influence in decisions that will directly affect their communities. The ACLU describes the September 2016 Community Control Over Police Surveillance (CCOPS) effort, which has the objective to ensure that "residents, through local city councils are empowered to decide if and how surveillance technologies are used, through a process that maximizes the public's influence over those decisions."[22] Since the implementation of the CCOPS efforts, over thirty cities have implemented the laws, with states like Maine and California even sponsoring statewide CCOPS legislation. Engaging community members and local leaders helps to integrate diverse voices into the conversation about the use of AI for policing and provides a space for people to learn about the technology and offer suggestions for improvement. Police forces need to make decisions that help improve their communities and not further perpetuate bias, but in order to know what might make the most positive impact, they need to directly listen to their communities.

The influence this type of technology has on individuals and communities grows every day, for better or for worse. While we can find benefits of AI in some industries, like health care, manufacturing, and retail for example, the risks associated with these systems cannot be ignored. The institutionalized and internalized biases that exist in the United States have huge impacts on AI, especially when these systems are used by police forces to make decisions that can directly impact the livelihood of individuals and communities. This essay has discussed some of the existing harms associated with the intersection of AI and policing, like the failures of Amazon's Rekognition facial recognition tool and the use of "dirty data" in predictive policing tools. While there may be future potential for police forces to use facial recognition and predictive policing to improve safety, there are currently too many existing biases in the data that is used to inform AI systems to confidently say that the AI used by police forces is positively impacting the United States. AI is already a part of our daily lives, and this is not going to change, but in order for police forces to use this technology for the betterment of society, there needs to be change in the way AI is used in policing. Through federal and private regulation, the critical assessment of relationships with AI vendors, creating diverse teams with diverse perspectives, and incorporating feedback from the public and community leaders, there may be a way forward for AI policing tools. AI is here to stay, but when lives are at stake from its use, there needs to be more forethought and critical analysis on its impacts.

An Analysis of the Indian Adoption Project and Current Migrant Family Separation Policies

AUTHOR: Amanda Phillips

PUBLISHED: June 2020

WRITTEN: December 2018

KEYWORDS: Misinformation; Disinformation; Native Americans; Family Separation; Migrant Families; Indian Adoption Act of 1985; Immigration; Government Policies.

ABSTRACT:

This paper discusses the devastating failures of the U.S. government to properly implement information management principles during the enactment of family separation policies, both as part of the Indian Adoption Project of 1958 and the separation of migrant families in 2018. Like Native American tribes have experienced for the last 50+ years, the children of asylum seekers and other migrant families have been separated from their loved ones; through information management failures, many of these children have been systematically deprived of their parents and culture as a result. Consequently, a new generation of vulnerable children face the increased risk of experiencing cultural genocide due to the U.S. separation policies resulting in a loss of fundamental cultural knowledge systems, languages, and identities.

Introduction

The United States (U.S.) has practiced family separation as official policy since its foundation. Separation of migrant parents from their children on the southern U.S. border is the most recent iteration and echoes Native American child removal over the past centuries. Native American families were forcibly separated by U.S. assimilation policies first through Native American boarding schools and then by the Indian Adoption Act in 1958.[1] Migrant families face separation under current immigration laws where families are reclassified as adults and unaccompanied minors and sent to different detention centers.[2] Family separation has caused great suffering by those affected by these policies.

The suffering caused by family separation has been further exacerbated by information management failures. Critical failures of information management in family separation have occurred in three pivotal ways. First, the U.S. government strategically used disinformation (false information deliberately spread) to maintain the legality of their family separation policies. Secondly, information managers failed to properly process and manage data, leading to catastrophic data loss in both policies. Lastly, the failure of essential information management has led to a loss of culture and personal knowledge for those affected, as well as their communities. Understanding how information management has been applied to family separation both historically and presently is essential. It has implications for the role of data in developing policies, the importance of maintaining personal data and may give valuable insight into how information management can be used in the future to mitigate harm.

Native American Family Separation through the Indian Adoption Project

Family separation of Native American children began formally in the 1860s when children were taken from tribes and placed into boarding schools.[3] These boarding schools were specifically designed to deny Native Americans their culture and force "assimilation through total immersion" in which they would "kill the Indian and save the man."[4] Students were stripped of personal information, required to forgo all Native American language or cultural practices.[4] The devastating effects of this practice are still felt by many Native American tribes today.[19]

When boarding schools became cost-prohibitive, the U.S. adopted another form of assimilation by placing Native children for adoption or foster care outside of the tribe. This program was formalized in 1958 as the Indian Adoption Project by the Bureau of Indian Affairs and administrated by the Child Welfare League of America.[5] For many of these children, there was ample opportunity to be raised in a tribal community or with tribal members, but preference was given to white, nuclear families.[1] By 1970, it was estimated that 20 to 35 percent of Native American children in the U.S. were placed in foster homes, adoptive homes, or institutions, 85 percent of which were outside of their respective tribe.[6]

In 1978 the Indian Child Welfare Act (ICWA) was enacted, which allocated tribes exclusive jurisdiction when a child is either a ward of the tribe or resides on a reservation.[1] While the law does not bar non-Native Americans from adopting or fostering Native American children, preference is given to the tribes for adoption or foster placement.[7] Despite this law, there is still a disproportionately large number of Native American children in the foster care system.[4] In 2018, ICWA was struck down as unconstitutional by a federal judge in Texas, claiming that it gives Native American families preferential treatment, thereby violating the Fifth Amendment. The Cherokee Nation has filed a stay and plans to appeal the decision.[8]

Migrant Family Separation at the U.S. Southern Border

On May 7th 2018, a "zero tolerance" policy for illegal entry to the U.S. was announced by Attorney General Jeff Sessions and Immigration and Customs Enforcement Director Thomas Homan.[9] As part of the zero-tolerance policy, parents found crossing illegally are criminally prosecuted.[2] Migrants referred for criminal prosecution are sent to a federal jail; under U.S. law, children cannot be held in federal jail, consequently, children are registered as "unaccompanied minors" and separated from their parents.[10] The law does not recognize a minimum age for unaccompanied minors and the ages of separated children range from zero years to seventeen years.[11] On June 20th of the same year, President Trump signed an executive order to end family separation but faced the task of reuniting the 2,000 families that were split during the enforcement of the zero-tolerance policy.[12]

During this period, children were detained in facilities meant for short-term holding or placed in short-term foster care assignments.[13] Parents were given inaccurate information when initially separated and during the reunification process.[11] Some migrants, including unaccompanied minors, have been deported without their family, making reunification vastly more complicated.[14] Emotional, physical and sexual abuse have been reported in detainment shelters and several studies confirm that this type of separation can have significant long-term trauma on children.[13] At this time, 200 or more children are classified as ineligible for reunification and their future remains unclear.[12]

Information Management Failures in Family Separation

Information management can be understood as the "management of the processes and systems that create, acquire, organize, store, distribute and use information."[15] Information must be effectively managed throughout its entire lifecycle, which includes the occurrence, transmission, processing, management, and usage of data.[16] Information managers are tasked with matching information needs to the design and delivery of information systems to allow for effective and efficient information use. The family separation policies failed in utilizing information and information management in a myriad of ways.

Strategic Use of Disinformation in Family Separation

A key element of family separation by the U.S. government is that it exists within a legal framework. Floridi defines information as data and meaning; data requires syntax to understand its meaning and the data must comply with the semantics of a chosen system. Misinformation occurs when semantic content is false, whereas disinformation occurs when the source of misinformation is aware of its nature.[16] Misinformation and disinformation have occurred at great length for both Native American families and migrant families, primarily used nefariously with communication by officials and legal documentation.

Legal documents are understood as factual semantic information, in which the signatory understands the content as well-formed, meaningful and veridical data.[16] However, migrant parents were given legal documents to sign in English, without translation and were told by border patrol agents that signing would allow for reunification with their children.[14] Some migrant parents report being told that they "would never see their children again" or were physically forced to sign legal documents by Border Patrol agents.[17] In reality, these documents were an agreement to be deported without their children.[2] Once a family member has been deported without their children the chances of reunification are significantly lowered, potentially resulting in permanent separation.[18]

A similar tactic has been used to control Native American tribes beginning with the first treaty systems and continues today with legal documents surrounding Native American children.[3] While Native American adoption documents did not have an official language barrier, the legal framework and specialized language of the documents did not allow for the signatories to have factual semantic information or a meaningful understanding of the documents contents.[16] Rather, many parents signed away their parental rights after caseworkers informed them that it was a temporary foster placement.[3] Native American mothers were denied information about due process, not given access to attorneys or informed of their legal rights.[6] It was common practice to notify parents of hearing notifications by placing them in a local paper, often one that was not available on the reservation, rather than contacting biological parents directly.[5]

These are examples of disinformation employed as a strategy to enforce a legal family separation policy. By not arranging for an interpreter or circumstances that would allow a full comprehension of the document, or simply verbally providing disinformation, policy officials failed to provide information that complies with the semantics of the environment. The presented information was rendered false and was thus manipulated to express an illusion of legality in their policies.[16] This represents a critical failure in the occurrence and transmission of data in the information life cycle, as information became false at the occurrence level due to a lack of veridical data and strategic use of disinformation. Then, factual information failed to be transmitted to the necessary parties, significantly impacting family's reunification efforts.

In both cases, the signed legal documents were held as proof of unfit parentage when parents attempted to regain parental rights or reunify with their children. The legal documents are paraded as a measurement of a parent's lack of love and care for their children, ultimately used as a tool to prove that their children should be surrendered into a government system.[17] Through coercion and disinformation, the government was able to both ensure the legality of their policy and make it significantly more difficult for parents to regain custody of their children.[18] By failing to produce or transmit information with semantic content, information managers in reference to family separation critically failed at the first two steps in the information lifecycle, to the severe detriment of families.

Information Processing and Management Failure in Family Separation

The third element of the information life cycle is processing and management which includes collecting, validating, modifying, organizing and storing information.[16] When the U.S. was tasked with reuniting separated migrant families, critical failures in the database system for handling family units were illuminated. In the database, Customs and Border Protection have categories for "family units" and "unaccompanied alien children", but no categories for the children removed from families and sent to separate shelters.[10] Instead, these children were entered into the database under the category "deleted family unit." When that database merged with the Department of Health and Human Services, there was no deleted family unit classification and the data linking parents to their children was lost.[10] As a result, the U.S. failed to organize and store essential data about the individuals taken as wards of the state.

The attempted fixes for this database failure were ineffective, and the means of collecting data highly problematic. Several files simply contained a written note with parent's names and alien numbers as the only information linking parents to children.[12] Young children's testimony was served as a replacement for the information that the U.S. government failed to store, which proved to be unreliable as many children were too young or too afraid to provide accurate information.[10] In many cases, parents and children were forced to undertake DNA testing to prove parentage and allow for reunification, submitting personal genetic data to an organization that has already proved untrustworthy.[18] Migrants are now held responsible for producing the information that they never had access to from the occurrence.

Native Americans also faced difficulty with databases holding their personal information. The Indian Adoption Project required at a minimum the name and tribal affiliation of the child, as well as the name and address of the biological parents in an adoptee's records.[1] Unfortunately, in many cases, this data was not accurately collected, and the adoption programs failed to send the collected information to the Secretary of the Interior, the supposed custodian of this data.[19] For the records that are intact and accurate, accessing them remains a significant challenge for many Native American adoptees, representing a failure in the usage of the information.[16] Many of the documents are protected under closed adoption law and adoptees are not given access to their original birth certificate or tribal data.[5] In some cases, adoptees are required to take DNA tests to prove ancestry, a measure that is not consistent with tribal measures of affiliation.[19] Adoptees can petition for access to the data but is mostly considered ineffective.[19]

In both methods of family separation, initial thought was given to occurrence and transmitting important personal data when individuals became wards of the government.

However, with the substantial information management failures, it is clear that no foresight was given in how this data may be accessed or used in the future. The data management policies illustrate that the focus was on separation without consideration of reunification. As a result, migrant families face significant difficulties in reunification, while Native American adoptees have struggled in discovering their personal data and ancestry.

Information Management Failure Results in Community and Cultural Loss

Lastly, these policies greatly affected individual's and communities' abilities to use cultural data, the final step in the information life cycle. The United Nations defines the forcible transfer of children from one group to another with the intent to destroy a group as genocide.[20] For Native American children, the Indian Adoption Program expressly attempted to assimilate Native Americans with the goal of "kill the Indian, save the man" paired with an explicit attempt to move Native American children to non-Native homes.[3] As a result, Native American children placed in foster care or adoption were stripped of their culture, in the majority of cases were not allowed to participate in cultural events, speak their language or in some cases, even made aware of their tribal ancestry.[20] When many Native American adoptees discover their heritage, they have difficulties in Native communities, where blood quantum, clothes, language, and attendance of ceremonies are elements for being recognized as a tribal member, rather than phenotype.[21]

Floridi posits that information has intrinsic worthiness and denying an individual of their infosphere is an instance of evil.[16] This refers to not only personal data, which was mismanaged through disinformation and database failure as discussed above but the role of culture and language in an infosphere. Native American culture utilizes stories to encode and share traditional knowledge.[23] LaRoche, a Sicangu Lakota tribal member, shares his experience when his grandfather, a victim of the boarding school program, refused to share the Lakota language when it could not be preserved in entirety.[22] Hence the information mismanagement through the family separation system resulted in a loss of personal information for individuals, but also the loss of something greater for their community. Tribes lost a significant portion of the generation they would traditionally transfer knowledge and culture to, with implications for cultural genocide.[23]

While the current migrant family separation does not have the same legacy effects that Native American tribes face, Native American experiences stand as a warning. Under the zero-tolerance system, children must be placed into either foster care homes or shelters funded by the Office of Refugee Resettlement within 72 hours.[11] As reunification becomes increasingly difficult, further exacerbated by the information management failures discussed above, the amount of time migrant children spend in foster care and detention centers increases. U.S. officials have determined that 200 or more children are not eligible for reunification or release and State courts are legally able to grant custody of migrant children to American families, without notifying parents.[14]

Migrant children also face a loss of language; many foster homes and detention centers do not include Spanish-speaking guardians.[12] Furthermore, a significant number of young children come from Honduras and Guatemala, speaking rare Indigenous languages.[24] These children are young enough that they are still learning their language, the longer they stay in foster care or shelters, the higher the likelihood that they will lose their original language in entirety. In the case of one toddler placed in a foster home in 2015 after being separated from her mother while seeking asylum, her loss of the Spanish language was used to support her foster parent's guardianship, rather than being returned to her mother.[18]

As both groups lose the base of their knowledge transfer systems, the impacts are widespread. Indigenous languages contain more than their linguistic qualities, but also the thought processes embedded in the language, when the language is lost, the knowledge system contained within the language is also lost. Fishman advances the extinction of language goes beyond what we can learn from its qualities and encompasses the "destruction of a rooted identity."[25] With a loss of culture comes a devastation of self-worth, limiting human potential and reducing the ability to solve social problems, including poverty and substance abuse.[26] Ultimately, the continued loss of children from a community and resultant loss of information, be it personal, community or cultural knowledge can serve as genocide, and the destruction of a way of life for distinct population segments.

Conclusion

The failure to properly handle family separation and the information surrounding it had catastrophic effects through the Indian Adoption Project and migrant family separation. As information managers responsible for data throughout the information life cycle, family separation policies failed in all four elements. The U.S. failed to properly occur and transmit data when presenting legal documentation as disinformation. Data ceased to be information when the U.S. transmitted information that was not veridical, failed to provide the necessary semantic information and falsely promised parents that signing documents would result in reunification. They failed in the processing and management of data by creating incomplete or false databases, as well as denying individuals access to their personal data. Lastly, the U.S. denied migrants and Native Americans the ability to use their data by impacting the ability to practice culture and speak their native language. As Native American and migrant children are kept away from their parents and culture, the risk of an entire group losing important knowledge systems, languages and identities increases, risking cultural genocide.

Information management and the failures therein take an already abhorrent practice and made it markedly worse. Understanding how information management was used and misused to support unjust policies will aid in identifying future conflicts. All policies of family separation are doomed to fail due to the mismanagement of personal and cultural data and the inability to carry out such policies without serious deleterious effects on those involved. At a minimum, measures should be taken to ensure that a loss of personal and cultural information is reduced. It is imperative that any future policy separating parents from their children include a robust information management system that prioritizes reunification rather than separation, to preserve personal and cultural information.

B Corporations: Purpose-Driven Business for the Good of All

AUTHOR: Rochelle Robison

PUBLISHED: May, 2021

WRITTEN: June, 2021

KEYWORDS: B-Corporations; Business Community; Shareholder Value.

ABSTRACT:
This paper discusses how B corporations, or benefit corporations, have risen in the past 15 years in response to a growing recognition that business can be profitable and purpose driven. Given the rise in socially consciousness and the business community's outsized impact on daily lives around the globe, this is the time to reassess how for-profit businesses are incorporated, including their responsibility to stakeholders, not just shareholders.

We are in a time of upheaval that calls for a new way of thinking and approaching the ills of the world, from COVID-19 to racism to environmental destruction. As a nation, I believe all of us are called upon to reflect on the changes we need to make in our personal lives, what we stand for, and what we need to fight against to make a more equitable, just, and sustainable world, now and for future generations.

Given the rise in socially consciousness and the business community's outsized impact on daily lives around the globe, this is the time to reassess how for-profit businesses are incorporated, including their responsibility to *stakeholders*, not just shareholders. The move to a more socially sustainable and conscious way is possible. It starts with expanding obligations beyond maximizing value for shareholders, to being socially and environmentally conscious to stakeholders, including employees, the environment, and the community at large.

B corporations, or benefit corporations, have risen in the past 15 years in response to this growing recognition, that business can be profitable *and* purpose driven. A B corporation is a type of for-profit corporation that, in addition to profit, is required to "create benefit for society as well as shareholders."[1] Unlike traditional corporations, Benefit Corporations must by law "create a material positive impact on society; consider how decisions affect employees, community and the environment; and publicly report their social and environmental performance using established third-party standards."[2] As of June 2020, 36 states and Washington, D.C. have passed legislation allowing for the creation of benefit corporations with 5 more in the process of considering legislation.[3]

B corporations are a variation of traditional corporations, or C corporations, but they differ in two significant ways. First, C corporations are *only* obligated to maximize long-term shareholder value. The board of directors has broad discretion to consider the business' best interests, but they have a fiduciary responsibility to shareholders, not to broader stakeholders. As noted, B corporations have a broader obligation to their employees, their suppliers, the community, and the environment. Second, while traditional corporations distribute quarterly and annual financial reports, they are not obligated to distribute *benefit* reports to their shareholders and stakeholders. B corporations must distribute these benefit reports annually, which is meant to keep the corporation accountable and transparent in describing how the B corporation has benefitted the public.[4]

Traditional corporations have not always prioritized maximizing profit. In *The Corporate Conscience*, Thomas O. Melia makes the case that corporations were designed to serve public interests starting with Roman law. The pivotal change in American law came with the 1919 case, *Dodge v. Ford Motor Company*. The Michigan State Supreme Court ruled in favor of minority shareholders, declaring that "a business corporation is organized and carried on primarily for the profit of the stockholders," and ruled Ford could not use the proceeds of the company for the benefit of customers and workers at the expense of shareholders.[5]

Another shift towards shareholders at the expense of the public interests and broader stakeholders came with the economist Milton Friedman's 1962 opinion piece in the New York Times titled "The Social Responsibility of Business is to Increase Its Profits." In it, Friedman wrote "There is one and only one social responsibility of business... to use its resources and engage in activities designed to increase its profits."[6] This short-sighted view of corporate stewardship arguably contributed to many instances of corporate abuse and malfeasance, including Enron and Worldcom in the 1990s and the Great American

Recession in the 2000s, with companies like Lehman Brothers and Washington Mutual collapsing and the American taxpayer footing the bill in the billions for companies deemed "too big to fail," like Bank of America and General Motors.

While other factors are certainly at play, another destructive effect of maximizing shareholder value exclusively has led to unprecedented levels of income inequality. Since 1978, the average CEO pay has grown a staggering 940% while the average worker pay has risen only 12%.[7] A focus on the bottom dollar leads to behavior that doesn't promote or encourage socially responsible behavior. In fact, markets, when left to work as intended, do not act morally or immorally—they are amoral—which does not support an ethical and socially connected society. As the corporate governance and ethicist, James Meacham noted, "Human beings are aspirationally ethical, markets are amoral, and businesses exist primarily for profit."[8] B corporations can bridge the gap to drive profits with purpose.

Another type of benefit corporation is a certified B corporation. Certified B corporations are assessed and monitored by a non-profit group called B Lab, founded in 2006. While many companies start out incorporating as B corporations, others go on to certify they are following the incorporated values to workers, customers, the community and the environment. It also creates a community for other B corporations to learn from companies in the community. Eight-two companies were certified in 2007 and today, there are more than 3,300 companies in more than 150 industries and 70 countries. Companies include Ben and Jerry's,

Athleta, Patagonia, All Birds, Eileen Fisher, Bombas, Warby Parker, Seventh Generation, Kickstarter, and Seattle-area companies like Cascade Engineering and MiiR. [9] The B corporation Declaration of Interdependence is compelling:[10]

We envision a global economy that uses business as a force for good. This economy is comprised of a new type of corporation - the B

Corporation - Which is purpose-driven and creates benefit for all stakeholders, not just shareholders. As B Corporations and leaders of

this emerging economy, we believe:

- *That we must be the change we seek in the world.*
- *That all business ought to be conducted as if people and place mattered.*
- *That, through their products, practices, and profits, businesses should aspire to do no harm and benefit all.*
- *To do so requires that we act with the understanding that we are each dependent upon another and thus responsible for each other and future generations*

This pledge clearly emphasizes the importance of stakeholders (workers, community, the environment) and focusing on long-term impact versus short-term gain. According to B Lab, companies certify for six main reasons: lead a movement, build relationships (with a community of like-minded leaders), attract talent, improve impact, amplify their voice, and protect their mission. Through all of this, the board of directors is required to balance profit and purpose, unlike traditional C corporations.

In addition to the B corporation movement, other influential business groups and leaders are seeing the need to "do the right thing" given the enormous power corporations have in modern society beyond returning profit for shareholders. They are also shifting their position as public sentiment has increased emphasis on the ethical and social responsibilities of the business community. In August 2019, the Business Roundtable announced five "Principles of Corporate Governance" in a new Statement on the Purpose of a Corporation.[11] It was signed by 181 CEOs. The principles include: deliver value to our customers; invest in our employees; deal fairly and ethically with our suppliers; support the communities in which we work; and generate long-term value for shareholders.

This is a significant change from a decades-long position of the Business Roundtable to elevate the shareholder above all else. In the announcement, CEOs such as Jamie Dimon of JPMorgan Chase & Co., said: "The American dream is alive, but fraying. Major employers are investing in their workers and communities because they know it is the only way to be successful over the long term. These modernized principles reflect the business community's unwavering commitment to continue to push for an economy that serves all Americans." President of the Ford Foundation, Darren Walker, said:

> *"This is tremendous news because it is more critical than ever that businesses in the 21st century are focused on generating long-term value for all stakeholders and addressing the challenges we face, which will result in shared prosperity and sustainability for both business and society."*

While this is a positive sign that business is seeing the need to expand the definition of responsibilities, it does not change the way most companies are incorporated. There are two gaps.

- First, the Statement on the Purpose of a Corporation is aspirational with no requirement to report or assess their pledge by a third party; B corporations pledge to report annually and the board of directors has a fiduciary responsibility to purpose and profit.
- Second, the Business Roundtable's statement notably does not address responsibility to the environment, which is a key tenet for B corporations. These companies have committed to use their B status to build a more sustainable and inclusive economy.

In the twenty-first century, it is good business to appear and do better for communities, workers, and the environment. Too many people are watching and voting with their dollars. "With consumers now looking to the corporate world to help them reduce their carbon emissions and cut down on the plastic filling our oceans, in 2020, the onus is firmly on businesses."[12] People are more socially conscious and want to invest in companies that not only look out for the bottom dollar and return on investment but also make socially and environmentally sustainable choices.

B corporations and certified B corporations can lead our country and the world to a more equitable and just society. As Rose Marcario, the CEO of Patagonia, stated: "The B Corp movement is one of the most important of our lifetime, built on the simple fact that business impacts and serves more than just shareholders -- it has an equal responsibility to the community and to the planet."[13]

Instagram and Mental Health — Profits or Positivity?

AUTHOR: Connor Tatman

PUBLISHED: September 2020

WRITTEN: December 2019

KEYWORDS: Social Media; Instagram; Reputational Risk; Mental Health

ABSTRACT:
This paper discusses the risks facing the picture-sharing application Instagram, a social media giant, as it explores ways to balance the mental health of its users and the way it currently generates its revenue, namely advertisement through direct sponsorship and marketing via social media influencers. If Instagram shifts its user experience away from "likes" being publicly visible, it must consider a number of potential risks to its current business model. The author identifies some of these risks, and potential steps to mitigate the exposure.

The average Instagram user spends approximately 26 minutes a day scrolling through the app.[1] That may seem like a trivial amount of time, but a mere 26 minutes equates to roughly *1/48th* of a person's life. If you subtract a typical eight hours of sleep from that equation, the number increases to *1/32nd* of a person's life. With over a billion users around the world, an incredibly large number of people are spending a significant portion of their lives looking at pictures on their phones that others have posted. Plus, this metric does not consider the amount of time that many of these people spend on similar social media platforms such as Facebook, YouTube, and Snapchat. For an activity like social media that people are spending so much time on, it is not surprising that there may be some unintended psychological effects. With talks of the correlation between social media and mental health being ever present in the news, Instagram has decided to be proactive on the issue by declaring that they will remove likes from their platform.

Taking a step back, it is important to first answer the question: what exactly is Instagram? Instagram is an application where users can post and edit pictures and videos, view posts by nearly any other user, and interact with friends. The service began back in 2010, and is one of the fastest growing picture applications in history, garnering over a million users within the first two months of launch. The app started to grow even faster after 2012 when Instagram was purchased by Facebook, increasing by tens of millions of users per year.[2] Another interesting fact about Instagram is how popular it is among teenagers. Despite Facebook being the most used social media platform in the world, teenagers say that they use Instagram far more often than Facebook. In fact, in a recent study 35 percent of teens say that Instagram is their favorite social media platform while only 6 percent prefer Facebook.[3] A similar study was recently conducted in Great Britain, known as the

#StatusofMind survey, where hundreds of teens were interviewed and their mental health was analyzed in regards to using popular social media apps. The results were not what Instagram was hoping for. In fact, Instagram received marks for the highest levels of anxiety, depression, bullying, and FOMO (the fear of missing out).[4]

Instagram CEO Adam Mosseri and his team have come under public scrutiny for "providing" an atmosphere where young people are exposed to larger-then-life photographs, many of which are photoshopped. Instagram has been talking about how to improve this situation for the past couple of years, but until early November 2019 no real solutions had been proposed. In a recent interview with Tracee Ellis Ross at the Wired 25 Summit, Mosseri stated that a small percentage of users in the U.S would begin to see posts in their feeds without like ratings.[5] How exactly would disabling likes help with the mental illness crisis? Neuroscientists seem to think that the answer lies in mental hooks caused by the usage of social media. When someone sees that another user has liked or commented on their post, the gut reaction from that person is that of positivity and fulfilment. Dar Meshi, a cognitive neuroscientist from Michigan State University, points out that humans are "hardwired to find social interactions rewarding", and at its core, Instagram runs off of social interaction.[6] Meshi states further that the area of the brain that is stimulated while having these interactions on Instagram is the same area that is stimulated when people gamble or have sex.

So, if Instagram is comparable to addictive activities and associated with degrading mental health, will removing likes really solve these problems? Mosseri seems to think so.

After conducting tests in Canada, Japan, and Brazil, the Instagram team liked what they had seen and decided it was time to move into the U.S. market. Slowly. It was emphasized heavily that the change would not be made overnight, and that only a small percentage of Instagram users in the U.S. would notice any changes in the coming weeks. This is a key factor in the implementation of Instagram's plan, and will be discussed in depth later. Mosseri stated that the mission is to, "try and reduce anxiety and social comparisons, specifically with an eye towards young people," which at face value seems to be an entirely positive goal for both Instagram and the greater community.[7] However, upon closer examination there are several areas where Instagram is exposing itself to a significant amount of risk with no clear contingency plans in place.

First, let us assume that the plan to remove public likes is successfully implemented across the entire app in the U.S. In this scenario, users are able to see how many likes their own posts get, but all other posts that they view do not display likes at all (which is what Instagram is proposing for the long run). Naturally, Instagram would want to have some metrics to show off their success, but this is where they run into a big problem. If their goal is to improve the mental health of their users, they need a way to measure that the mental health of their users is improving with the implementation of hidden likes. Measuring mental health is neither cheap nor easy to do,[8] and with no clear plan in place to quantify their success, Instagram is exposing itself to a potential procedural control failure. Before an investor decides to invest in an asset, they carefully consider the cost of the investment and the potential payoffs of that investment. For a corporation like Instagram, their plan would only reward them with a reputational boost which is nearly impossible to accurately quantify. The cost on the other hand is quite real.

Social media influencer marketing is on track to surpass being a $5 billion dollar market by the end of 2019.[9] Although this figure is split between all social media networks, the majority share belongs to Instagram. With an impressive 3.21 percent engagement rate compared to 1.5 percent across all other social networks,[10] it is clear that Instagram has developed a platform that is incredibly appealing to advertisers and shoppers alike. The #ad which is typically used for most sponsored brand deals between corporations and Instagram influencers has seen rapid growth in the past few years,[11] and with a general rule of one cent of ad revenue per follower, hundreds of thousands of users are making money off of advertising on Instagram. Instagram's plan to hide public likes puts this entire online ecosystem in jeopardy.

There are two major ways that advertising is conducted on Instagram. The first being direct sponsored ads that appear in users feeds and have *sponsored* tags at the bottom, and the second being user promotions where the advertiser uses an influencer as a delivery method. One thing that both of these advertising methods have in common is their dependency on likes. Because of how delicate the situation is, it would be extremely wise for Instagram to use a RACI model or some similar tactic in order to outline and access the risk associated with their plan before informing the public. It might seem blatantly obvious that advertisers should be thoroughly taken into consideration before deciding to hide likes, but Instagram has seemingly done little public outreach to such corporations. Of course, it is possible that Instagram has done research and outreach behind closed doors, but even if this was the case, other advertisers would like to see examples of how Instagram will interact with advertisers in the absence of likes, highlighting yet another potential procedural control failure. In fact, in the same interview as previously discussed, Mosseri stated, "We're going to put a 15 year-year-old kid's interests before a public speaker's interest," making it very clear that influencers and therefore advertisers are not the company's priority.

A brief application of an RACI model will highlight not only who is involved in the decision to remove public likes, but also will show the potential snowball effect that could occur as a result of poor planning. Responsibility and accountability both belong to Mosseri and his team since he is spearheading the plan. Next, consultation should involve conversations with influencers, advertisers, and users alike which Instagram has failed to do effectively thus far. The fact that Instagram has more or less ignored the input of influencers, who are largely responsible for the rapid growth and success of the platform over the years, has a lot of people very upset with the actions of the company. In a recent interview with *Business Insider*, Canadian influencer Kate Weiland expressed her concerns with how she has seen a significant drop in user interaction (less likes, comments, and ad interaction) which makes it extremely difficult to determine what type of content is the most successful.[12] In a country like Canada which has already seen widespread implementation of hiding public likes, users don't interact with as much content, influencers are nervous about their futures on the app, and advertisers have far less confidence not only in the influencers that they sponsor, but the longevity of the platform in general. The final step of the model that Instagram has also largely ignored is informing the appropriate stakeholders, which it has done at a minimal level.

With so much at stake on the business side, Instagram's decision to start hiding public likes shows how much value they place on the ethics behind their platform. Or is there another motive? Analyzing Instagram's recent compliance trends can assist in answering this question. Loosely defined as following the laws and ethical practices that apply to an organization, compliance can be a helpful tool in analyzing why a decision was made. To start, let us take a brief look into Instagram's recent legal complications or lack thereof. In the public domain there are, at the time of this writing, no major lawsuits that involve Instagram being sued due to issues related to mental health. So, if Instagram is government compliant, they must feel that they are not living up to the ethical standards that their company desires. This is a trend that has been developing with companies in the past decade, especially with companies that have a great deal of interaction with the public. The benefits to a company's reputation can be significant when they have a proper moral and ethical code in place, but is that really the right move for Instagram at this time?

The two most important factors that Instagram should take into account in their decisions going forward are that they have already announced that they have begun implementing their plan, and that they have taken very little user feedback into account thus far. By asking everyday users, influencers, and advertisers what they think about the decision to make likes private, Instagram could learn some valuable information that could save them time and money. Perhaps people think the solution will be ineffective and interrupt their user experience? This could very well be the case, but even if this is true it would be foolish to pull the plug before the plan has been thoroughly tested. Once the percentage of people that are a part of the hidden likes initiative is greater than the current 2 to 3 percent, and Instagram has a clearer image of the public reception, that would be the ideal time to reevaluate the risk of continuing with their plan.

At this point, assuming that Instagram is being careful in implementing the hidden like policy, it becomes a win-win situation for the company and leaves it with two foreseeable outcomes. Option one is that the majority of US users dislike the change, and Instagram can revoke the changes while having concrete evidence that they are trying to make ethical changes to make their platform a safer space for its young users. Option two is that the majority of the users like the changes, in which case Instagram can gain a reputational boost from their initiative on the mental health crisis and continue to pave the way for social media companies in this sector. Such a small change in a picture app has the potential to send shockwaves through the entire industry. Other social media sites like Facebook and YouTube have also begun to experiment with similar plans,[13] and if Instagram is able to successfully execute their plan to hide likes by slowly including more people while surveying the user experience, they just might change the standards for social media companies on mental health.

The Global Paradox of Digital Divides in a Shrinking Village

AUTHOR: Gabriel McCoard

PUBLISHED: June 2021

WRITTEN: May 2020

KEYWORDS: Digital divide; information and communications technologies

ABSTRACT:

This paper discusses the duality of how the evolution of information and communications technologies (ICTs) has resulted both in greater connectedness (the "global village") and greater inequalities in access to that connectedness (the digital divide). The paper examines some of the root causes for this current state, and some of the various efforts that have been made to address the disconnect. Ultimately, the idea of a "global village" certainly exists, but the author asks how much of the world is included in that village, and whether the village is the same one for everyone.

Advancements in information and communications technologies (ICTs) have made numerous technologies more accessible, affordable, and easy to use. In doing so, this collection of communication technologies—including the internet, wireless networks, cell phones, computers, software—have resulted in two related but seemingly contradictory notions. First, that the evolutionof ICTs has enabled the emergence of a "global village," where people from across the globe are able to connect instantly with each other online, regardless of their physical location. And yet at the same time, the digital divide remains undeniable as many areas of the world remain disconnected from these ICTs, since not all nations (or segments of populations) have equal access to digital technologies, nor are they always equipped to take advantage of these "solutions."

"The new electronic interdependence recreates the world in the image of a global village," remarked media philosopher Marshall McLuhan in the early 1960's, giving popular rise to the concept of communication technology as a shrinking force.[1] "Today, after more than a century of electric technology, we have extended our central nervous system in a global embrace, abolishing both spaceand time as far as our planet is concerned."[2]

As ICTs allowed communication to become exponentially faster and cheaper in relatively short time periods, fissures began to crack the edifice of inter-connectedness, as disparities in access to ICT emerged in what came to be known by terms such as "information inequality," "computer literacy," and "participation in the information society."[3] Ultimately, the term "digital divide" won out, which Del Hazeley defined as "'the gap between those who do and those who do not have access' to digital technology, computers, and the Internet wherein the term access is defined as the motivational, material, mastery and manipulative access to technology."[4] As such, the "Digital Divide" assumes certain gaps in technical capacity and internet connections, "leading to gross inequality of accessibility and usage between the developed world and that of developing nations," but also to internal divides within the same nation.[5]

Global inequality has been a worldwide phenomenon for generations; in more recent years a vast array of governments, inter-governmental organizations, non-governmental organizations, corporation, and the like, have launched campaigns to address the disparities between and within nations. Many of these players, however, have launched their objectives with an internalized agenda and certain assumptions about the "on-the-ground" reality of many nations that are not accurate. Organizations seeking to address these gaps, as is often the case in international development, do so for their own agendas without comprehending or appreciating the situation.

Both Facebook and Google have recently, with various partners, began to lay undersea cables toexpand internet connectivity throughout the world.[6] Some estimate that collectively, Google, Microsoft, Facebook, and Amazon currently own or lease half of all global undersea bandwidth.[7] Google itself spent $30 billion by 2018 to expand its cable capacity.[8]

Reasons why a digital divide exists are less clear than metrics of deployment of specific hardware or network access. At the turn of the 21st Century, the United Nations (UN) devised the Millennium Development Goals ("MDG"), eight barometers of development. While the MDGs strove for such things as improved education and better access to health, the final Goal is most relevant. That goal, "Develop a Global Partnership for Development" called for multiple actors (notably UN member countries) to support development goals, and technological deployment fell under its auspices.[9] The2015 final MDG report outlined progress (or lack thereof) towards each goal. Among the successes, per the UN, was the percentage of the world able to access the internet, or "internet penetration," which increased from 6 percent in 2000 to 43 percent in 2015.[10] Cellular-mobile phone access, as measured by subscription access, increased to 7 billion from 738 million in 2000, such that by 2015, 95 percent of the world's population was covered by a mobile signal.[11] The UN concluded, however, that while access to greater services was growing, so was the divide between those who had it and those who did not, due in part to such barriers as cost and "national backbone" to provide bandwidth, such that while 97 percent of the population in well-to-do countries had internet access, only 64 percent of the poorest nations did.[12]

Explaining the gap requires understanding several contributing factors. One 2007 survey found thata variety of determinants explain the gap between users and non-users, even while use of internet technologies increased overall.[13] These factors influence each other, and include per capita income, pricing of services, population age, levels of education, and percentage of population living in urban areas.[14] Other specific factors included productivity of ICT equipment, reliability of electricity, overall infrastructure, and human capital factors (among others, education and computer literacy).[15]

While the UN cites that the MDGS were largely successful, they expired by their own mandate in 2015 upon the launch of the 17-point Sustainable Development Goals, or SDGs, an interconnected"blueprint to achieve a better and more sustainable future for all" by 2030.[16] While the full extent ofthe 17 goals are outside the scope of this treatment, Goal Nine, "Build resilient infrastructure, provide inclusive and sustainable industrialization and foster innovation," [17]applies to notions of minimizing the digital divide and bringing more people into the global village. (The change in the goal structure can also lead an observer to wonder whether the changes are semantic or substantive.) A summary on implementation progress states the following:

> *Innovation and technological progress are key to finding lasting solutions to both economic and environmentalchallenges, such as increased resource and energy-efficiency. ...[M]ore than half of the world's population is now online and almost the entire world population lives in an area covered by a mobile network. It is estimated that in 2019, 96.5 per cent were covered by at least a 2G network.*[18]

The United Nations Economic and Social Counsel, in April 2019, updated several SDG metrics, among them:

- 53.6% of individuals, or 4.1 billion people, use the Internet, ranging from only 20% in Oceania (excluding Australia and New Zealand) and 26% in sub-Saharan African to 84% in Europe andNorthern America and 87% in Australia and New Zealand;

- Fixed-broadband continued to increase, with almost 15 fixed-broadband subscriptions for every 100 inhabitants, ranging from 33.6 in developed countries to only 11.2 in developing countries;

- There were virtually no fixed-broadband connections in least developed countries, due to high cost and lack of infrastructure.[19]

Having quantitative data is one thing, understanding what it means is another. Garrido and Fellowspropose four elements of to assess the effectiveness goals related to "Development and Access to Information" (DA2I).

1. Access to information and communication infrastructure;
2. social context of use;
3. capabilities (such as a population's knowledge, skills, and resources); and
4. the legal and policy landscape.[20]

These four benchmarks can be used regardless of what is being analyzed, be it a specific technology, a group of people, an entire nation, and so forth.[21]

Technology, of course, does not exist in a vacuum; its adoption and use requires an individual to be able to access it and be sufficiently skilled in its use. Many factors influence an individual's ability to do this. Jan A.G.M. van Dijk put forth a "relational" theory, which attempts to balance an individual in relation to other actors, helps to contextualize the challenges.[22] As the author stated, "All too often, the metaphor of the digital divide suggests a yawning gap and the absolute exclusion of certain people."[23] There, instead, relationships, between people, between technology, between different people and different technologies, etc. that result in either the presence or absence of a digital gap. Prime units are not individuals but rather the positions of individuals and relationships that surround them, making inequality the results of differences between these groups.[24] Thus, while the physical hardware is without a doubt important, so is the social structure determining how, or if, it can be used.

Many of the undersea cables being laid are intended to connect various regions of Africa.[25] That continent without a doubt has given rise to many impressive tech developments, especially those using mobile phone, rather than computer, technology.[26] These successes, as Hazeley detailed, were developed locally and in response to local situations.[27] They have, however, been few and far between, as the region continues to be plagued by various impediments, while mobile phones have inherent computing weaknesses compared to computers.[28] Similarly, the Continent has seen the rise of a number of tech incubators, mostly centered on a few coastal cities. These hubs, however, face several challenges, including lack of infrastructure, access to capital, and scant legal frameworks to guide innovation.[29]

Reflecting on experiences in India, researcher Kentaro Toyoma's succinctly articulated the disjunction between quantifiable expectations of technology deployment and reality. He cited two factors that gave rise to the "Information and Communication for Development" (ICT4D) movement: 1) international development players eager to find new solutions to longstanding problems in the developing world, and 2) the tech industry's dual interest in emerging markets and philanthropy.[30] As he stated, "… technology's effects were wholly dependent on the intention and capacity of the people handling it," specifying that regardless of design, technology "is only a magnifier of human intent and capacity. It is not a substitute."[31]

TMS Ruge, the founder of Hive Colab, Uganda's first tech hub, expressed that philanthropical notions without an understanding of local needs "…erode the ability to deal with this problem." He posed the question, "wouldn't it be better to invest money into indigenous companies…therefore maintaining a sustainable business…?"[32] While his remark, made over a decade ago, specifically referred to Western celebrities distributing mosquito nets instead of encouraging the development of local industries to meet problems as local define them, applies equally to technological initiatives based on certain presumptions.[33]

Technology that is incongruent with a community's ability to learn and leverage—considering infrastructure, extraneous factors of electricity reliability, and education—is unlikely to succeed longterm. Any organization, whether a government agency, a non-profit, or a global corporation, that pushes a specific quantifiable objective, especially when those managing it have limited time in- country and approach a project from the viewpoint of their own expectations, will likely not succeed.

While increased bandwidth is certainly needed throughout much of the world, it remains to be seenif undersea cabling initiatives will reduce the digital divide. There is no doubt that there is a village. The question is how much of the world is in that village, or whether they are in the same village.

The Dubious Merits of Meritocracy

AUTHOR: Melanie Keane

PUBLISHED: September 2019

WRITTEN: March 2019

KEYWORDS: Criminal Justice; Societal Bias; Meritocracy; Equality

ABSTRACT:

This paper discusses the prevalence and impact of the social norm of meritocracy in a variety of social contexts, including the workplace and in the criminal justice system. The paper explores the substantial body of research that reveals how meritocracy is associated with increased acceptance of inequality as well as negative attitudes.

"The criminal justice system in the U.S. treats you better if you're rich and guilty than if you're poor and innocent."[1] So said United States Senator and 2020-election Presidential candidate Cory Booker after the sentencing of political consultant Paul Manafort for fraud and tax evasion to 47 months in prison. In the wake of the sentencing, Booker and other policy experts criticized the short term as unjust due to its leniency, particularly given that federal sentencing guidelines recommend 19 to 24 years in prison for such crimes.[2]

To Booker, the sentence reveals a deep-seated flaw in the United States criminal justice system that favors the wealthy and condemns the poor, thereby violating our nation's creed of "liberty and justice for all." According to

Booker, "you can tell a lot about a country by the way it incarcerates."[3] He exemplifies this point by citing trends in countries like Russia to imprison political opposition, trends in countries like Turkey to imprison the media, and trends in the United States to incarcerate "the poor, the addicted, the mentally ill, the survivors of abuse and sexual assault, and black and brown people."[4]

Indeed, social scientists have discovered that ethnic minorities are incarcerated to a much greater extent than whites, despite similar rates of criminal behavior between groups across a variety of offenses.[5] Specifically, African Americans, Puerto Rican Americans, and Native Americans represent the highest incarceration rates of any ethnic group, thereby suggesting a disproportionate impact of criminal justice on certain populations.[6] A series of studies extending from 1998 to 2004 assessed the impact of race on criminal sentencing among black and white defendants, and discovered that the former tend to receive harsher criminal sentences, including a greater likelihood of being sentenced to death.[7]

Also worth noting is the degree to which incarceration occurs in the United States relative to other countries. According to the International Center for Prison Studies, one-third of all women incarcerated in the world in 2013 were based in the United States.[8] Although the First Step Act represents bipartisan consensus that reform is necessary to the nation's criminal justice system, enduring progress will require a level of examination that extends beyond the language of law into the social, cultural, and psychological factors that breed inequality. The goal of this paper is therefore to explore such factors in the context of ethical frameworks.

Considerable research has been conducted to assess the prevalence and impact of implicit bias in a variety of social contexts, much of which reveal daily patterns of discriminatory attitudes and behavior toward racial and ethnic minority groups. With regard to law enforcement, for example, studies reveal that black individuals are shot by police more quickly and frequently than white individuals – a phenomena referred to as "shooter bias."[9] In studies of the "trolley dilemma," homeless and drug addicted individuals are generally perceived by participants as more "acceptable" to sacrifice than individuals of higher social status,[10] and in the context of health care, studies reveal patterns of discriminatory practices toward black and other ethnic groups.[11]

Although considerable attention is paid to the impact of implicit prejudice in these studies, less investigation seems to surround the underlying factors that form group-based prejudice. Through what lens do we perceive, justify, and perpetuate status differences among racial and ethnic groups? The course of this research has led me to consider one factor in particular: the social norm of meritocracy.

Cambridge Dictionary defines meritocracy as "a social system, society, or organization in which people get success or power because of their abilities, not because of their money or social position." Meritocracy has been exalted at both ends of the political spectrum in the United States for creating an 'even playing field' that provides citizens with equal opportunities to achieve social mobility and economic success. As such, meritocracy is widely perceived to be an impartial system that affords social status and rewards to individuals on the basis of their talent and hard work rather than sex, race, or social class.[12] As researcher Gonçalo Santos Freitas cites, meritocracy "encourages people to work hard and reach their potential, which will result in benefits not only for the individual but also for society, as it reduces corruption and improves rates of economic growth."[13]

Not only is meritocracy extoled in theory, research suggests that it is considered by most Americans to represent a common practice. A 2016 study of social attitudes by the Brookings Institute indicates that 69 percent of Americans agree with the statement that "people are rewarded for intelligence and skill."[14] The response represents the highest percentage of 27 participant countries and illustrates the extent to which Americans believe that economic rewards follow the merits of effort, intelligence, and skill.[15] Of course, adoption of meritocracy is not exclusive to the United States. According to a 2009 survey of British social attitudes, 84 percent of respondents consider hard work to be 'essential' or 'very important' to the attainment of success.[16]

As a social ideal, meritocracy follows the "Fairness or Justice Approach," which argues that all individuals should be treated equally.[17] However, as moral philosopher Tom Regan states, an ideal moral judgment is just that – an ideal. Despite its perceived virtues, a substantial body of research reveals that meritocracy is associated with "higher justifications and stronger acceptance of inequality," as well as negative attitudes toward low status groups.[18] For example, a 2015 experiment revealed that participants demonstrated considerably less support for programs that attempt to reduce social inequality when primed with status-legitimizing beliefs.[19]

A similar study conducted by economists at the University of Minnesota and Maastricht University in the Netherlands revealed that subjects who participated in games of skill were less inclined to redistribute prizes than participants who engaged in games of chance.[20] A comparable study by Beijing Normal University discovered that participants in a game of skill were more likely to support earned entitlements if they were on the receiving end, suggesting a tendency to evaluate merit in self-serving ways.[21] Finally, three experiments conducted among 445 participants revealed that managers in meritocratic organizations tend to distribute greater rewards to male employees over equally qualified female employees.[22] By contrast, such bias was not identified among organizations that did not explicitly adopt meritocracy as a core value. The experiments found that managers tend to evaluate candidates based on who they *feel* has the greatest potential or most closely mirrors themselves – even if they are unaware, thus perpetuating the status quo through implicit bias.[23]

Taken in the context of criminal justice, meritocracy may engender unfavorable decisions toward low status groups, who are more likely to be considered guilty and sentenced to harsher penalties than high status groups.[24] Multiple studies reveal a pattern of bias in criminal and legal decisions due to stereotypical associations between race and certain crimes.[25] Participants of one study, for example, were found more likely to attribute a defendant's behavior to external factors if the crime was not typical of his or her race. Conversely, participants imposed more severe penalties on defendants who were charged with crimes perceived to be typical of their race.[26]

The collective findings of these studies are both surprising and ironic, given the 'even playing field' that meritocracy intends to promote. According to Castilla and Benard, a "paradox of meritocracy" occurs due to an inflated sense of judiciousness that accompanies merit-based practices, along with a general failure to examine implicit bias.[27] In the context of social reform, meritocracy can engender an indifferent if not punitive attitude toward poor and marginalized populations whose misfortune is haphazardly attributed to personal defects rather than systemic issues and, of course, the vagaries of chance.

In terms of rationale, meritocracy ignores the perennial function of chance in the equation of one's success or failure, and appeals to uncritical assumptions that "the rich are rich because they are talented and hard-working, and the poor are poor because they are ineffective, lazy and weak.[28] As a consequence of these assumptions and the ensuing belief that social status is a reflection of one's merit, meritocracy often serves to legitimize status differences and justify the status quo.[29]

In the context of more recent events, the authenticity of meritocracy has been called into question following a college admissions scandal announced in March 2019 by the Justice Department in which wealthy parents paid millions of dollars in bribes from 2012 to 2018 to place their children in prestigious universities.[30] Therefore, from the perspective of ethical frameworks, while meritocracy may rhyme with the approach of "Fairness and Justice," history reveals a pattern of the opposite.

Worth noting is that the term meritocracy was coined by British sociologist and politician Michael Young in a dystopic novel that he published in 1958 entitled *The Rise of Meritocracy*.[31] The novel was intended as a social satire that depicts a world in which social class is replaced by a hierarchy that rewards individuals based on rigid testing standards, which ultimately reestablishes the old class system and leads to revolt. According to the author one year before his death, the book was intended to be a warning.[32]

In basic terms, meritocracy poses a problem due to the fact that, as philosopher Alain de Button succinctly stated in a 2009 TED Talk, "we are surrounded by snobs."[33] De Button defines a snob as "anybody who takes a small part of you [be it merit-based or otherwise] and uses that to come to a complete vision of who you are." He further suggests that while society in the United States embodies a spirit of equality – often in the name of meritocracy – its history reflects deep inequalities that carry profound psychological implications.

For example, De Button cites a correlation between "a society that tells people they can achieve anything and the existence of low self-esteem," which is reflected in rising rates of suicide and depression among developed countries with individualistic cultures such as the United States. As a consequence of meritocracy and the emphasis placed on individual success or failure, "Your position in life seems not accidental but merited and deserved, which makes failure seem devastating."[34]

Given the substantive issues related to meritocracy, society may benefit from complimenting the Fairness and Justice Approach with something akin to the Common Good Approach, which states that "the interlocking relationships of society are the basis of ethical reasoning" and that "respect and compassion for all others -- **especially the vulnerable** -- are requirements of such reasoning."[35]

Within society, differences of elevation among people are inevitable. However, differences in social rank should not be random or unjust as this would likely lead to class struggles. By adhering to the Common Good Approach, individuals may be more inclined to support laws that promote the welfare of everyone as opposed to an elite minority. Through this perspective, society may be more capable of identifying "common conditions that are important to the welfare of everyone," including underrepresented populations, which studies reveal are often more vulnerable to systemic abuse.

Given the complexity and deeply-embedded nature of these issues, no single solution is likely to be effective, although the first, most practical step would seem to be acknowledging the dubious merits of meritocracy itself. Philosopher Richard Rorty speculated that the best chance we have of social reform is to eschew the dogma that only ideology can replace ideology, as well as the assumption that there must be one theoretical solution to problems of social injustice.[36] This, he argues, may encourage more reformist experiments.

SECTION FOUR

Targeted Organizational Risks

PAPER	AUTHOR
Accenture's Technology Vision 2020 for Innovative DNA	Sophia Werner
Amazon Prime Air: A Disaster Waiting to Happen?	Greyson Fields
Apple's Security & Privacy Practices	Raphael Kyle Caoile Manansala
Deepfakes on Instagram: Mitigating Event and Process Risk	Kate Peterson
GDPR Enforcement and Google's €50 Million Fine	Alex Osuch
Huawei Company Risk Management	Bingyan Wang
Kyoto Animation Arson Attack Risk Analysis	Bingyan Wang
NASDAQ's Exploration into Blockchain Technology	Allessandra Quevedo
The Evolution of Aadhar in India	Ashritha Dsouza

Accenture's Technology Vision 2020 for Innovation DNA: Can It Better Both Revenue and User Security?

AUTHOR: Sophia Werner

PUBLISHED: May, 2021

WRITTEN: May, 2020

KEYWORDS: Accenture; Consulting; Innovation; Cybersecurity

ABSTRACT:
This paper discusses how over three fourths of C-level executives believe that the stakes for innovation have never been higher. Yet, the world has also seen a rise in concern and expectation for handling security and privacy. Accenture's Technology Vision 2020 pushes for ideas that will take C-level companies' innovation in the right direction. It is a vision that advocates for constant innovation realized on a systems level and commoditized beyond its original purpose. As long as Accenture communicates that the company's brand image should be at the pinnacle, that innovation is done meticulously, and that updates are frequent, Technology Vision 2020 may also help reach the security and privacy levels the world has begun to demand as well.

There is no question the world has seen a digital take over in the last few decades. C-level companies have created a smattering of information, technology, and data focused "C" positions (CIO, CISO, etc.) and actively account for an innovation budget in their yearly reviews. In fact, over three fourths of executives believe that the stakes for innovation have never been higher.[1] Yet, the world has also seen a rise in concern and expectation for handling security and privacy. 92% of consumers feel companies are responsible and should be proactive in protecting their data.[2] As the world goes into the new decade, Accenture pieces together recommendations for how their clients can continue to increase their bottom line - Technology Vision 2020. A vision that pushes constant innovation realized on a systems level and commoditized beyond its original purpose. I believe Accenture's recommendation will increase company revenue and address security concerns in turn - so long as Accenture communicates that the brand image is at the pinnacle, innovation is done meticulously, and updates are frequent.

This paper will begin with a description of Accenture's Technology Vision 2020, specifically its most risky pillar, followed by an assessment of how supported an idea it is, and then transition to the security risks that underlie the specific pillar's vision, and why I believe that despite the risks, the successful implementation of the Accenture Technology Vision 2020 can and will increase both revenue and security.

Accenture's Technology Vision 2020 states that in order for their clients to continue to lead into the new decade, these companies must "redefine the intersection between people and technology," look to the future rather than "playbooks from the past" for their technology solutions, and resolve these disconnects.[3] The plan is broken into five pillars, but "Innovation DNA: Create an Engine for Continuous Innovation," the final pillar, acts as the backbone with the most revenue potential.

Innovation DNA speaks to the "DNA" or underlying systems, software, and technologies that determine how a company will grow. The three "building blocks" that create this unique company DNA are maturing digital technologies, scientific advancements or partnerships, and emerging distributed ledgers, artificial intelligence, extended reality, and quantum computing (DARQ). Maturing digital technologies can be thought of as advanced transformations similar to Starbucks loyalty and membership programs - technologies that companies could make a profit from or create commodities out of their advancements. Scientific advancements allow for Accenture's clients to partner with or utilize scientific breakthroughs to achieve a greater competitive advantage.[4] One example being Warner Bros. partnering with Project Silica to store and retrieve the entire 1978 "Superman" movie on quartz glass.[5] Finally, DARQ provides clients marketable, consumer digestible, and relevant technological advances that their consumers expect and desire.[6] Accenture firmly believes these three factors merged with the current core competencies of a business will not only differentiate their clients from competitors but also potentially craft entirely new markets, and they have the statistics to support them.[7]

In 2018 Accenture conducted a 8,356 company survey of C-level executives that compelled them to create "Innovation DNA." In the study those companies deemed "leading" adopted technologies that supported architectural decoupling and outpaced competitors 97% to 30%. They were also, on average, two and a half times more likely to adopt DARQ technologies.[8] Meanwhile "laggard" companies, those who did not advance or only advanced to fill point-solutions, experienced two to three times *lower* revenue growth than those that implemented DARQ and architectural decoupling advancements as system wide solutions.[9][10] If that was not reason enough James Wilson explained that this achievement gap is only set to exponentially widen in the next few years. By 2023 the revenue gap could be as wide as forty-six percent.[11] With all of this data it is no wonder Accenture recommends building an innovative and unique DNA backbone. The potential for increased revenue is obvious. The potential for security breaches, though, can seem almost as apparent at first glance.

Every step in building Accenture's proposed innovative DNA backbone holds cybersecurity challenges and risks for Accenture clients. Commoditizing mature digital technologies exposes a company's software to potential threats by involving third parties and outside influences. Not to mention the risk for misuse of a product to fill unintended needs by the purchaser.[12] Partnerships with outside research for scientific advancement and competitive advantages involve the risk of misaligned security and privacy requirements between partnering researchers resulting in (occasionally unintentional) insecure solutions, and DARQ adoption holds a myriad of OWASP Top Ten vulnerabilities, potential lawsuits, and even more outside/third party misalignment possibilities. Coupling all of these risks with a lack of federal regulation or legislation on the legal implementation of the three backbone elements pose serious security challenges.

When it comes to commoditizing individual mature digital technologies, Accenture clients have experienced risks and security advancements. For example, as Starbucks commoditizes their membership and loyalty application, they make their product more reliable, scalable, and cost-effective, but they also cause disruption in the market - one that attracts attackers.[13] This forces Starbucks to take their security seriously through steps such as their current bug bounty hunt, hiring outside security vendors, and keeping the most private information (security architecture, engineering, and United States app development) in-house.[14] Commoditizing their technologies pose a threat. Accenture and Starbucks realized and received the true revenue potential because they took the risks with planned steps to protect themselves and their customers.

Similarly, adopting mature technologies is becoming essential to companies' bottom lines. Data analytics and big data investments are nearly universal among every Fortune 1000 company today, and 94% of respondents from a NewVantage Partners Big Data and AI survey admit using a cloud service (84% with multi-cloud storage).[15] With the adoption of cloud services and outside data analytics companies comes the potential for weaknesses unbeknownst to the hiring company. Accenture combats this with their excellent relationships and interview process to recommend the best suited third-party mature technologies to their clients.

Facing the cybersecurity risks and pains associated with partnerships and scientific advancement are companies like Anheuser-Busch and Indigo Agriculture. They are "[leveraging] microbiology and data-driven analytics to make agriculture more sustainable and profitable," to improve farming margins.[16] These companies face the potential of leaked or stolen grower information such as addresses and other identifiable information. Their data analytics and collection mechanisms must be dually protected and shared across secure networks/lines.[17] They also deal with the impending challenge of transporting their findings and solutions to other countries where data protection and other cyber security laws are more advanced (think GDPR in the EU). While the agricultural sector is not the most at-risk for data leaks or attacks, Anheuser-Busch and Indigo Agriculture have taken precautions that are scalable and meaningful.

Finally, and most tangibly, the adoption of DARQ is the most publicized and therefore easiest to learn about and plan an attack by outside influences, but it also has some of the greatest protections. Facebook Reality Labs and Oculus paired AI image recognition with XR experiences to create their "Real World Index."[18] The obvious threats of playing indoors and outdoors in real-time captured images can manifest itself beyond cyberspace and into the physical realm if misused. Malicious actors can attack the system and create images unlike real-life and disrupt the business not to mention harm innocent users, and finally with such detail being focused on the formation of a new and market disruptive technology comes the chance for basic security measures to be forgotten. The chance for human error in every aspect is astronomical.[19] Yet, these companies are taking extreme caution, meticulously testing, and funding for security specifically because they have the time and energy to; that is the sole purpose of an innovation lab.

Looking at the potential for success and taking into account the number of risks, I recommend Accenture encourage their clients to first hold their brand at the center of all of their decisions. Every brand is founded on client/consumer trust, satisfaction, and loyalty. Failing to protect any system that underlies the basic DNA of the company, whether it releases consumer information or not, can cause catastrophic backlash not to mention potential legal battles.[20] Again, Starbucks cites their brand image as their driving force behind security measures, and the work they have done post-security breach in 2017 supports its effectiveness.[21]

Second, I recommend Accenture urge their clients to innovate intentionally. Intentional innovation sounds like an oxymoron. The two are usually mutually exclusive, but intentional innovation in 2020 means taking time during each decision and step to protect and secure the work. Often in the development world the creation and completion of an application comes before the securing of it. This human error is sited by all in the cybersecurity field as the number one cause of faults. Protecting and/or discussing security constraints throughout the process limits and accounts for much of the human error and allows a multitude of people (almost everyone from every team, planning, developing, debugging, etc.) to voice their opinions and identify a wider variety of threats.

The third and final recommendation I have is for Accenture to leave their clients with the understanding that any released or adopted technologies (mature, DARQ, or otherwise) be continuously monitored similarly to how Starbucks released their bug bounty. This active search and seizure of threats, bugs, etc. defend against cyber attacks as well as physical or legal battles. I would advocate for a full time security position or team (depending on size of adopted/released technology) for the first three to six months before weaning off as the company sees fit. Not one of Accenture's clients, or a product that has adopted any of these three DNA steps is Zoom. Yet, Zoom is quickly rising in the ranks because of its dedication to security and its ability to listen and respond to users providing updates and precautions that have strengthened their site. I feel if more companies were to do this the adoption or commoditizing process would go more smoothly.

All three aspects of a business's DNA backbone intermingles and poses risks sometimes as powerful as the benefits. I believe if Accenture pushes their companies to follow my three recommendations - innovate meticulously, update frequently, and hold the company's brand image above all else - the potential revenue and safety companies will bring into the new decade will be astounding.

Amazon Prime Air: A Disaster Waiting to Happen?

AUTHOR: Greyson Fields

PUBLISHED: July 2021

WRITTEN: December 2020

KEYWORDS: e-commerce; Amazon; supply chain; consumer behavior

ABSTRACT:
This paper discusses the potential rewards and numerous risks Amazon faces as the technology firm pursues the implementation of Prime Air, an ultra-fast e-commerce delivery solution. The successful operationalization of Prime Air will result in the speedy delivery of consumer goods via drones—but to achieve this, Amazon will need to mitigate public safety risks; physical property damage risks; and system integration and process coordination risks. Recommendations include applying the RACI tool—at a large scale—to increase the likelihood of Amazon succeeding in this innovation effort.

The COVID-19 pandemic made 2020 an unconventional year in many ways—it also allowed big-technology companies to be immensely successful. Stock prices soared to new heights and corporate revenues shot into the sky as many people spiraled into consumer spending frenzies after being couped up at home in a way never previously experienced by most. Amazon's stock increased 75 percent year-to-date in October 2020 compared to the same period in 2019,[1] as home-deliveries reached record highs. Amazon is a behemoth conglomerate that controls myriad facets of e-commerce, especially in America. Much of Amazon's success is attributed to the success of one particular business line: Amazon Prime.

A subscription to Amazon Prime unlocks many benefits for consumers, including Prime Video, Prime Music, and a growing list of other services. Most notably, it gives members access to free shipping on e-commerce purchases—regardless of dollar value—that promises two-day, one-day, or even same-day delivery. Many customers find the speed of delivery highly desirable and increasingly expect same-day delivery to be an option. A survey by consulting firm Invesp found that 56 percent of online customers between the age of 18 and 34 expect to have same-day delivery available. However, only 61 percent of customers are willing to pay more for same-day delivery.[2]

Does it stop there? What is the limit to delivery speed that customers desire and retailers will provide? In 2013, Amazon's CEO Jeff Bezos told "60 Minutes" that he expected drones would be flying deliveries to customers' homes within five years.[3] At the end of 2020, Amazon has continued exploration and investment into this delivery option that could further set itself apart from competitors. Prime Air is the "future delivery system" designed to deliver packages up to 5 pounds within 30 minutes using unmanned aerial vehicles (drones). The challenge will be implementing a service that can meet the expectations while also planning for and responding to Basel framework risks stemming from people, process, systems, and external events.[4] Prime

Air delivery includes multiple inherent risks that Amazon will need to address.

Risks to Public Safety

The deployment of Prime Air will require the use a fleet of drones capable of flying sufficiently long distances while carrying packages 5 pounds or less. Subsequently, these drones must be supported by a sufficient energy-source (e.g. a battery) that which would likely increase the weight of a drone. The drones would likely deploy from current Amazon fulfillment centers—at least in the beginning phases—which are often in dense population areas. If a drone were to malfunction and crash, the possibility of seriously injuring a person is extremely high. Drone delivery has faced large public and media backlash due to individual hobbyist drones injuring people. For example, a drone hit the top of the Space Needle in Seattle and knocked a woman unconscious.[5] Planning for public safety should be Amazon's number one priority to gain the public's trust, especially in its hometown of Seattle.

Risks to Physical Assets

Amazon will also need to plan to mitigate the risk of damage to physical assets—both the drones themselves and the packages that the drones are transporting. Amazon has invested heavily into the research and development of drone technology to ensure the innovation of drones capable of transporting packages of the size and of the distance it claims. It is uncertain if Amazon will manufacture the drones themselves or through a third party. Regardless, it's almost guaranteed that these drones will require a significant investment. Amazon should plan to include features such as the drones possessing high-definition cameras to record every aspect of the delivery if the drone is damaged or the package it is carrying is stolen/damaged/lost. As household drones have become more popular, a growing portion of the population has become wary of drones and their perceived purpose—some individuals have shot drones out of the air after becoming suspicious of malpractice.[6]

RISKS TO SYSTEM INTEGRATION AND PROCESS COORDINATION

Related to damage of physical assets, Amazon will also need to account for execution, delivery, and process management risk. The successful operation of Prime Air will depend on large, complicated information technology systems and the smooth interaction of many complicated processes working in tandem to successfully deliver the correct packages to the correct locations within the delivery window. This process would involve the loading of the package onto the drone, drone flight to the delivery location, drop-off of the package, and successful return to the take-off location. Amazon warehouses would have to segregate areas where this process will occur, possibly forcing Amazon to expand or purchase new land to host drone flights. A process of this size presents a large investment, many points of failure, and will require a large volume and velocity of data to operate an Internet of Things[7] "Smart Delivery" network. Furthermore, if there's any mishap during the delivery process, Amazon risks financial loss and reputational damage if service level Prime customers are not satisfied with the service or if a potential bad actor event disrupts the promised speedy drone delivery.

REGULATORY RISKS

While the desired new delivery process is speedy, the process of securing government approval is often much slower. One of the primary reasons it has taken Amazon so long to bring Prime Air to fruition is due to FAA oversight of the issue. The FAA, or Federal Aviation Administration, is the governmental entity that is responsible for regulating civil aviation to promote safety,[8] including commercial drone delivery. Amazon has been battling regulatory issues that prohibit the use of drone delivery for years. Although, in August 2020 the FAA cleared Amazon to move forward with its fleet of Prime Air delivery drones, granting certification under Part 135 of FAA guidelines.[9] This certification gives Amazon the ability to carry property on small drones "beyond the visual line of sight," which is currently a requirement for household drones. The FAA's main aspiration is to promote safety while encouraging innovation by enacting Part 135.

Participants of Part 135 must prove their concepts through a 5-phase certification process: pre-application, formal application, design assessment, performance assessment, and administrative functions.[10] Each phase must be completed before moving onto the next phase. Through this certification process, participants are awarded one of four types of certificates: Part 135 Single Pilot, Single Pilot in Command, Basic operator certificate, and Standard operator certificate.[11] The certification process is rigorous so that it can validate that pilots are adequately qualified to pilot drones. Although, Amazon would most likely have an automated flight path or something similar.

Recommendations

Considering the multiple angles of risk that Prime Air emulates, analyzing this issue from a conservative risk management point of view is the best approach. Applying the RACI tool, offer three recommendations are appropriate as Amazon moves forward with Prime Air delivery by implementing policies and procedures that will define who is responsible, who is accountable, who to consult, and who to inform.[12]

First, Amazon should continue investing or increase its investment into the safety of its drone fleet to mitigate its business and personal liability risk. In the case of a drone crash or accident, Amazon could expect to pay large settlements depending on the severity of the injury and incident. Safety should be the number one priority with this new method of delivery. By this, Amazon should enact an oversight team of managers that lead the development of safety features of the drones, the drone network, and deployment of drone deliveries. In addition, Amazon should have a team—if it does not exist already—to directly interact with the FAA to ensure that Amazon has met or exceed all requirements of Part 135, which would further validate the safety of the delivery process.

Second, Amazon should have preventative measures in the case of packages not being delivered and drones being damaged, reducing its damage to physical assets risk. The investment into development, manufacturing, and maintenance of these delivery drones is costly and is something that Amazon needs to protect. Applying the RACI tool to this issue will set clear boundaries around the process and people for which are responsible and accountable for package and drone assurance. As stated earlier, 61 percent of consumers are willing to pay for same-day delivery. For Amazon Prime, this would be the main selling point of Prime as customers will receive packages faster than ever before. It would be devastating to Amazon's Prime business in the case of customers using drone delivery but are unable to receive packages due to bad actors or external events. Furthermore, Amazon's investment into its drones will be significant. Thus, there must be protection and contingency plans in the case of drones or packages are damaged during delivery.

Third, Amazon must have a plan to minimize its execution, delivery, and process risk. It is expected that Amazon is investing heavily in the research and development of a drone flight network and software systems that will manage the tracking, takeoff, delivery, and return of the drones. This process will take a lot of time and money to train those responsible for it. Amazon should focus a large amount of its investment on ensuring that the delivery process of packages is as smooth, efficient, and operationally "bulletproof" as possible.

Conclusion

Amazon believes that Prime Air is the future of delivery services. In fact, multiple other companies are also bringing drone delivery as service offerings including Alphabet's Wing and UPS Drone Delivery.[13] In Amazon's situation, it is paying large sums of money of shipping costs, more than $47 billion over the last four quarters.[14] With Amazon Prime Air delivery, Amazon would reduce the costs associated with its current delivery services such as vehicles, drivers, and fuel. With this shift, Amazon could potentially save money but will face numerous risks. Most notably, Amazon will face: business and personal liability risk, damage to physical property risk, and lastly, execution, delivery, and process risk. Applying the RACI tool—at a large scale—Amazon can increase the likelihood that it will fly into the future of deliveries as a leader in ultra-fast e-commerce delivery solutions, similar to most of the areas of business it acquires.

Apple's Security & Privacy Practices

AUTHOR: Raphael Kyle Caoile Manansala

PUBLISHED: December 2020

WRITTEN: March 2020

KEYWORDS: Apple, security, privacy, artificial intelligence, privacy by design, Internet of Things, encryption, iPhone, iPad, iCloud, Apple Watch, HomePod, Home Kit, Siri, Hey Siri, Apple Maps, biometric authentication, MacBook

ABSTRACT:
Apple has become an industry leader – not just in the smartphone business – but also in its privacy and security practices. This happened by accident when the U.S. Government started demanding Apple weaken its iPhone operating system (iOS) for law enforcement to gain access to its data. Since its 2014 iteration of iOS, also known as iOS 8, Apple took an unprecedented step of introducing full-disk encryption as a feature dubbed as Data Protection when an iPhone user sets a passcode lock. This pioneered the idea in Silicon Valley that the data on smart technology devices like the iPhone belonging to its users. Apple has been known for its attention to detail. As we further explore its design decisions, we will see just how Apple took careful considerations in making decisions based on the security and privacy of its customers.

Privacy by Design

Apple's design principle of privacy by default is that which permeates Apple's technology by only collecting the minimum amount of data necessary in providing a product or service – known as data minimalization.[1] With the introduction of the iPhone 4S in 2011, this created a new sector in the technology industry for smart digital assistants like Siri. The development of Siri took severe considerations in the privacy of Apple's customers. The iPhone 6 added another feature called "Hey Siri" for the hands-free activation of Siri. When this feature is enabled on any Apple device, it uses an always-on, low-power processor for continuous on-device machine learning.[ii] The iPhone only sends the person's words to an Apple remote server after "Hey Siri" is detected locally and activated [2]. It does not send everything the device hears, and most of the listening data is stored temporarily on the device itself. Apple has addressed the complication of using an Apple Watch – a device with significantly smaller hardware – by having the "Hey Siri" detector to only run when the watch's motion coprocessor detects a wrist raise gesture that turns the screen on.[3] The onboarding process of setting up a new iPhone personalizes "Hey Siri" by helping the iPhone understand who to listen to for the prompt to reduce the false triggers when "Hey Siri" is spoken by someone else and cutting similar-sounding phrases. [iii] This "explicit enrollment" into Siri learning your voice is used to determine your voice under ideal conditions, and its ability to recognize your voice under other circumstances with varying ambient noises uses continuous learning that improves the more a user uses Siri. On Apple's server-side, it first checks what the first words are ("Hey Siri") and then sends cancellation signals back to the device if the server determines a false trigger, abandoning the proceeding data [iii]. Apple took on the challenge of voice recognition done locally on the iPhone for the sole purpose of preserving the privacy of its users. The alternative would have been to send all the recordings received on an iPhone to a remote server to recognize "Hey Siri," which is how Amazon's Alexa does all its speech recognition.[4] The question of "Is Apple listening and recording me all the time?" can be with a "Yes – but" or "Probably not," knowing that Siri is only listening after a confirmed "Hey Siri" activation or manually activated. Apple also took note of the motion and proximity sensors on their devices to determine implicit behaviors of when a user does not want Siri ever to be prompted. "Hey Siri" does not work when an Apple device is facing down or when it is covered, which includes when it is in your pocket or your bag. [5] Siri can only be prompted when it is out of your pocket or bag and is facing up. This, on top of Siri learning to only listen to the user for "Hey Siri," dramatically reduces the data stored on Apple's servers, overall.

Apple started adding biometric authentication to its devices with the introduction of the iPhone 5S (2013) using a fingerprint sensor called Touch ID and the iPhone X (2017) using facial recognition called Face ID. This biometric information is encrypted in the Secure Enclave that never leaves the device and uses on-device machine learning to improve its accuracy over time. The iteration of Face ID remains resilient to anti-spoofing and false matches by using a True Depth camera mechanism that projects over 30,000 infrared dots to create a 3D map of the user's face and capturing an infrared image [6]. With the use of on-device machine learning, it adapts to natural changes of the user's face, such as facial hair growth and fashion choices. This is way ahead of other Android competitors in the market. Most Android smartphones with facial recognition rely on 2D facial mapping methods, which can be fooled with a 3D-printed head.[7]

The most recent advancement on the MacBook side of Apple is its latest T2 security chip. This works similarly to the Secure Element found in iPhones, where it is responsible for the secure booting of the operating system and disk encryption. However, the MacBook lineup made from 2019 and later implemented a hardware microphone disconnect mechanism when the MacBook lid is closed.[8] The T2 security chip is responsible for disconnecting the microphone on a hardware level. This mechanism prevents any software – even with root or kernel privileges in the operating system – from activating the microphone when the lid is closed.[viii]

The most infamous move towards security and privacy by Apple is their introduction of full-disk encryption enabled by default in 2014 with the release of iOS 8. Part of this was in response to the revelation of U.S. Government domestic surveillance programs as well as law enforcement pressuring technology companies into unlocking their smartphones.[9] U.S. Government agencies have since turned to third-party hackers into unlocking iPhones via brute-force methods.[10] However, Apple has remained vigilant in patching these exploits that third-party hackers use with the introduction of USB Restrictive Mode, where USB accessories do not work on the iPhone, iPad, and iPod Touch after an hour of not being unlocked [11]. These are some of the significant steps Apple has taken in protecting their customers' data from government entities.

Internet of Things

With the introduction of the HomePod in 2018, Apple entered the Internet of Things market with a smart home speaker. Most notably, it brought along the privacy and security measures built around Siri and Apple's Internet of Things management program – Home Kit. A thorough evaluation conducted by the Common Sense Privacy Program for Education stated that the device is the best for privacy – scoring 79 out of 100 in the overall and scoring high marks in data rights, tracking, sharing, and security.[12] The one major drawback about the HomePod, and its lack of success compared to other virtual assistants, is that it offers limited features and integration. This is partly due to the way Siri is designed, as mentioned previously, where Siri's machine learning intelligence is done on the device itself as much as possible. The HomePod never sells user data, share to third-party markets, feature behavioral ads, feature third-party tracking, tracks users, nor create an advertisement profile on its users.[xi]

Home Kit is stored on the highest level of security with end-to-end encryption, stored separately per user, and protected until the user authenticates [13]. This level of protection is the same as that which the U.S Justice Department is trying to weaken in aid of law enforcement because they, too, cannot decrypt this information. Minimal information about the home configuration is provided anonymously to Siri, like room names, accessories used, and scenes needed for command recognition that are not tied to any Apple ID. The information is processed locally on the HomePod or authorized iPhone as much as possible without sending it to Apple's servers. When data is processed and stored on Apple's servers, it is tied to a random anonymized identifier that is only used to improve Siri – never shared or sold. By default, Apple does not retain audio requests unless the user opts in to improve Siri. When they do, the audio sample is disassociated with the random identifier after six months.[14] A HomePod can be sold or given away simply by removing the accessory or resetting the HomePod – since information is stored on a per-user device basis on their iPhone, iPad, or iPod Touch.

Fundamentals in Artificial Intelligence

What sets Apple apart from a lot of tech companies is that most of their artificial intelligence (AI) is done locally on the device. This approach also draws them back when compared to the advances their other competitors have made when they store most of their data collection on the server-side. There are many quirks that Apple has deeply considered in protecting the privacy of its customers with their integration of artificial intelligence. For example, Quick Type, Apple's text-prediction algorithm, uses AI to predict a user's language behavior.[xiii] The language processing of a user's syntactical idiosyncrasies is done directly on the device. This includes messages that Siri reads aloud is done in real-time without sending it to Apple's servers.[xiii] When AI is used on the server-side, this is done with an anonymized random identifier, and operations like predictive suggestions in search or Safari is tied to a random identifier that is generated every 15 minutes.

Unlike Google Maps and its associated services like Waze, Apple Maps does not keep a profile of user movements and searches. Location data is minimized on Apple's servers, such as where you parked your car is stored only on the device-side.[xiii] Apple does not have access to your day-to-day whereabouts and your ETA; your data is synchronized with end-to-end encryption where only the user can access this information. For Apple Maps' location data that is sent to its servers, such as traffic data for server-side AI processing, Apple obscures your location history to a less-exact one after 24 hours – known as location fuzzing.[xiii]

Unlike Facebook and Google Photos in handling photo recognition AI, facial recognition, scene detection, and object detection are done entirely on the device itself instead of iCloud.[xiii] The Photos app's For You section is on-device generated content that is featured, such as sharing suggestions (i.e., x-Person is in the picture. Would you like to share it with them?), highlighting memories of past photos from some number of years related to the current date (i.e. "n-Photo(s) taken n-year(s) from today"), and displaying featured photos (i.e., n-Photos are highlights taken at x-location and are of high quality).[15] Pictures sorted based on individual persons use on-device facial recognition. The Search feature allows users to search based on the environment of an image with on-device scene classification. Using the photo editor is based on on-device image processing to adjust and fine-tune an image; editing a picture does not require uploading it to someplace. The lighting effects of Portrait Lighting mode and blurring effects of Portrait Mode are done using on-device AI to deliver studio-quality effects. Most importantly, the analysis of all photos and videos are not available to third parties and third-party applications as well – they only exist on the device inside Photos.[xiv]

Unlike Google Chrome, Safari uses on-device AI to prevent cross-site tracking by default [xiii]. This is done by consolidating data on a per-website basis so that third-party content is not used to track users, and data from other websites do not "follow" users. Social widgets embedded into websites can track users, even when the user does not interact with them. Safari blocks social widgets by default that can be used for social media to follow you even when you do not click on them [xii]. Websites are also able to use tactical methods known as device fingerprinting by creating a pseudo-profile of a user based on their device and browser configurations like fonts installed and plugins used. Safari prevents advertisers and websites from creating a digital fingerprint of users by only presenting a simplified system configuration that looks identical to other Safari users [xiii]. In theory, the more users using Safari as their browser on any Apple device, the more robust this system becomes of having "more of the same" users browsing a website. A certain level of anonymity is achieved by having a digital version of what Apple describes as "herd immunity."[16]

Apple's Potential Flaws and Recommendations for the Future

While Apple does implement privacy and security measures further than most of its competitors, there is still room for improvement in fortifying the security and privacy protections the company promises. As mentioned previously, Apple is vulnerable to all government demands internationally. In other words, the U.S. Government is not the only country wanting Apple to weaken its security and privacy mechanisms. Apple does comply to their fullest extent in aiding law enforcement investigations and government agencies by providing data Apple has on its servers. Apple has attempted to make everyone aware of this by publishing a transparency report. In their most recent January-June 2019 report, the U.S. Government has requested Apple on data for "4,796 devices; 918 financial identifiers; 3,619 accounts; 206 emergencies."[17] Apple has responded to 206 emergencies involving imminent danger of death or physical harm, such as missing persons. Apple has provided the government 918 financial identifiers involving payment card and gift card transactions, especially in cases of fraudulent transactions. Apple has provided information on 3,619 accounts, which include their Apple ID, email address, and content data; content data being data stored on Apple servers – on iCloud – such as emails, photos, iOS device backups, contacts, or calendars. (Content data on iCloud is arbitrary to the device's iCloud settings). All these numbers total to the 4,796 devices whose data has been handed over to the U.S. Government. We must take note that this report is only within six months and on the U.S. alone; the numbers are different for other foreign government entities and at different periods. My recommendation is to be prepared to counter these government demands. While some reasons for any government or law enforcement to demand Apple for data they have on its customers could be justifiable, there are some reasons where they are not. For example, the Chinese government has forced Apple to remove apps that aid Hong Kong protestors.[18] This puts Apple into a partisan conflict with Hong Kong and China's "one country, two systems," where Hong Kong citizens do have the right to assemble while mainland Chinese citizens do not.

Due to the U.S. Government's pressure on Apple to weaken its security and privacy policies, Apple has withdrawn its plans of implementing end-to-end encryption to iCloud data.[19] While all of Apple's user data is encrypted in iCloud and transit, Apple has the decryption key for some parts of iCloud on its users, which is what Apple provides to government agencies, as mentioned previously. With the lack of end-to-end encryption, this makes Apple users susceptible to government surveillance and rogue Apple insider actors. At this moment, on-device AI processing, Siri information, Home data, Health data, iCloud Keychain (password manager), Quick Type Keyboard learned vocabulary, payment information, screen time (the amount a user spends on apps), and Wi-Fi passwords are the only data that Apple cannot decrypt.[20] While data stored locally on Apple devices are inaccessible to Apple and difficult for government entities, this mechanism should be implemented across all iCloud data as well. Messages are an interesting caveat where Messages are end-to-end encrypted so long as iCloud backup is turned off because the encryption key for Messages is included in the backup.[XX] My recommendation to most Apple users is to limit the data they have on iCloud to only their contacts (because this is important), perhaps their calendar (because this may be used often by users), and the categories that are guaranteed to be encrypted from Apple or other entities. Apple device backups should be done locally on a Mac or Windows device where the user should opt-in to encrypt their backup as well – this method is not decryptable by Apple or government entities. Apple, as a company, should reconsider its plans of encrypting iCloud backups to where they cannot decrypt it – perhaps once the US Government eases their pressure on the company – as iCloud backups are convenient. For users that do opt-in to iCloud backing up their data, it is essential to consider how much data is stored and decryptable on iCloud. While some of the critical data sets are protected even from Apple, app data that is backed up into iCloud is vulnerable. The vital data inside third-party apps (apps not made by Apple or end-to-end protected from Apple) are susceptible to this, such as password manager apps, two-factor authenticator apps, messaging apps, cloud storage apps, health-related apps, financial-related apps, and shopping apps.

Conclusions on Apple's Closed Garden of Security and Privacy

What sets Apple apart from other companies is its use of security and privacy by design across all its ecosystem of Apple devices. This closed garden that Apple controls for their customers' safety, privacy, and peace of mind has made it easier for Apple to advance in privacy and security. Unlike other companies, Apple can govern and update its software and hardware, while their competitors usually have less control with one or the other. This allows them to take down apps quickly, roll out security patches ubiquitously, and end-of-life support on their devices is unprecedented. For example, the iPhone 6S – released in September 2015 with iOS 9 - is expected to be still able to receive updates well into September 2021 with iOS 14.[21] In its lengthiest end-of-life support, the iPhone 5S – release in September 2013 – and the second-generation iPad Mini – released in November 2013 – still got updates on its older iOS 12 operating system in early 2020. In contrast, only 10.4% of Android devices are running Android 9 (codenamed "Pie") nine months after its release in 2019 – the majority of which are only on devices purchased between 2018 and 2019 [22].

Since Apple's public defiance of the US Government demanding Apple to weaken its existing security and privacy standards, it has become Apple's selling point that data belongs to their customers, and they respect and encourage data autonomy. Most of the sources used in this research cite Apple's own published white papers and transparency reports on security and privacy design. While Siri is behind in comparison to the capabilities of Amazon Alexa or Google Assistant, most AI processes are done and stored locally as much as possible, preserving the privacy and security of users. The company has carefully considered privacy based on implicit human behavior of not wanting to be listened to by their virtual assistant, such as when an iPhone is facing down, in their bag or pocket, or when a MacBook is closed. Biometrics are responsibly stored only locally inside a secure element whose keys are only possessed by the user. Safari is leading the way for a more private smartphone browsing experience. Location data sent to Apple Maps, such as traffic data, are anonymized and then fuzzed 24 hours later to a much less precise location; some location history like where you park your car is never sent to Apple. Internet of Things has been responsibly implemented using end-to-end encryption, and much of this data stays on the local devices themselves and inaccessible to Apple on their servers. Albeit the company is far from perfect, there are still a lot of technology companies that can learn from Apple's design principles.

Deepfakes on Instagram: Mitigating Event and Process Risk

AUTHOR: Kate Peterson

PUBLISHED: January 2021

WRITTEN: February 2020

KEYWORDS: Social Media; Instagram; Deepfakes; Information Integrity

ABSTRACT:

This paper discusses the rising level of risk stemming from deepfakes—videos modified using highly sophisticated technology—and the challenge that arise when these are widely and rapidly shared on social media platforms. Specifically, this analysis focuses on the external event and process control failures related to deepfakes on Instagram as well as suggestions for their mitigation.

Introduction

One of the main themes of *Threat Horizon 2019* is Distortion, or the loss of "trust in the integrity of information."[1] Over the past few years, social media companies have come under fire for their role in allowing the spread of both misinformation and disinformation,[2]

---

[2] Per dictionary.com, misinformation is "false information that is spread, regardless of whether there is intent to mislead," while disinformation is "deliberately misleading or biased information; manipulated narrative or facts; propaganda."

with the Facebook company encountering intense scrutiny. According to former Special Counsel Robert Mueller's investigation, Russia-affiliated actors used Facebook-owned social media platforms to sow discord within the United States prior to the 2016 presidential election.[2] The upcoming 2020 election has renewed concerns regarding the spread of falsified and modified online content by foreign actors. Complicating matters is the rise of "deepfakes"—videos modified using advanced artificial intelligence (AI) technology. Recent media reports indicate that Instagram—a photo and video-sharing platform acquired by Facebook in 2012[3]—will likely be the social media site of choice for such abuse in 2020.[4] While 2016 events highlight the company's struggle to manage operational risk in a variety of ways, this analysis will focus on external event and process control failures related to deepfakes on Instagram as well as suggestions for their mitigation.

Deepfakes and Risk

First, we need to understand deepfakes and why they are problematic. If we adhere to the taxonomy detailed in "An Animal Kingdom of Disruptive Risk" by James Lam, we can describe deepfakes as Gray Rhinos, or "known unknowns." Lam explains that "[w]ith gray rhinos the main culprit is inertia: companies see the megatrends charging at them, but they can't seem to mitigate the risk or seize the opportunity."[5] In the case of deepfakes, such AI has been in use for years, primarily by film companies who have had the financial means to invest in expensive technology. Technological advancements, however, have facilitated popular access to deepfake software, like FaceSwap,[3] and concerns related to manipulated video first surfaced in 2017 when pornographic deepfakes appeared on Reddit.[6] Further, evolving AI technology used to create modified videos has improved rapidly, making it difficult to identify deepfakes without the assistance of additional AI systems. Experts worry that deepfakes could be used to disrupt the 2020 election, citing the edited video of House Speaker Nancy Pelosi,[4] which was widely circulated on social media.[7]

EXTERNAL EVENT RISK

Indeed, external event risk on Instagram stems from its content-sharing nature. Most social media sites advertise themselves as a way to connect and communicate with others. In the case of the Facebook company, foreign actors, likely motivated for geopolitical reasons outside the control of social media corporations, took advantage of this ability to share unverified content with a wide audience. Based on social media use during the 2016 election cycle, we can conclude that social media users were unaware of the prevalence of falsified content or of any attempts to lead voters astray. In fact, according to the Mueller Report, Internet Research Agency (IRA) operatives, from their offices in Russia, were able to organize and promote events within the United States.[8] And while the focus has been on the Facebook site itself, IRA operatives had higher levels of user engagement on Instagram, according to a New

---

[3] FaceSwap is open source deepfake software. See www.faceswap.dev for more information.

[4] This video was manipulated simply by slowing down the audio. Advanced AI technology could make manipulated videos more difficult to identify.

Knowledge report. [9] Looking to the future, it is likely that a variety of groups—both foreign and domestic—will attempt to propagate disinformation via deepfakes on Instagram to influence voters.

PROCESS RISKS

In addition to the risk posed by external events like foreign interference, ambiguous processes regarding content moderation have created significant risk within the Facebook company. Per Lam, operational risk can arise from documentation processes: "Improper or insufficient documentation may result in miscommunications between the parties to a contract, creating additional, unnecessary risks if there is a dispute."[10] While Instagram's community guidelines cover topics ranging from self-harm to intellectual property rights,[11] Instagram has been reticent to remove "fake" content, with the Facebook company CEO, Mark Zuckerberg, citing free speech issues.[12] These concerns are certainly valid; regulation of social media content, whether by the government or private companies, has the potential to lead to increased censorship, monitoring, and surveillance. That said, Facebook and Instagram have failed to address falsified or manipulated content like deepfakes in a consistent and timely manner. Indeed, the company developed a deepfake policy as late as January 2020.[13] Per the new policy, the Facebook company prohibits media if:

- It has been edited or synthesized – beyond adjustments for clarity or quality – in ways that aren't apparent to an average person and would likely mislead someone into thinking that a subject of the video said words that they did not actually say. And:

- It is the product of artificial intelligence or machine learning that merges, replaces or superimposes content onto a video, making it appear to be authentic.[14]

The company clarifies that this policy does not apply to satirical videos or parodies yet fails to explain how satirical or parody videos will be defined and identified by either AI technology or human fact-checkers. While Instagram currently labels videos that have been flagged by fact-checkers as false information, it is also unclear as to whether parody and satire deepfakes will be flagged in some manner. From Jonathan Swift's *A Modest Proposal* to *The Onion* of today, satire can be a powerful tool to subvert or expose corruption. Identifying satire, however, requires close attention. It is unclear from this policy how moderators will distinguish parodies and satirical videos from deepfakes destined to mislead. Nor is it clear if users will be notified that a deepfake has been approved as satire or parody.

Mitigating Risks

While impossible to eliminate the threat of deepfakes altogether—Instagram is a platform based entirely around photo and video-sharing—the Facebook company can mitigate event and process risk by fighting disinformation with better information. First, the Instagram platform should feature media literacy content, which should appear regularly via the Instagram feed as well as Instagram Stories. Second, the Facebook company should sponsor and invest in media literacy education by working closely with public libraries, community centers, local governments, and non-profit organizations. These events should be free, public workshops or courses taught by educators and librarians and should cover media literacy, critical thinking, and distinguishing fact from fiction. In addition to supporting media literacy efforts, the Facebook company should come up with a standard definition for what constitutes a parody or satire video and develop robust standard operating procedures around distinguishing these videos from deepfakes designed to mislead. Once a video has been identified as either a parody or a satirical video, it should be labeled as such so that it is not misinterpreted as authentic video footage.

Investing in education efforts around media literacy as well as creating a standard to designate approved content would show that Facebook and Instagram are committed to both avoiding a repeat of history and strengthening free speech.

GDPR Enforcement and Google's €50 Million Fine

AUTHOR: Alex Osuch

PUBLISHED: November 2019

WRITTEN: March 2019

KEYWORDS: Google; GDPR; European Union; Data Breach; Data Privacy; Data Security

ABSTRACT:

Since on May 25th, 2018, Data Protection Authorities across Europe have begun to process thousands of complaints and data breach reports under the European Union's (EU) General Data Protection Regulation. Numerous investigations into violations large and small are underway. Information organizations can benefit from an up-to-date understanding of how the results of these investigations will set precedents for future enforcement. In the case of Google, improper consent acquisition during the Android phone activation process earned the company a record-setting €50 million fine from CNIL, the French Data Protection Authority. The implications of this ruling suggest thorny design issues with which all information organizations operating within the EU must contend.

Introduction

Since the enforcement of the European Union's (EU) General Data Protection Regulation (GDPR) began in May 2018, the speculative anxiety over compliance within information organizations has become a concrete reality. This new reality is not an idle one. Between May 2018 and February 2019, there were approximately 59,000 total data breaches self-reported to data privacy authorities (DPAs) by organizations operating in the EU.[1] They ranged from small leaks to major incidents affecting millions of people. While investigations and penalties will follow for many of these breaches, it is unlikely that there will be sufficient resources to prosecute every single case. As such, it remains to be seen whether the efforts of DPAs will tend towards investigating highly visible cases or towards closing as many cases as possible across all types of organizations. An even bigger concern is how to determine which elements of GDPR will trigger the most complaints and inquiries. Although breaches are the most commonly discussed type of event, they are just one way to incur penalties, and self-disclosure is just one way to catch a regulator's eye.

An examination of the largest GDPR penalty to date, the €50 million fine imposed on Google by the French DPA Commission Nationale de l'Informatique et des Libertés (CNIL), can help unpack some of these other issues. As we will see, choices in product design can be just as risky as a data breach, and the implications of this risk goes far beyond faulty security controls. This discussion will summarize and use the articles of GDPR—in a non-exhaustive way—as a lens to explore the findings against Google, the relevant enforcement mechanisms, and what the future could hold for information organizations operating in the EU.

Elements of Enforcement

Article 4 defines the terms of the regulation, and it is probably the most important article for understanding the GDPR as a whole. The first paragraph defines what is being protected: "personal data," being "any information relating to an identified or identifiable natural person ('data subject')."[2] The paragraph goes on to specify the types of signifiers that could identify a data subject, but, without listing them here, it is safe to say that personal data under the regulation is a very broad category. The same can be said for data subjects, who only need natural personhood and have personal data within the EU to qualify; data subjects do not need to have EU citizenship or even reside in the EU.[3] From the standpoint of U.S. privacy regulations, the importance attributed by the EU to data subjects as stakeholders and personal data as a protected asset is exceptional.[4]

The rest of Article 4 defines concepts, entities, processes, and events that relate to how organizations and data subjects interact, including, for example, a notably robust definition of consent: "any freely given, specific, informed and unambiguous indication…[that] signifies agreement to the processing of personal data relating to him or her."[5] The two other definitions worth highlighting at the outset of this discussion are "data processor," which is an individual or organization that performs operations (e.g. "collection," "structuring," "use," "dissemination," etc.) on personal data, and the even broader category of "data controller," which is an individual or organization that decides on "the purposes and means" of processing personal data.[6] More terms from Article 4 will be referenced in discussing GDPR enforcement as they become relevant. It is recommended that anyone interested in data privacy read Article 4, at the very least, because it succinctly articulates the framework through which this regulation views the world of information management.

Article 51 specifies that each member of the EU establish an independent "supervisory authority" to oversee enforcement.[7] This is important in relationship to data controllers and processors, who, as defined in Article 4, must have a "main establishment" somewhere in the EU if they work across more than one state.[8] It follows that wherever the main establishment is located, the supervisory authority or DPA in that state will typically work with the organization. Because of their history in incentivizing multinationals with tax breaks, Ireland plays host to most of the large tech organizations' main establishments.[9] As we will see in Google's case, however, it is possible for a controller's main establishment to be ruled as residing outside of the EU, at which point any DPA can potentially head up an investigation.[10] By design, an organization operating in compliance with their local DPA should satisfy compliance requirements under any DPA, but not all DPAs are temperamentally aligned.[11]

Article 77 defines the right of data subjects to submit complaints when they feel their personal data has been affected by an infringement as a result of data processing.[12] This article is of special interest to the enforcement of GDPR, since the complaint process seems to trigger just as many investigations as self-reported incidents and DPA-led inquires. Between May 2018 and January 2019, DPAs in the EU as a whole received over 95,000 complaints from individuals and groups, with 30,000 of those happening in

January alone, and there is no reason to think that the trend will plateau in the near future.[13] Information organizations are required to create Data Protection Officer (DPO) positions under Article 37, mainly for ensuring internal compliance, but a strategically thoughtful organization will value the ability of this role to respond to data subject concerns as well.[14] The opportunity to head off a concern that could otherwise become a complaint to a DPA should be seized.

Article 83 defines the conditions for imposing fines. The first paragraph delivers the key criteria for what an effective penalty should be under GDPR: "effective, proportionate and dissuasive."[15] So far, DPAs have chosen to err on the side of moderation in deploying fines. After Google, the next highest fine has been a €400,000 penalty by the Comissão Nacional de Protecção de Dados (CNPD) against a Portuguese hospital for mishandling data under Article 5, which refers to processing principles like "minimisation" and "accuracy," and Article 32, which refers to securing data.[16] This penalty could have been in the millions of euros, but Portugal's DPA decided that a number of factors mitigated the severity of the issue, including the hospital's cooperation with the investigation.[17] For its part, the Data Protection Commission (Ireland's DPA) has described advisory and punitive investigations as equally important for its regulation of the multinational technology companies headquartered within its borders.[18] It is not difficult to imagine, however, that as time goes on and organizations continue to fall out of compliance with GDPR, the fines may begin to intensify.

Google

Perhaps the most notable GDPR penalty thus far, and certainly the one to make the most headlines, is the fine levied by the CNIL against Google. At €50 million, it is again much lower than what the French DPA could have pursued (which could have been in the billions), but it represents the highest amount yet imposed.[19] Although the fine was announced on January 19th, 2019, the initial complaints were submitted to the CNIL only days after the enforcement took effect.[20] Despite having their European administrative headquarters in Ireland, the CNIL decided that Google's decision-making with regards to their data processing was conducted outside of the E.U, and so it was determined that they had no main establishment within the EU insofar as one would be needed to address the complaints.[21] This allowed the CNIL, rather than Ireland's DPC, to take up the case, although it should be noted that the CNIL conferred with several other DPAs to cooperatively determine this course of action.[22]

The main organization behind the complaint submission was La Quadrature du Net, a digital freedom advocacy group, which assembled more than 12,000 complaints and submitted them as a group complaint.[23] The other group submitting a detailed complaint on behalf of several data subjects was the Austrian organization noyb ("none of your business").[24] Article 80 established the ability for public interest organizations to represent data subjects in this way.[25] The strategy for scaling up complaints (presumably effective in the face of immense DPA workloads and the limited resources of individuals) seems to have been effective, and it will likely continue to figure into enforcement actions in the future.[26]

The focus of the complaints and the final finding of violation concerned the way in which Google handled the acquisition of consent during the activation process of mobile equipment using the Android operating system; users were required to create a Google account in order to use their phones, and part of this process involved consenting to Google's privacy policy.[27]

Article 13 defines the types of information that must be provided to a data subject when personal data is collected, including details about the controller and the conditions of processing the data, as well as the rights of the data subject with respect to this arrangement.[28] The CNIL found that Google's account creation design dispersed this information in a way that made it difficult for users to find, in some cases requiring five or six actions to access, and that many of the descriptions of purposes for processing were too vague. [29] They also found, in certain cases, that the time period for data retention was not provided.[30] Interestingly, the CNIL acknowledged the tremendous scope of Google's processing as an obstacle for providing transparency.[31]

The takeaway is that organizations must find a way to comprehensively describe their use of data, even when said use is incredibly complex and difficult for a given organization to account for.[32] This is a truly difficult design task. The problem could, however, even be the reverse: data processing that cannot be described in the "concise, transparent, intelligible and easily accessible form" that Article 12 calls for may find itself on the chopping block.[33] Looming the background of this decision is Article 30, which mandates (albeit in an often loose "where possible" way) the keeping of records for any processing conducted on personal data.[34] As seen in U.S. case law, numerous organizations have been found to have violated their privacy policies after gaining consent from users, and it could be the case that Google keeps their policy vague in order to dodge the difficulty of properly auditing it.[35] Google certainly understands the value of their information when it comes to billing their customers, but maintaining transparency towards regulators and consumers must be a trickier question. It has to be said that posing these questions about the nature Google's processing systems is necessarily speculative, but their defensiveness does indicate some deeper issue with how their business works.

Article 6 defines the basis upon which the processing of personal data is legal. Much of the article is concerned with defining allowances for law enforcement and the public good, but in Google's case, as in most cases related to Article 6, point (a) of the first paragraph is key: "the data subject has given consent to the processing of his or her personal data for one or more specific purposes."[36] The CNIL found that Google had not properly established this legal basis for using personal data in their ad personalization services.[37] The first aspect of this finding relates to Google's Article 13 violations, since users were not clearly informed about the specific processing taking place across all of Google's services in support of ad personalization.[38] More substantive is the fact that Google designed the checkbox for displaying personalized ads to be pre-ticked, and users were also required to tick a single checkbox the acquired consent for all forms of processing.[39] This goes against the specific and unambiguous elements of consent as described in Article 4, as well as the "clear affirmative action" element described in Recital 32, both of which would presumably prohibit pre-ticked boxes and mandate discrete boxes (whether through a full list or intuitively nested lists) for each processing purpose.[40]

The complaint lodged by noyb argued further that Google's failure highlighted an "imbalance of power" between the data subject and Google.[41] They argued that because Google required acceptance of the privacy policy in order to use the phone, the Android ecosystem is so prevalent (%85 of all smart phones), and so many apps are limited to the Android or iOS ecosystem, users are were unable to freely give consent, and were instead coerced under a "clear imbalance" between processor and data subject as described in Recital 43.[42] The CNIL declined to take up or discuss this argument. While convincing in a certain sense, the argument would call for a fairly radical penalty and subsequent restructuring of the company's services. It's likely that the CNIL felt that a carefully focused ruling with a significant but not undue penalty would serve their purposes better. And yet, broad critiques of consent acquisition are more threatening to Google's way of life than other challenges the organization faces, such censorship of what it indexes, as in the case of Holocaust denial material in Germany and France, or when governments block specific apps, such as Pakistan blocking Blogger.[43] This conflict over consent acquisition design could be symptomatic of a larger antipathy between massive information organizations and European DPAs that seems difficult to reconcile.

The CNIL cited Google's business model, complex processing capabilities, and ubiquity for French data subjects as proper reasons for imposing a visibly large fine.[44] One can hear echoes of the issues at stake in Katell's discussion of algorithmic profiling regarding the impact of personalized ads on individuals and social well-being.[45] Yet, €50 million is clearly below the maximum (4% of annual global turnover revenue) for high-penalty articles like 6 and 13.[46] The amount seems especially minuscule when compared to the nearly €10 billion in fines Google has received in the EU since 2017 for anti-trust violations.[47] It seems that the CNIL, as well as other observers in this case, felt that the fine was appropriately dissuasive, in that it ought catch the attention of other organizations hoping to move ahead with business-as-usual.[48] In any event, Google is appealing the CNIL's decision on the grounds that its design was sufficient and that the ruling has a chilling effect on innovation.[49] These arguments do not appear to be particularly novel, so it remains to be seen if they will bear fruit, but the results of this litigation may shed further light on how the CNIL came to its decision.

As Google has yet to amend the process, the CNIL notes that "the violations are continuous breaches of the Regulation as they are still observed to date."[50] Add in the fact that both noyb and La Quadrature du Net's complaint submissions were part of a privacy campaign against other major information organizations, and it becomes clear that Google's penalty will not be the last.[51] Indeed, La Quadrature du Net's public statement on the ruling emphasized their disappointment with the amount fined and a desire to see more rulings and maximum penalties.[52]

Conclusion

In their annual report, the DPC listed a number of ongoing investigations ("statutory inquiries") against major corporations, including Facebook, Instagram, WhatsApp, Apple, and Linkedin.[53] Six of these were for complaint-triggered Article 6 violations, with another three relating to privacy policies and terms and conditions, and still another three relating to personalized advertising.[54] As an organization not dissimilar to the ones the DRC is currently investigating, Google's penalty for these same infractions does not bode well. Indeed, Helen Dixon, head of the DRC, explained that she would soon be distributing draft decisions for these investigations to other data regulators in the EU, presumably as one of the last steps in the process.[55]

Simply put, every information organization is going to face the questions posed by the ruling against Google. How does an organization with supermassive processing capabilities convey their activities to the average person? How can accelerating trends in data science be reconciled with GDPR? What if it is not possible to do so? Does GDPR really seek, as Google's argument for appeal suggests, to put a halt on innovation and roll back economic advancement? DLA Piper's enforcement report forecasts "that 2019 will see more fines for tens and potentially hundreds of millions of euros."[56] One imagines that in the next couple years, these hard questions will provoke very high-level strategic decisions, and the impact could reshape the global information economy.

Huawei Company Risk Management

AUTHOR: Bingyan Wang

PUBLISHED: July 2020

WRITTEN: December 2019

KEYWORDS: Communications Technology; Operational Risk; Global Operations

ABSTRACT:
This paper discusses the system and external event risks faced by the global communications technology company Huawei in recent years. For this company—whose mission is to "bring digital to every person, home and organization for a fully connected, intelligent world" —the author explores the increased areas of risk exposure and provides potential recommendations for risk management.

Introduction

Huawei Technologies Co. ("Huawei") is a privately-owned communications technology company founded in Shenzhen, China in 1987 by Ren Zhengfei that produces and sells communication equipment. At the end of 2018, Huawei had more than 188,000 employees. Huawei's products and internet solutions have been applied to more than 170 countries around the world, serving forty-five of the world's top fifty operators and one third of the world's population.[1] Huawei's vision is to "bring digital to every person, home and organization for a fully connected, intelligent world."[2] As it grows, the company faces more challenging risks from both inside and outside the company.

The four primary areas of operational risk have been defined as inadequate or failed processes, people and systems, and external events.[3] This paper will focus on Huawei's operational risks related to systems risks and external events.

Systems Risks

System risk covers instances of both disruption and outright system failures in both internal and outsourced operations. Examples of system risks at Huawei include the area of human resources (HR) management systems and the company's employee stock ownership plan (ESOP).

Overall, inefficient HR functions will inhibit the effective operation of any company. Huawei's growth over the years has resulted in a large and complex company structure, and the risks have subsequently increased related to the tasks related to managing close to 200,000 employees across the globe. Like most engineering-based businesses, Huawei depends heavily on its primary resource, the employees who work to create the products and services that are delivered to customers. Ren Zhengfei has said that "Resources can be exhausted; only culture endures. Huawei does not have any natural resources to depend upon. What we do have is the brainpower of our employees. This is our oil, our forests, and our coal."[4] The company also has a reputation of having an extremely competitive culture between employees. For a global company like Huawei, the HR systems will heavily impact the operations of the company, which support activities including recruiting & hiring, compensation & benefits, performance management, and managing personnel complaints and issues. Ren Zhengfei expressed concern that "Our current structure is too complex. The work progress becomes slow. We may need a system reformation."[5] Without a modern and streamlined HR management function (and supporting systems), Huawei will face increased levels of risks. The HR strategy is critical for recruiting and retaining employees; failure in the HR systems could have significant impacts on the operations of the company.

Another area of risk for the company arises from the home-grown employee benefit plan at Huawei, which is structured as an ESOP. The founder of Huawei created the company's ESOP in the late-1980s, which at the time was an innovative system designed to let employees own approximately 99% of the company stock.[6] The goal of setting up employees to be the owners of the company is to encourages employees to pursue the same goals in pursuit of the company survival and success instead of merely focusing on personal wages. The ESOP has received commendations from outside the company and has been credited for positive aspects of the company's development. Based on the ESOP model, people who do not work for Huawei cannot buy its stock; employees who are invited to participate must buy an allotment of shares with their own money. The share price of stock is determined once a year (connected to the valuation of the company), instead of being set on the open stock market.[7] Therefore, employees share in the potential benefits (increased company value) and potential risks (loss of wealth). However, as employees become wealthier, they may lose motivation to work as hard in the past. When an employee leaves, most of the time the company must repurchase back stock, creating an increased risk to cash flow if unexpected levels of employee departures occur. In recent years, Huawei has experienced a higher resignation rate, that increases the risks to the company required to repurchase stock from departing employees.[8]

External Events

By definition, companies typically have no control over the risks related to external events. Since the company decided to "bring digital to every person," Huawei is focusing on expanding its market further after they successfully dominated in the Chinese market. The decision to expand in U.S and European markets has increased the risk exposure of the company to more external events.

For example, Huawei has been accused of introducing technological "back doors" in its products to provide clandestine access to mobile-phone networks, as requested by the Chinese government.[9] Huawei denied these allegations. Ironically, the U.S. government has put increasing pressure on other technology companies in recent years to build methods to allow law enforcement to circumvent mobile phone security measures. Despite this hypocrisy, the U.S. began implementing a series of business restrictions on Huawei to prevent them from expanding in the U.S. market; telecommunications provider AT&T has kept Huawei products out of its domestic networks.

The cybersecurity allegations from the U.S. government have also been influenced by the trade war between U.S. and China. Banning products from certain countries can be a political strategy and protect the domestic companies at the same time. Meng Wanzhou, CFO of Huawei and the daughter of Ren Zhengfei, was arrested in the Canadian airport as requested by U.S. authority under the charge of violating the sanctions against Iran in December 2018.[10] The charges against Huawei and Meng Wanzhou show the increased risk facing Huawei when it comes to external events and political controversies. The risks come from not only the trade war but also the technology competition. In the theory of enterprise risk management, the larger the investment, the bigger the risks. The breaking innovation of 5G and the popularity of Huawei are two factors in the increased level of scrutiny the company faces from external forces. The unsuccessful expansion into the U.S. market reveals the obstacles and pressures that the company may have when it comes to external event risks. The potential impact of these risks include economic and reputational loss, as well as the increased risk of becoming embroiled in lawsuits.

Recommendations

Through the identification of these particular areas of risk, there are a number of recommended risk mitigation efforts identified below. In order to manage risk across the whole enterprise, one strategy is to manage risk "with the five Ts," [11] which are: tolerate, treat, transfer, terminate, and take advantage. The risk mitigation methods in this part of the paper will be based on those strategies.

For the internal risks from the system problems, the company should treat the risk by improving the current HR management systems. One reason that problems exist is the legacy systems currently in place, potentially hindering the company from benefiting from the cultural diversity its global operations present. The company could conduct an operational assessment of its HR management functions, in order to support more efficient operations and systems. In terms of the ESOP, the company could perform a repurchase liability study on a regular basis.

For external events, the focus must be on mitigating the potential negative impact when the inevitable risk event takes place (since there is almost no control on the likelihood of a negative event taking place). When facing political-related issues, the company could choose the "tolerate" strategy, since these forces are beyond its control.[12] Another strategy would be to "watch for emerging opportunities, as well as threats."[13] "Taking Advantage of the Opportunity Inherent in the Risk" is a strategy also suggested when facing external issues. Facing certain frustrations can have a positive effect to encourage employees; the setback can be used as a promotion to encourage the company to innovate new solutions. Additionally, Huawai can continue to pursue other markets, in order to continue its expansion strategy while letting the U.S. political environment to inevitably continue to change focus.

Conclusion

With the mission to "bring digital to every person, home and organization for a fully connected, intelligent world," Huawei strives to improve its products and expanding its market. In this process, risk management is critical to navigate and complete the company performances. The company may face risks from various dimensions, but effective risk management can increase risk awareness, risk identification, and risk mitigation in order to drive towards continued success.

Kyoto Animation Arson Attack Risk Analysis

AUTHOR: Bingyan Wang

PUBLISHED: April 2021

WRITTEN: December 2019

KEYWORDS: Workplace Safety; Reputational Risk; Artson; Employees Safety

ABSTRACT:
The paper conducts an assessment of the risk conditions leading up to the 2019 arson of Kyoto Animation's Studio 1 building, which killed 36 people and injured 33 more. The risk conditions included reputational risk and multiple types of operational risk, and some of the various preventative controls that failed to prevent this tragedy. The analysis includes suggestions for lessons learned going forward for companies of all types.

Introduction

In Kyoto, Japan on July 18th, 2019 at Kyoto Animation's Studio 1 building, a man poured gasoline around the studio and set it on fire. People in the neighborhood heard the sound of the explosion, and saw the fire coming from the building. The accident completely burned the Kyoto Animation Studio from the first through the third floors, killed 36 people, of which 33 were company employees. The incident injured an additional 33 people. The police later arrested the suspect, Shinji Aoba, who claimed his novel was plagiarized by the company. The man was injured in the fire and was taken to hospital for burn injury treatment.[1]

Significance

This incident became global news, as Kyoto Animation is a well-known Japanese acclaimed anime studio with thousands of anime fans. Kyoto Animation's philosophy states that, "since inauguration, our principles are 'Make a challenge,' 'Do the best,' 'Produce required works' and 'Keep our corporate as a humanitarian one.' We value people."[2] The company made high-quality animate productions including the Melancholy of Haruhi Suzumiya, Clannad, and Violet Evergarden.[3] The Studio 1 building that was burned was built in 2007 and was mostly used by animation production staffs. The 33 artists killed in the incident were considered to be the backbone elites in the animation creation industry. The fire destroyed most of the studio's manuscripts and digital archives reserved from the last 40 years.[4] The Museum of Kyoto Researcher Kiyotaka Moriwaki told the reporter: "Those are people who are passionate about animations and have quite high skills. This studio created dreams and hopes for young people."[5] Condolences also came from many people overseas. Apple CEO Tim Cook tweeted: "Kyoto Animation is home to some of the world's most talented animators and dreamers – the devastating attack today is a tragedy felt far beyond Japan. KyoAni artists spread joy all over the world and across generations with their masterpieces."[6] To Japan, the severity of the incident was measured by the loss of 36 lives, the loss of art, the mystery of the murderer, and by the impact on the animation industry, which many consider one of the most important cultural symbols in Japan.

Risk Analysis

This event created a heavy loss. In order to mitigate the risk in the future to prevent similar incidents, this paper will identify the risks involved in this event and provide suggestions to more animation companies. The risk analysis will focus on the Kyoto Animation's reputation risk and the company's control failure in the area of human error and external events from the safety side in this incident.

REPUTATION RISK

The reputation is everything to a company. Protiviti gives the definition of the reputation risk in the atrial of *Board Oversight of Reputation Risk* – "reputation risk is the current and perspective impact on earnings and enterprise value arising from negative stakeholder opinion[7]." Failure to regulate the reputation risk will bring negative impact to the company. The Kyoto Animation always has a good reputation gained from the quality productions. Anime fans, people in the animation industry, politicians, news reporters and many others who are concerned about this incident from all over the world cared about this tragedy and its after-stories. Japanese people living nearby went to the studio site and sent their condolences to the incident. At the same time, people started to discuss the company's plagiarism—the suspect told the police that the company stole his novel.

The Kyoto Animation responded to this accusation. The attorney of the Kyoto Animation confirmed that the company had received the novels from a person named

Shinji Aoba in the annually solicited novel submissions. However, his novel did not pass the first round of the contest. "We have confirmed that it has no similarity to any Kyoto Animation works," he added.[8]

Besides the conformation form the attorney, no evidence was found that the company plagiarized. The motivation for the suspect sets the fire and mentioned about plagiarism was unclear. Police announced Shinji Aoba had mental illness and pointed out that he might have unilateral hatred for Kyoto animation.[9]

The clearance of plagiarism is a good result for the company. "It takes many good deeds to build a good reputation, and only one bad one to lose it," said Benjamin Franklin.[10] The popularity of this incident from the public could have destroyed the company's reputation if the plagiarism allegations were found to be true.

Operational risk failure: External event

This external event is a man-made disaster and showed a big safety risk that the company failed to prevent. External events often have common risks,[11] and the risk factors in this event include design and construction flaws of the building, inadequate training, and flaws in the law policies.

First, the construction of the building promoted the growth of the fire. The first to third floors of the studio were penetrated by a spiral ladder. The chimney effect caused the flames and smoke to rise rapidly. After sneaking into the entrance gate on the first floor, Shinji Aoba spilled and ignited gasoline. The location where he ignited gasoline was considered to be near the spiral staircase. A Kyoto Prefecture police investigation found that a fire broke out in the Kyoto Animation First Studio building. The investigation shows the building has a gate leading to the roof level. The gate was able to be opened from the inside of the building. The police believed that due to the violent fire condition, most people failed to escape from that gate in time.[12]

Second, inadequate fire drill training gave victims less chances to survive. About 70 people were working in the building at the time of the incident. On the second floor, 21 of 32 people survived mostly by jumping from the veranda. The report shows 19 corpses were found on the third floor, stacked on top of each other on the stair way to the top of the building.[13] People tend to follow others at the time of emergency. However, the people's misjudgment of the situation on the third floor may have contributed to the factors that resulted in so many deaths.

Third, flaws in the law policies indirectly caused the incomplete fire prevention system. The Studio 1 building was equipped with fire prevention equipment including fire extinguishers, fire alarms, and a smoke barrier. The fire prevention system had passed the inspection by the Kyoto Municipal Fire Bureau in October 2018. However, the automatic sprinkler system and indoor fire hydrant were not installed since the law did not require that "office buildings" to be installed those items.[14]

The fire started at 10:30 AM, with the fire department alerted to the condition around five minutes later at 10:35. However, the fire caused severe damages in a very short period of time. Of the 70 people in the studio, 33 people died. If one of the risks was realized earlier, the loss may not have been as severe.

OPERATIONAL RISK FAILURE: HUMAN ERROR

Human error contributed in a significant way to the failure of the preventative controls in place. The company's security system did not detect the security risk that later resulted in serious consequences. The company has policies and equipment for physical safety. However, the people in charge of implementing the processes for these policies failed to follow the procedures and made the tragedy possible. The Studio 1 building had security cameras installed, including at the front entrance and the entrances and exits for staff. The company policy requires that both employees and visitors are checked in and out; staff are required to use their employee ID cards to enter the building, and visitors must be verified before entering the building. These doors would be locked at night and the shutters would be closed. However, since employees and visitors go in and out during the daytime, the entrance was always keep opened during the day.[15]

The tragedy had a chance to be prevented. The company president Hideaki Hatta admitted that the company had received many anonymous threats before the incident. The threats did not attract the company's attention because as a big animation producer, the company receiving threats is almost a normal thing. However, the threats should give the company some signs to improve its security system. Besides the threats, the suspect had explored the surrounding environment and practiced the attack a few times before July 18th, unknown to the company.

On July18th, NHK TV station would visit the company for a press interview. For the convenience of reporters, staff, and other important visitors accessing the building, the first-floor entrance was opened for everyone. The suspect came into the building with 40 L of gasoline, five knifes, and a hammer on a hand cart. Unfortunately, the security did not notice his entrance and did not catch his suspicious behavior leading up to the building being set on fire. Human error made the suspect able to get in the building and complete the attack.

Suggestions & Analysis of company reactions

Hazards and vulnerabilities shown in this incident can exist in many other companies, too. After the incident, Kyoto Animation performed good reactions for the company to move forward. The paper will analyze the company's aftermath reactions and give suggestions to all animation companies to prevent a similar tragedy happen in the future. The academic project, *Managing Risk Across the Enterprise,* provided five steps risk management to mitigate risks, including tolerate, treat, transfer, terminate, and take advantage.[16] The recommendations will be given based on those methods.

First, the reputation risk caused by plagiarism issue should be terminated from the source. Ladipo Adeosun, a business scholar, stated the importance of the corporate reputation: "Reputation matters and it explain why customers choose company product or service in preference to competitors offering. It makes the difference between success and failure."[17] If the company does have plagiarism behaviors, it should terminate the risk, since the loss of reputation is a high risk. In the current case, where the company was being suspected of plagiarism, the company should treat the risk by stating the truth. Kyoto Animation hired an attorney to speak for the company. At the same time, the president of the company spoke out against the allegations to make the truth transparent. The company reaction convinced the public and increased the company's credibility.

Second, companies can treat the risks from external events by establishing a fire prevention program. Animation companies tend to reserve large volume of combustible materials including paper materials and paintings. An incident of fire will cause serious consequences if many combustibles present. In this case, the fire prevention should be considered by more animation companies. The academic report also provided an efficient way to build such programs. Companies can consider the following ways: appoint a risk manager to lead development of tools, including workshop and scale tools; provide staff training including fire drills; develop a risk manual or guide for employees to learn; create risk tables and registers to document consequences or likelihood of such dangers; create a risk website or some other reporting mechanism; and keep tools simple and management practical.[18]

Third, treating the risk of human error by seeking better human resources regulations to make sure people are following procedures. On the one hand, the company policy should be complete and specific. The Kyoto Animation can build more complete security system and specify the security policies for both regular working days and days that are open for visiting. In the case of Kyoto Animation, even the company has the entrance policies for visitors, the security guard did not follow the procedures. Thus, one the other hand, the company should also adopt more efficient human resources management methods for employees to follow the right policies.

After Story

Reports from Japan's NHK show that in the past 20 years, the number of victims in Japan's fire casualties has been single digits. In 2019, this arson in Kyoto is the worst arson in Japan in 18 years.[19] Although companies are always trying to avoid risks, sometimes the management of risks can bring positive effects. Enterprise risk management is defined as "positive or negative effects of uncertainty or variability on agency objectives."[20] Under the pressure of asset and human loss, the company properly reacted after the incident and brought positive effects. The company president decided to build a memorial park at the site, compressing the deepest respect for lost lives in the incident. John Ledford, president of the American anime licensor Sentai Filmworks, led a founding online to support Kyoto Animation. People raised more than 1.63 million dollars on the third day which was more than twice the target amount.[21]

In their philosophy, Kyoto Animation states they "value people"[22] and they try to "do the best" on their work. The company shows its strong culture by the implantation of these values. Condolences were from many countries and people were willing to help using their own efforts. The incident reflected the company's positive reputation and successful reputational risk management efforts. Kyoto Animation is teaching the importance of managing the company reputation. Meanwhile, risks can come from everywhere. It's important for companies to realize the importance of risk management on the safety side and be prepared for unexpected situations.

NASDAQ's Exploration into Blockchain Technology

AUTHOR: Allessandra Quevedo

PUBLISHED: February, 2021

WRITTEN: March, 2020

KEYWORDS: COVID-19; pandemics; supply chains; pharmaceuticals

ABSTRACT:

As NASDAQ Inc. continues to explore the integration of Blockchain technology to both the private and public markets, it is no secret that this technology has the power to truly make a transformative impact in how businesses are structured and how they do business. Whether it is NASDAQ's enterprise Blockchain platform or whether it is the future of trading on the NASDAQ stock exchange as a whole, the technology promises a more efficient form of performing trade settlements and transactions— while reducing the number of individuals who need to be 'hands on.' Blockchain promises for a more optimal form of conducting business; one that is more transparent and promotes trust between investors.

As a company at the forefront of the emerging global markets and economies, it is no surprise that the NASDAQ company, or NASDAQ Inc. would invest in a technology that has the potential to transform the way business transactions are performed. To preface, NASDAQ Inc.

runs the NASDAQ exchange, which is the second largest stock exchange in the world (by market cap).[1]

The adoption of this emerging technology, however, might not be surprising to some. In recent years, Blockchain technology has begun to emerge as is its own identity; one separate from cryptocurrency—which one might instinctively refer to. Blockchain is more than just cryptocurrency. Rather, a new form of data storage and distribution. This form of technology has the potential to alter the structure of today's capital markets and the way businesses conduct trades and transactions worldwide through this new Distributed Ledger Technology (DLT).[2]

Before I begin a closer analysis into NASDAQ Inc.'s current integration of Blockchain technology and research, I will preface a history on the company itself, the current stock market system, Blockchain technology and the value it provides to the market, then challenges this form of technology faces. Each component of this larger system has greater implications beyond just the NASDAQ stock exchange—when applied to the rest of the world and other stock changes around the globe.

The evolution of the finance and banking industry is now coupled with the race to adopt emerging technologies in order to cut costs and operate with efficiency. But banks are not the only players looking at Blockchain technology. NASDAQ Inc. "is a holding company, that engages in trading, clearing, exchange technology, regulatory, securities listing, information and public and private company services."[3] It operates under the following umbrellas: Market Services, Corporate Services, Information Services and Market Technology. The Market Services, in particular deals with equity derivative trading and clearing and cash equity trading, and trade management services businesses. NASDAQ stands for National Association of Securities Dealers Automated Quotation System. The NASDAQ stock exchange trades stocks from major companies such as Apple, Amazon,

Microsoft, and Facebook.[4] Long before the automated trading process occurred, transactions occurred in person—on a trading floor.[5] However, the birth of the NASDAQ allowed traders to do business on an automated quotation system—which allowed brokers and traders to see prices of trades and stocks in 'real' time.[6] In 1987, a stock market crash caused some market traders difficulty to pick up their phone for trades, so they launched a small program that allowed for electronic entry. The benefits of this method led to a large percentage of the world's exchanges to be converted to this method.

As for the functions of the NASDAQ, it now contains about 3,200 publicly traded companies. The variety of companies that are traded on this market include a range from capital goods, to healthcare to public utilities. NASDAQ Inc. runs 26 exchanges for equities, bonds, derivatives and commodities in the United States, Scandinavia, and the Baltic region.[7] Because the NASDAQ has no trading floor, the exchange itself is a 'dealer's market' so brokers buy and sell stocks through the market, rather than making purchases from each other. The automated trading system also allows trades to be made through an automatic execution based on the parameters set by the trader.[8] This area, however, still currently require the need for intermediaries, such as other personnel to handle complex trades and the paperwork to ensure that trades are executed fairly and are legally compliant with the parameters set by each party's contracts.

Given the previous overview of NASDAQ Inc. and the NASDAQ stock exchange, it is also important to understand how the current trading system works. While each stock exchange is different, at the NASDAQ, buyers and sellers trade with a dealer instead of each other.[9] The process of completing trades and exchanges can be referred to as a cumbersome and costly process. There are numerous risks involved when exchanging information between two institutions or parties and the steps needed to complete the trade process and complete post-trade settlements and custody is one that required the intervention of multiple individuals.[10] Transactions typically require the need for parties doing a transaction or settlement to acquire intermediaries, to evaluate the paperwork and undergo the verification process. There is a pre-trade, trade, post-trade and custody of assets process that is layered with complexities.[11] Thus, the current process for completing these transactions requires a lot of added costs to the trade itself. Participants have to spend much more money on the investment process.

In addition to the time and the difficulty it takes to evaluate the paperwork, the current market systems typically run on a centralized database that stores all of their digitized assets.[12] This poses a large threat, as the centralized database could be targeted by hackers or a natural disaster. If any of that data is harmed, that is a huge loss to institutions. The maintenance of a central database is also expensive. It requires a lot of storage and framework in order to support all of that data in a centralized location.[13] And finally, the traditional form of data distribution lacks transparency—especially when one party is unable to receive immediate document changes, and it cannot compare the decisions of other participants involved in the exchange/settlement process. This is an issue largely because if there are any errors—it may become difficult for other parties to immediately address it.[14] Thus, it would add time to the settlement process, as this back and forth will need to occur through the intermediaries.

Many of these issues can be addressed through the implementation of Blockchain technology. To introduce Blockchain technology, a brief definition, states it as a "relatively new kind of data-base that has become a prominent solution for storing digital information more securely."[15] In other words, Blockchain technology is a ledger-based information system. Meaning, as information is created, it is evenly distributed across all nodes of that particular Blockchain network. Blockchain allows information to never be deleted or tampered with.[16] This is especially important in record keeping, and in the world of finance, it shows all of the information regarding a particular transaction or contract. The information is timestamped, and once an individual request to add information to the Blockchain, each node in network is aware and must approve of the change. This makes it harder to re-write old information or delete it.[17] Much of the information that is created into a block will be available for each player to have access to. Thus, applying this to the world of finance and banking, this form of Distributed Ledger Technology (DLT), proposes many solutions to the industry's existing problems.

The use of Blockchain technology within the stock markets proposes a lot of potential to cut costs and perform business operations and trades more efficiently. The use of Blockchain would mean that trades could happen more efficiently because the data needed to verify the transaction would be accurate and complete.[18] It typically takes both parties between three or more days to complete transactions due to the intermediaries, operational trade clearance and the regulations with which the trade must comply.[19] Much of the data needed in transactions are buried in-between spreadsheets from each party. The reduced need for the lack of intermediaries would greatly maximize the profit margins for both parties involved. The technology allows this process to be automated and it opens up transparency between the parties at a more instantaneous rate than before. The direct exchange of information and business transactions thus reduces the need for third party involvement.[20] The transferring of financial information and the exchange of assets, can be seen as closely aligning with Blockchain's core transformative impact.

To summarize, the advantages of Blockchain technology offer a lot of cost effective and automated settlement and transaction process. Reduced costs—during the trade and settlement process and after, through the reduction of other unnecessary processing fees, the automation of ownership transfers after trades, increased transparency between financial institutions, and a probable increase in investment and liquidity, would help markets operate faster and would require the need for less regulation.

In addition to the positive potential impacts Blockchain has to offer to stock markets and the finance industry, there are still a lot of challenges that these institutions need to overcome. One of the main concerns, is implementing a system to update how Blockchain technologies add information to existing information block. Current methods, are when Blockchain miners process either Bitcoin transactions or require the use for complex algorithms to store new information as a new hash to be added to the Blockchain block, they are rewarded (with typically a Bitcoin) by solving optimization problems from those who want to have their transactions processed.[21] The form of payment encourages a distributed number of miners to add the information to the network's Blockchain. However, the large influx of transactions and trade deals introduces a new challenge: who's transactions will be processed first, in what order, and what fees of payment or incentives can we give miners to sort this information.[22]

The current financial market is uncertain in how to implement this on a wide-scale network. Who will become the miners, which institutions will take on the computing power needed for this? These are some of the few questions people still have. In addition, the scalability size in general will require planning.[23] In order for all institutions to be able to support that much data—processed through all the players in a Blockchain network, there needs to be planning on that institution will build the database storage capacity to withstand all of that information processing. Rather than having one central database, each institution or player in the network also needs to seek and expand their processing and data storage power.[24] This poses another unique problem for the expanse of Blockchain technology as a whole. How will the boosted needs of computer power and processing power affect its impact on the earth. CO2 emissions will be even more so than before.

Lastly, in order to successfully scale Blockchain technology, another obstacle to overcome are the legislation and regulation policies surrounding Blockchain technology. Because of it's potential to scale across the globe—with NASDAQ Inc. operating with corporations outside of the United States—governments should also be prepared to enact a unilateral set of regulations for cross- border transactions pertaining to be Blockchain specific.[25] One of the reasons why some of the current legislation doesn't quite work is because these current processes of committing the trade, the post-trade procedures, settlement process, etc. are all separate, whereas Blockchain would essentially merge and streamline the layers to this process into one. It has traditionally operated separately, but with Blockchain, law makers and policy regulators need to understand how the technology works and the larger implications of utilizing this technology at a large scale.[26]

In the U.S. alone, only about half of the states have enacted any Blockchain legislation at all.[27] And much of the regulations in place refer to the investment of cryptocurrencies and warning businesses in making decisions to adopt this new form of payment. A lot of the regulations themselves aren't surrounding the technology adoption or usage—which serves as a constant reminder of how the success of Blockchain technology relies on the public and its users to be able to identity apart from Bitcoin and cryptocurrency in general. And lastly, a vast majority of countries' laws are in place regarding institutions and industries that are built with a centralized structure—with a singular seat of control and responsibility.[28] This means that a lot of the laws and regulations operate under a top- down approach. Making it easier to pinpoint individuals on a specific level or status if something goes wrong in the information exchange or the trade settlement. The need for a whole new set of regulations is needed to traverse the unclear waters of Blockchain technology's capabilities and limitations.

To summarize, the challenges Blockchain faces in its adoption into the stock market are: the complexity of the networking system—the breadth and scale of the institutions that become key players in a large network, the storage constraints; each key player in the network has to be able to withstand the computing power and to process complex transactions and trades, and the mechanisms of updating the Blockchain network itself remain unclear and remain a challenge, and finally, a universal compliance and regulatory policy for these complicated business transactions have not yet been established.

With the challenges aside, NASDAQ Inc. has been working on Blockchain research and has funded various Blockchain projects and startups from as early as 2013. Since NASDAQ Inc. is an industry leader in developing innovative securities transaction methodologies, they announced its first private securities transactions using Blockchain technology in 2015.[29] Chain.com, was the first to use the Blockchain ledger platform. The implications of this technology could mean that institutions could settle transactions apart from the traditional settling system. In 2015, NASDAQ Inc. also launched a LINQ, the private share-trading platform that additionally allowed unlisted companies to represent their shares digitally.[30] LINQ is the first platform from an established financial services firm to demonstrate how asset trading could be managed digitally through the use of Blockchain-based platforms. Frederick Voss, NASDAQ Inc.'s lead on Blockchain strategy, believes the inefficiencies of current exchange suites for entrepreneurs and investors give LINQ a competitive edge that will encourage trading on private platforms.[31] Voss and Global Software Development Director, Alex Zinder, also emphasize Blockchain's ability to remove the need for pen and paper or spreadsheet- based data entry. This, to them, appears to be the biggest benefit of Blockchain technology.

In addition to the global trading platform and the business services Nasdaq Inc. provides, Nasdaq Inc. launched a venture investment program in 2017 called Nasdaq Ventures. This program is dedicated to "discovering, investing and collaborating on new technologies."[32] The investments provided by Nasdaq Ventures can range from $1 million to $10 million. One of the main areas of investment focus, are in Blockchain. Nasdaq Venture's goals for Blockchain Technology are in "creating faster and more transparent financial solutions by advancing innovation in Blockchain and digital transfer." Nasdaq Ventures has invested in a handful of Blockchain startups, in hopes of finding ways to automate business processes and transactions made between organizations. Other startups include startups specializing in cryptocurrency and cryptography.[33] But most importantly, Nasdaq Ventures has a particular focus on Symbiont, a Blockchain platform for building networks. NASDAQ Ventures invested roughly $20 million in Symbiont, making it the largest investment for a Blockchain startup to date.[34]

As NASDAQ Inc. continues to explore the integration of Blockchain technology to both the private and public markets, it is no secret that this technology has the power to truly make a transformative impact in how businesses are structured and how they do business. Whether it is NASDAQ's enterprise Blockchain platform or whether it is the future of trading on the NASDAQ stock exchange as a whole, the technology promises a more efficient form of performing trade settlements and transactions—while reducing the number of individuals who need to be 'hands on.' Blockchain promises for a more optimal form of conducting business; one that is more transparent and promotes trust between investors. It shares information on the trades happening, and it allows members of each network remain informed about the deals happening around them. On the other hand, Blockchain technology still has a long way to go. Problems with scalability, computing and storage capability across all actors in a Blockchain network, and the legal and regulatory issues that remain unfulfilled by the governments. NASDAQ's research and interest in Blockchain technology surely establishes them as one of the top companies in the industry; pioneering for advancing technologies. However, I believe that this is a long and hard battle to face—as there needs to be a greater understanding of the technology and the overall implications of it through business and financially. Blockchain is truly a transformative technology—however, at this time, the question that remains is in the scalability of the technology worldwide.

The Evolution of Aadhaar in India

AUTHOR: Ashritha Dsouza

PUBLISHED: February 2020

WRITTEN: May 2019

KEYWORDS: Biometrics; Personal Identifiable Information

ABSTRACT:
The Aadhaar program was envisaged as a biometric-based unique identity number that could improve the delivery of welfare benefits and limit the scope of fraudulent activities. But as the project progressed, it faced challenges from various stakeholders such as government bodies from different levels and citizens This paper analyzes and identifies the gaps in processes and external events of the Aadhaar project and suggests ways to address those gaps.

Over the last several decades, the world has slowly transitioned from traditional paper-based identification systems to digital identification systems. In India, an inability to prove one's identity was the biggest challenge preventing the marginalized sections in accessing benefits and subsidies given by the government. "Prior to 2010, the landscape of identification in India was fragmented."[1] The previous system of multiple identity documents issued by various Indian government agencies caused complications in the distribution of funds and subsidies, duplication of efforts and extreme inconvenience to individuals. To tackle and address these problems, the Indian government launched the Aadhaar project in 2009.

Aadhaar was envisaged as a biometric-based unique identity number that could facilitate citizens' access to welfare. Since it was thought to be a more reliable identity proof, "the union and state governments made Aadhaar compulsory to avail a series of essential services including opening and accessing bank accounts, passports, cell phone services"[2]. According to the Unique Identification Authority of India (UIDAI), as of 2018, "a total of 121 crore Aadhaar cards have been issued."[3] Since its inception, the rising significance of Aadhaar has been accompanied by a lot of challenges and risks.

Initially, the Aadhaar project was supposed to revolutionize the identification mechanism. But as the project progressed, it faced challenges from various stakeholders such as government bodies from different levels, technical partners, citizens and equipment suppliers. Using the traditional operational risk framework, my paper analyzes and identifies the gaps in processes and external events of the Aadhaar project and suggests ways to address those gaps.

External Events

This category identifies the "external issues that could affect the performance"[4] of the Aadhaar project. "Aadhaar's design is based on a centralized database called the Central Identities Data Repository that stores every individual's demographic and biometric information."[5] Centralized identity databases, however, have been controversial, because of the inherent security risks and policy concerns. There have been multiple reports suggesting bogus and fake entries in the Aadhaar database. Moreover, there is a huge concern over the accuracy of biometrics, since the thumb impression and iris of those who are involved in manual labor could get changed or damaged. Failing the biometric identification test has led to the exclusion from welfare programs of the poor and the homeless. The 2018 UIDAI statistics, which revealed that the Aadhaar project suffered a 12 percent failure rate,[6] supports the above point. This indicates that many people equivalent to the population of many countries were denied welfare benefits that they were actually entitled to. The combination of making Aadhaar mandatory and not providing alternatives for establishing identity excluded those it had actually set out to make better off.

Furthermore, The Aadhaar Act of 2010 stated that no external entity could request confidential demographic information such as name, address, phone number, etc.[7]. However, as the ecosystem developed, many companies like Paytm used Aadhaar data to verify customer information. Since there are no specified controls on storage and retention of the data, data collected by such companies through Aadhaar can be accessed by them in the future.

Processes

When Aadhaar was being developed and launched, several complex legal questions emerged concerning fundamental and constitutionally guaranteed rights, along with mass surveillance. Due to the outdated legal framework, the privacy and rights of the people, who have enrolled in the system cannot be guaranteed. Individuals may be tracked or put under surveillance without proper authorization using the authentication and identification records in the Aadhaar database. Such records will typically also contain information on the precise location, time, and context of the authentication or identification and the services availed. Additionally, a proper communication channel to report issues in the Aadhaar portal or data breaches has not been communicated to the people. This further leads to non-reporting of vulnerabilities and increases the mistrust of people in Aadhaar. For instance: according to The Aadhaar Act of 2016, only UIDAI authorized officers could file a criminal complaint about violations under the Act· This means that any law-abiding citizen cannot initiate action to report fraudulent activities and would have to completely depend on the UIDAI for any action against fraudulent actors.

Another prominent deviation was that photocopies of the Aadhaar card were accepted by security personnel as a proof of identity at railway stations and airports, without authenticating the data from the UIDAI system. Due to non-implementation of this provision of The Aadhaar Act of 2016, any fraudster with a genuine citizen's name and Aadhaar number can take such a copy and enter high-security areas.

Based on the challenges discussed above, it is clear that the Aadhaar project is not doing well in many dimensions. The below mitigation process uses certain "elements of the

Operational Risk Resilience Model"[8] to address the gaps in the processes and external events.

Awareness and Risk Assessment

This process improves the effectiveness of risk control systems, which helps UIDAI to monitor and minimize ongoing risks. For instance, valid identification mechanisms should be identified in case the Aadhaar authentication fails. There is no hard-and-fast rule for technology to improve its functioning. UIDAI must "develop strategic IT infrastructure which can enable the entire populace to benefit equitably."[9] While the transition phase is being realized, public services should not be affected. Additionally, the Indian government must set up an effective communication channel and address the concerns of its citizens satisfactorily

Treatment Through Prevention and Detection

The Indian law has always been considered traditionalist in its approach. As the technology infrastructure improves, there is also a greater need to add provisions in the existing laws and create an enabling legal framework for data protection. One of the main components where Aadhaar could have performed significantly better was if the implementation of a Data Protection Act was achieved on time. This could have helped in setting effective data measures and standards and also in maintaining the faith of the citizens of India in the project.

Response and Recovery

The response and recovery mechanisms are aimed at containing an event immediately when it occurs. One of the biggest risks, which was identified, was the security of the system. To fortify the security of the system and prevent future data leaks, UIDAI could proactively seek incident reports about flaws or vulnerabilities from consumers. Such reports could help UIDAI address issues in the system, which were not looked at earlier. Also, the data leak through the Aadhaar project highlights the importance of training people to appropriately handle biometric data. This would involve developing a strong compliance framework and ensuring that the officials are knowledgeable about the framework.

Aadhaar has added tremendous value to the lives of many Indians, yet in many cases, it has failed to assuage the fear of citizens. The Indian government offers key lessons for governments across the world to incorporate the "best practices" to establish an effective digital identification system.

References

COVID-19 Vaccine Supply Chain Risks

[1] Paris, Costas. "Supply-Chain Obstacles Led to Last Month's Cut to Pfizer's Covid-19 Vaccine-Rollout Target." *The Wall Street Journal* 3 Dec. 2020. Accessed Dec. 2020 <www.wsj.com>.

[2] Murray, Brendan. "The World's Supply Chain Isn't Ready for a Covid-19 Vaccine." *Bloomberg*. 24 Jul. 2020. Accsssed Dec. 2020 <www.bloomberg.com>.

[3] Leonard, Matt. "What We Know about Pfizer's Coronavirus Vaccine Distribution Plan." *Supply Chain Dive*. 11 Nov. 2020. Accessed Dec. 2020 <www.supplychaindive.com>.

[4] Murray, Brendan.

[5] Ibid.

[6] Searle, Annie. "Third Party Risk." INFO 312 Enterprise Risk Management lecture, University of Washington. 2 Nov. 2020.

[7] Mancini, Donato Paolo. "Logisticians Grapple to Map out 'Cold Chain' for Vaccine Campaign." *Financial Times*. 8 Oct. 2020. Accessed Dec. 2020 <www.ft.com>.

[8] Griffin, Riley. "Another Challenge for Vaccine Makers: Keeping It at Minus-112 Degrees." Bloomberg. 20 May 2020. Accsssed Dec. 2020 <www.bloomberg.com>.

[9] Kaplan, Deborah Abrams. "The Role of Freight Forwarders in Distributing the Coronavirus Vaccine." *Supply Chain Dive*. 30 Nov. 2020. Accsssed Dec. 2020 <www.supplychaindive.com>.

[10] Nagurney, Anna. "The Challenges of Vaccine Cold-Chain Distribution Must Be Met to End the Pandemic." *Global Biodefense*. 5 Oct. 2020. Accssed Dec. 2020 <www.globalbiodefense.com>.

[11] Curtis, Patchin and Mark Carey. *Risk Assessment in Practice*. Committee of Sponsoring Organizations of the Treadway Commission. Oct. 2012. Accessed Dec. 2020 <www.deloitte.com>.

[12] Rahhal, Natalie "Pfizer Will Only Ship HALF Its Planned 100m Covid Vaccine Doses by Year-End." *Daily Mail Online.* 4 Dec. 2020. Accessed Dec. 2020 <www.dailymail.co.uk>.

[13] Leonard, Matt. "What We Know about Pfizer's Coronavirus Vaccine Distribution Plan." *Supply Chain Dive.* 11 Nov. 2020. Accessed Dec. 2020 <www.supplychaindive.com>.

[14] Ibid.

[15] Mehrotra, Kartikay. "Unknown Nation-State Attacking Vaccine Cold Chain in Phishing Scam, IBM Finds." *Bloomberg.* 3 Dec. 2020. Accessed Dec. 2020 <www.bloomberg.com>.

[16] Ibid.

[17] Zaboeva, Claire et al., "IBM Uncovers Global Phishing Campaign Targeting the COVID-19 Vaccine Cold Chain." *Security Intelligence.* 3 Dec. 2020. Accessed Dec. 2020 <www.securityintelligence.com >.

[18] Ibid.

[19] Ibid.

[20] Searle, Annie. "Terrorism & Technology." INFO 312 Enterprise Risk Management lecture, University of Washington. 23 Nov. 2020.

[21] Kaplan, Deborah Abrams "The Role of Freight Forwarders in Distributing the Coronavirus Vaccine." *Supply Chain Dive.* 30 Nov. 2020. Accessed Dec. 2020 <www.supplychaindive.com>.

[22] Hopkins, Jared. "Covid-19 Vaccines to Be Stored Secretly Under Tight Security." *The Wall Street Journal.* 21 Oct. 2020. Accessed Dec. 2020 <www.wsj.com>.

[23] "INTERPOL Warns of Organized Crime Threat to COVID-19 Vaccines." INTERPOL. 2 Dec. 2020. Accessed Dec. 2020 <www.inerpol.int>.

[24] Ibid.

[25] Murray, Brendan.

[26] Kaplan, Deborah Abrams.

[27] "Developing COVID-19 Vaccines May Not Be Enough: Turning Vaccines into Vaccinations." PricewaterhouseCoopers. Oct. 2020 Accessed Dec. 2020 <www.pwc.com>.

[28] "IBM Releases Report on Cyber Actors Targeting the COVID-19 Vaccine Supply Chain." Cybersecurity and Infrastructure Security Agency (CISA). 3 Dec. 2020. Accessed Dec. 2020 <www.us-cert.cisa.gov>.

[29] Kaplan, Deborah Abrams.

ESD—System Under Fire

[1] Annie Searle, "What Are Controls?" Enterprise Risk Management INFO 312 lecture at the University of Washington, presented October 11, 2020.

[2] Hilary Tuttle, "How the NSA's First CRO is Integrating Risk Management Into National Security." *Risk Management.* December 1, 2015. Accessed Oct. 2020 <www.rmmagazine.com.com>.

[3] Senior Manager at Microsoft Dynamics 365 Fraud Protection Team, discussion on vulnerable ESD Technology Systems, interviewed on October 20, 2020.

[4] Ibid.

[5] Tom Lee, "The Worst Government Website We've Ever Seen?" *Sunlight Foundation.* April 19, 2011. Accessed Oct. 2020 <www.sunlightfoundation.com>.

[6] Caroline Sinders, "Why the Government Sucks at Making Websites." *Gizmodo.* June 20, 2018. Accessed Oct. 2020 <www.gizmodo.com>.

[7] Wyatt Andrews and Anna Werner, "Healthcare.gov Plagued by Crashed on 1st Day." *CBS News.* October 1, 2013. Accessed Oct. 2020 <www.cbsnews.com>.

[8] "Unemployment Benefits Fraud." Employment Security Department - Washington State. N.D. Accessed Oct. 2020 <www.esd.wa.gov>.

[9] "Information Technology Contracts." *BidNet.* N.D. Accessed Oct. 2020 <www.bidnet.com>.

[10] Meyer, Robinson. "The Secret Startup That Saved The Worst Website In America." *The Atlantic.* July 9, 2015. Accessed Oct. 2020 <www.theatlantic.com>.

[11] "What Is Phishing." *KnowBe4*. N.D. Accessed Oct. 2020 <www.phishing.org>.

[12] Son, Nick and Christopher Lietz, "Cybersecurity and the Board of Directors – Tips for Securing Support for your Cyber Risk Management Program." (Seattle: Coalfire, 2016). Accessed Oct. 2020 <www.coalfire.com>.

[13] "Unemployment Insurance Phishing Fraud Alert." Office of Inspector General for the U.S. Department of Labor. N.D. Accessed Oct. 2020 <www.esdorchardstorage.blob.core.windows.net>.

[14] "Phishing Facts." *PhishingBox*. N.D. Accessed Oct. 2020 <www.phishingbox.com>.

[15] Peypoch, Ramon. "Preventing Phishing Attacks: The Dangers of Two-Factor Authentication." Agari. June 8, 2020. Accessed Oct. 2020 <www.agari.com>.

Essex Lorry Deaths: A Tragedy of Human Smuggling

[1] "Human Trafficking, Smuggling and Slavery" The Crown Prosecution Service Accessed 1 Dec. 2019. <www.cps.gov.uk>

[2] "Essex lorry deaths: Driver appears in court on manslaughter charges" Channel 4 News Accessed 1 Dec. 2019. <www.youtube.com>

[3] "GDP per capita (current US$) – Vietnam" World Bank. Accessed 1 Dec. 2019. <data.worldbank.org>

[4] "About Us" Immigration Enforcement. Accessed 1 Dec. 2019 <www.gov.uk >

[5] "About Us" Border Force. Accessed 1 Dec. 2019 <www.gov.uk >

[6] "People-smuggling checks at UK ports inadequate, hauliers say" The Guardian. Accessed 1 Dec. 2019 <www.theguardian.com>

[7] "Why do people risk their lives to get to the UK?" bbc.com. Accessed 1 Dec. 2019 <www.bbc.com >

[8] "Your options if you're in the UK illegally" Citizens Advice. Assessed 1 Dec. 2019 <www.citizensadvice.org.uk>

[9] Greenfield, Nunez-Neto, Mitch, Chang, and Rosas. "Human Smuggling from Central America to the United States: What Is Known or Knowable About Smugglers' Operations and Revenues?". Homeland Security Operational Analysis Center operated by the RAND Corporation, 2019. <https://www.rand.org/pubs/research_briefs/RB10057.html>

[10] "Ask a North Korean: smuggling goods and helping escapees across the Yalu River" NK News. Accessed 1 Dec. 2019 <www.nknews.org>

[11] *Trafficking in Persons Report. p.481-p.484* United States Department of State Office to Monitor and Combat Trafficking in Persons. Accessed 1 Dec. 2019 <www.state.gov>

[12] *A Global Report on Trafficking in Persons.* UNODC. Accessed 1 Dec. 2019 <www.unodc.org>

[13] *2018 Global Slavery Index.* Minderoo Foundation. Accessed 1 Dec. 2019 < www.globalslaveryindex.org>

[14] "Essex lorry deaths: UK must bear responsibility, says Chinese state media" The Guardian. Accessed 1 Dec. 2019 <www.theguardian.com>

[15] *Trafficking in Persons Report. p.481-p.484* United States Department of State Office to Monitor and Combat Trafficking in Persons. Accessed 1 Dec. 2019 <www.state.gov>

[16] Smith and Erwin. "Role & Responsibility Charting (RACI)" Project Management Forum, 2005

IoT & SCADA Risk in Smart Grids

[1] Lea, Perry. Internet of Things for Architects: Architecting IoT Solutions by Implementing Sensors, Communication Infrastructure, Edge Computing, Analytics, and Security. Packt Publishing. 2018. Pg. 15.

[2] Russel, Brian and Van Duren, Drew. *Practical Internet of Things Security.* Packt Publishing. 2016. Pg. 57.

[3] *CRASHOVERRIDE: Analysis of the Threat to Electric Grid Operations.* Dragos Inc. 12 Jun. 2017. Accessed Feb. 2019. <www.dragos.com>. Pg. 10.

[4] Business Blackout: The Insurance Implications of a Cyber Attack on the U.S. Power Grid. Lloyd's of London. 6 Jul. 2015. Accessed Feb. 2019. < www.lloyds.com>. Pg. 23.

[5] Russell and Van Duren. 2016. Pg. 5.

[6] Blume, Steven W. *Electric Power System Basics for The Nonelectric Professional.* 2nd Ed. 2017. Hoboken: John Wiley & Sons, Inc. Pg. 2-3.

[7] Pansini, Anthony J. *Power Transmission and Distribution.* 2nd Edition. The Fairmont Press. 2005. Pgs. 6, 29, 99.

[8] Pansini. 2005. Pgs. 5, 30.

[9] Blume. 2017. Pg. 147.

[10] Pansini. 2005. Pgs. 127.
[11] Thomas, Mini and McDonald, John D. *Power System SCADA and Smart Grids*. CRC Press. 2015. Pg. 1.
[12] Interagency International Cybersecurity Standardization Working Group. *Interagency Report on the Status of International Cybersecurity Standardization for the Internet of Things (IoT)*. National Institute of Standards and Technology. Nov. 2018. Accessed Feb. 2018. <www.nist.gov>. Pg. 4.
[13] Lea. 2018. Pg. 109.
[14] Lea. 2018. Pg. 283.
[15] Lea. 2018. Pg. 30.
[16] Boyes, Hugh et al. "The Industrial Internet of Things (IIoT): An Analysis Framework." *Elsevier B.V.* Oct 2018. Computers in Industry 101: 1-12. Pg. 3.
[17] Yi, Peizhong et al. "Distributed Opportunistic Scheduling for Building Load Control." In Xiao, Yang. Editor. *Security and Privacy in Smart Grids*. CRC Press. 2013.Pg. 88., Thomas and McDonald. 2015. Pg. 217-218.
[18] *NIST Special Publication 1500-201: Framework for Cyber-Physical Systems: Volume 1, Overview*. National Institute of Standards and Technology. Jun. 2017. Accessed Feb. 2019. <www.nist.gov>. Pg. 5.
[19] Russell and Van Duren. 2016. Pg. 48.
[20] Thomas and McDonald. 2015. Pgs. 205, 208.
[21] Thomas and McDonald. 2015. Pg. 6.
[22] Thomas and McDonald. 2015. Pg. 162.
[23] Thomas and McDonald. 2015. Pg. 44.
[24] Pansini. 2005. Pg. 2.

[25] Li, Zhao et al. "Advanced Metering Infrastructure and its Integration with the Distribution Management System." In Xiao, Yang. Editor. *Security and Privacy in Smart Grids*. CRC Press. 2013. Pg 102-103.

[26] Synder, Aaron F. et al. "Smart Meters and Advanced Metering Infrastructure." In Borlase, S. *Smart Grids*. CRC Press. 2018. Pg. 449-450.

[27] Li, Zhao et al. 2013. Pg. 103.
[28] "Table 10.10. Advanced Metering Count by Technology Type, 2008 through 2017." *Electric Power Annual 2017*. U.S. Energy Information Administration. 22 Oct. 2018. Accessed Mar. 2019. <www.eia.gov>.
[29] Li, Zhao et al. 2013. Pg. 105.

[30] Li, Zhao et al. 2013. Pg. 105.

[31] *Advanced Metering Infrastructure and Customer Systems: Results from the Smart Grid Investment Grant Program.* Office of Electricity Delivery and Energy Reliability. Sep. 2016. Accessed Mar. 3. 2019. <www.energy.gov>. Pg. 20.

[32] Snyder et al. 2018. Pg. 455-456.

[33] Yu, Xinghuo and Xue, Yusheng. "Smart Grids: A Cyber-Physical Systems Perspective." *Proceedings of the IEEE.* Volume 104, Issue 5. May. 2016. Accessed Feb. 2019. <www.ieee.org>. Pg. 1063.

[34] Li, Zhao et al. 2013. Pg. 110., Yue and Xue. 2016. Pg. 1059, 1066.

[35] Advanced Metering Infrastructure and Customer Systems. 2016. Pg. 25.

[36] Advanced Metering Infrastructure and Customer Systems. 2016. Pg. 25-26.

[37] Advanced Metering Infrastructure and Customer Systems. 2016. Pg. 26-27.

[38] Advanced Metering Infrastructure and Customer Systems. 2016. Pg. 29.

[39] *Advanced Metering Infrastructure: Utility Trends and Cost-Benefit Analyses in the NEEP Region.* Northeast Energy Efficiency Partnerships. 2017. Accessed Mar. 2019. <www.neep.org>. Pg. 9, Pg.18.

[40] Advanced Metering Infrastructure and Customer Systems. 2016. Pg. 28.

[41] *Seattle City Light 2019-2024 Strategic Plan.* Seattle City Light. N.d. Accessed Mar. 2019. <www.seattle.gov>. Pg. 6., Kroman, David. "City Light's 'smart meters' are $17.4M over budget." *Crosscut.* 27 Jun. 2018. Accessed Mar. 2019. <www.crosscut.com>.

[42] Snyder et al. 2018. Pg 452.

[43] Advanced Metering Infrastructure and Customer Systems. 2016. Pg. 22.

[44] Advanced Metering Infrastructure and Customer Systems. 2016. Pg. 10.

[45] Li, Zhao et al. 2013. Pg. 108.

[46] Thomas and McDonald. 2015. Pg 264.

47 Thomas and McDonald. 2015. Pg 280-281.

48 *Assessment of Demand Response and Advanced Metering.* Federal Energy Regulatory Commission. Dec. 2017. Accessed Mar. 2019. <www.ferc.gov>. Pg. 20.

49 Giaconi, Guili et al. "Privacy-Aware Smart Metering: Progress and Challenges." *arXiv.* 1802.01166v4. 24 May. 2018. Accessed Mar. 2019. www.arxiv.org. Pg. 3.

50 Russell and Van Duren. 2016. Pg. 34.

51 Giaconi, Guili et al. 2018. Pg. 7.

52 *Naperville Smart Meter Awareness v. City of Naperville.* No. 16-3766 (7th Cir. 2018).

53 "Privacy Win! US Court Says Fourth Amendment Protects Smart Meter Data" *Privacy International.* 24 Aug. 2018. Accessed Mar. 2019. <www.privacyinternational.org>., *Naperville Smart Meter Awareness v. City of Naperville.* Pg. 12-13.

54 Odendahl, Marylin. "Ruling in smart meter case highlights privacy concerns." *The Indiana Lawyer.* 6 Mar. 2019. Accessed Mar. 2019. <www.theindianalawyer.com>.

55 Sobczack, Blake and Behr, Peter. "Duke Agreed to Pay Record Fine for Lax Security — Sources." *E&E News.* 1 Feb. 2019. Accessed Mar. 2019. <www.eenews.com>.

56 *CIP-003-6 – Cyber Security – Security Management Controls.* North American Electric Reliability Corporation. 2014. Accessed Feb. 2019. <www.nerc.com>. Pg. 1-2.

57 "Seattle City Council adopts nation's strongest law to protect utility customer personal data." *Washington ACLU.* 6 Aug. 2018. Accessed Mar. 2019. <www.wa-aclu.org>.

58 "Advanced Metering: More Power in Your Hands." *Seattle City Light.* Mar. 2016. Accessed Mar. 2019. <www.seattle.gov>. Pg. 1-2.

59 *City of Seattle Privacy Impact Assessment: AMI.* City of Seattle. 17 Apr. 2017. Accessed Mar. 2019. <www.seattle.gov>. Pg. 3-4.

60 *City of Seattle Privacy Impact Assessment: AMI.* 2017. Pg 11.

61 Lea. 2018. Pg.160-161.

62 Russell and Van Duren. 2016. Pg. 28.

---

[63] Al-Ali, A.R. & Aburukba, Raafat. "Role of Internet of Things in the Smart Grid Technology." *Journal of Computer and Communications.* 03. 229-233. 2015. Accessed Mar. 2019. <www.researchgate.net>. Pg. 231.

[64] Foreman, James Christopher and Gurugubelli, Dheeraj. "Cyber Attack Surface Analysis of Advanced Metering Infrastructure." *The Electricity Journal.* 28.1: 94-103. 2015. Accessed Mar. 2019. <www.arxiv.org>. Pg. 4.

[65] Russell and Van Duren. 2016. Pg. 163-164

[66] Zillner, Tobias. "Zigbee Exploited: The Good, The Bad and The Ugly." *Cognosec.* 6 Aug. 2015. Accessed Mar. 2019. <www.blackhat.com>. Pg. 3-4.

[67] Higgenbotham, Stacey. "How to Design a Smart Apartment System that Works." *StaceyOnIoT.* 25 Jan. 2019. Accessed Mar. 2019. <www.staceyoniot.com>.

[68] Lea. 2018. Pg. 436.

[69] Lea. 2018. Pg. 437.

[70] Ronen, Eyal et. al. "IoT Goes Nuclear: Creating a ZigBee Chain Reaction." *IEEE Symposium on Security and Privacy.* 2017. Accessed Jan. 2019. <www.eyalro.net>. Pg. 13.

[71] McCullough, Jeff. "AMI Security Considerations." *Elster.* 2010. Accessed Mar. 2019. <www.elster.com>. Pg. 4.

[72] Foreman and Gurugubelli. 2015. Pg 4-5.

[73] Foreman and Gurugubelli. 2015. Pg 4.

[74] Foreman and Gurugubelli. 2015. Pg 3.

[75] *Advanced Metering Infrastructure and Customer Systems.* 2016. Pg. 69.

[76] "What is a DDoS Botnet?" *Cloudflare.* N.d. Accessed Mar. 2019. <www.cloudflare.com>.

[77] Cloudflare. N.d.

[78] C. G. J. Putman, Abhishta and L. J. M. Nieuwenhuis. "Business Model of a Botnet." *26th Euromicro International Conference on Parallel, Distributed and Network-based Processing (PDP),Cambridge*, pp. 441-445. 2018. Accessed Mar. 2019. <www.arxiv.org>. Pg. 1.

---

[79] Boddy, Sara and Shattuck, Justin. *The Hunt for IoT: The Growth and Evolution of Thingbots Ensures Chaos.* 4th Edition. F5 Networks. 13 Mar. 2018. Accessed Feb. 2019. <www.f5.com>. Pg. 7.

[80] "IDC Forecasts Worldwide Technology Spending on the Internet of Things to Reach $1.2 Trillion in 2022." *IDC.* 18 Jun. 2019. Accessed Mar. 2019. <www.idc.com>.

[81] Lea. 2018. Pg 443.

[82] Lea. 2018. Pg 443.

[83] Lea. 2018. Pg 443.

[84] Lea. 2018. Pg 444.

[85] *Internet of Things DDoS White Paper.* Electricity Information Sharing and Analysis Center. 24 Oct. 2016. Accessed Jan. 2019. <www.eisac.com>. Pg. 7.

[86] Fong, Kim et al. *rIoT: Quantifying Consumer Costs of Insecure Internet of Things Devices.* University of California, Berkeley, School of Information. 9 May. 2018. Acessed Jan. 2019. <www.ischool.berkeley.edu>. Pg. 22.

[87] Soltan, Soleh et al. "BlackIoT: IoT Botnet of High Wattage Devices Can Disrupt the Power Grid." *Proceedings of the 27th USENIX Security Symposium.* USENIX. Aug. 2018. Accessed Mar. 2019. <www.usenix.org>. Pg. 20.

[88] Soltan et al. 2018. Pg 16.

[89] Soltan et al. 2018. Pg 24.

[90] Soltan et al. 2018. Pg 24. Fong et al. 2018. Pg. 14.

[91] Blume. 2017. Pg 54.

[92] Blume. 2017. Pg 59.

[93] *United States Electricity Industry Primer.* Office of Electricity Delivery and Energy Reliability. Jul. 2015. Accessed Feb. 2019. <www.doe.gov>. Pg. 16.

[94] *United States Electricity Industry Primer.* 2015. Pg. 18.

[95] Thomas and McDonald. 2015. Pg. 137.

[96] Thomas and McDonald. 2015. Pg. 160.

[97] Blume. 2017. Pg 149.

[98] Thomas and McDonald. 2015. Pg. 161-162.

[99] Blume. 2017. Pg 69.

[100] Thomas and McDonald. 2015. Pg. 162.

[101] Blume. 2017. Pg 192.

[102] Huang, Yih-fang et al. "State Estimation in Electric Power Grids: Meeting New Challenges Presented by the requirements of the Future Grid." *IEEE Signal Processing Magazine*. Sep. 2012. Accessed Feb. 2019. <www.ieee.org.com>. Pg. 38.

[103] Huang et al. 2012. Pg.39.

[104] Thomas and McDonald. 2015. Pg. 18.

[105] Thomas and McDonald. 2015. Pg. 198.

[106] Hao, Jingping et al. "Cyber Security of Smart Grid State Estimation: Attacks and Defense Mechanisms." In Sun, Hongjian et al. (Eds). *Smarter Energy - From Smart Metering to the Smart Grid.* Institution of Engineering and Technology. 2016. Pg. 305.

[107] Thomas and McDonald. 2015. Pg. 196.

[108] Hao et al. 2016. Pg. 312.

[109] Hao et al. 2016. Pg. 310.

[110] Hao et al. 2016. Pg. 317.

[111] Singer, P.W. and Friedman, Allan. *Cybersecurity and Cyberwar: What Everyone Needs to Know.* Oxford University Press. 2014. Pg. 115.

[112] Singer and Friedman. 2014. Pg 117.

[113] Singer and Friedman. 2014. Pg 115, 120.

[114] Iqbal, Asif et al. "Digital Forensic Readiness in Critical Infrastructures: A Case of Substation Automation in the Power Sector." In Matoušek, Petr and Schmiedecker, Martin., Eds. *Digital Forensics and Cyber Crime: 9th International Conference, ICDF2C 2017, Prague, Czech Republic, October 9-11, 2017, Proceedings.* 2018. Accessed Mar. 2019. <www.springer.com>. Pg. 122-123.

[115] Iqbal et al. 2018. Pg. 126.

[116] Iqbal et al. 2018. Pg. 127.

[117] Hilt, Stephen et al. *Exposed and Vulnerable Critical Infrastructure: Water and Energy Industries.* TrendLabs. 30 Oct. 2018. Accessed Feb. 2019. <www.trendmicro.com>. Pg. 12-14.

[118] "What is Shodan?" *Shodan.io* n.d. Accessed Jan. 2019. <www.shodan.io>.

[119] Master OTW. "SCADA Hacking: Finding SCADA Systems Using Shodan." *Hackers Arise.* 30 Jun. 2016. Accessed Jan. 2019. <www.hackers-arise.com>.

[120] Hilt et al. 2018. Pg. 21.

[121] Radvanovsky, Bob and Brodsky, Jake. "Project SHINE: What We Discovered and Why You Should Care." *SANS Institute.* 24 Feb. 2015. Accessed Jan. 2019. <www.sans.org>. Pg. 7.

[122] Hilt et al. 2018. Pg 41-44.

[123] *21 Steps to Improve Cyber Security of SCADA Networks.* The President's Critical Infrastructure Protection Board. 2002. Accessed Feb. 2019. <www.hsdl.org>. Pg. 5.

[124] Hilt et al. 2018. Pg 45.

[125] Ong, D. "ICS/SCADA Cybersecurity and IT Cybersecurity: Comparing Apples and Oranges." *Atilla Cybertech.* 8 Dec. 2017. Accessed Feb. 2019. <www.attilatech.com>. Pg. 11-12.

[126] Wang, Yongge. "Smart Grid, Automation, and SCADA System Security." In Xiao, Yang. Editor. *Security and Privacy in Smart Grids.* CRC Press. 2013. Pg 257., Russell and Van Duren. 2016. Pg. 50.

[127] "Venezuela's Maduro: Blackout Due to Cyber-Attack, Infiltrators." *Al Jazeera.* 9 Mar 2019. Accessed Mar. 2019. <www.aljazeera.com>.

[128] Torchia, Christopher. "Venezuelan government targets Guaido as some power returns." *The Washington Post.* 12 Mar. 2019. Accessed Mar. 2019. <www.washingtonpost.com>.

[129] Leetaru, Kalev. "Could Venezuela's Power Outage Really Be A Cyber Attack?" *Forbes.* Mar 9. 2019. Accessed Mar. 2019. <www.forbes.com>.

[130] Dragos. 2017. Pg. 4.

[131] Dragos. 2017. Pg. 22.

[132] Dragos. 2017. Pg. 23.

[133] Zorz, Zeljka. "Keeping on Top of ICS-Focused Hacking Groups, Defenses." *HelpNet Security.* 2 Mar. 2018. Accessed Feb. 2019. <www.helpnetsecurity.com>.

---

[134] *Alert (TA17-163A): CrashOverride Malware.* The National Cybersecurity and Communications Integration Center. 27 Jul. 2019. Accessed Feb. 2019. <www.us-cert.gov>. Pg. 1-2.

[135] *TLP: White – ICS Defense Use Case No. 6: Modular ICS Malware.* Electricity Information Sharing and Analysis Center. 2 Aug. 2017. Accessed Feb. 2019. <www.e-isac.com>. Pgs. 1-2, 23.

[136] *Alert (TA18-074A): Russian Government Cyber Activity Targeting Energy and Other Critical Infrastructure Sectors.* The National Cybersecurity and Communications Integration Center. 15 Mar. 2019. Accessed Feb. 2019. <www.us-cert.org>. Pg 10.

[137] *Critical Infrastructure Protection: Additional Actions are Essential for Assessing Cybersecurity Framework Adoption.* United States Government Accountability Office. Feb. 2018. Accessed Feb. 2019. <www.gao.gov>. Pg 16-17.

[138] *Cybersecurity Strategy: 2018-2020.* U.S. Department of Energy. 2018. Accessed Mar. 2019. <www.energy.gov.>., *Multiyear Plan for Energy Sector Cybersecurity.* U.S. Department of Energy. Mar. 2018. Accessed Mar. 2019. <www.energy.gov.>.

[139] Whittaker, Zack. "U.S. Threatens to Reduce Intelligence Sharing if Germany Doesn't Ban Hauwei." *TechCrunch.* 11 Mar. 2019. Accessed Mar. 2019. <www.techcrunch.com>., Russell and Van Duren. 2016. Pg. 29.

[140] Lea. 2018. Pg 7

[141] *Independent Study Pinpoints Significant Scada / Ics Cybersecurity Risks.* Fortinet. 7 May. 2018. Accessed Mar. 2019. <www.fortinet.com>. Pg. 4.

[142] Coburn, Andrew et al. *Solving Cyber Risk.* John Wiley & Sons Inc. 2019. Pg. 101

Water in Trouble

[1] "Water & Sanitation." UNICEF USA. N.D. Accessed Mar. 2020 <www.unicefusa.org>.

[2] "Critical Infrastructure Sectors." CISA. N.D. Accessed Mar. 2020 <www.cisa.gov>.

[3] "Water and Wastewater Systems Sector-Specific Plan - 2015." CISA. 2015. Accessed Mar. 2020 <www.cisa.gov>.

4 *2017 Infrastructure Report Card.* American Society of Civil Engineers. Mar. 2017. Accessed Mar. 2020 <www.infrastructurereportcard.org>.

5 Kopaskie, Andrea. "Public vs Private: A National Overview of Water Systems." *Environmental Finance Blog*, the University of North Carolina at Chapel Hill. 9 Oct. 2016. Accessed Mar. 2020 <www.efc.web.unc.edu>.

6 Columbia Water Center. "The State of Water in America." Earth Institute, Columbia University. Mar. 2011. Accessed Mar. 2020 <www.blogs.ei.columbia.edu>.

7 *2019 State of the Water Industry Report.* American Water Works Association, 2019.

8 *Buried No Longer: Confronting the U.S. Water Infrastructure Challenge.* American Water Works Association. 2018. Accessed Mar. 2020 <www.awwa.org>.

9 Tabuchi, Hiroko. "$300 Billion War Beneath the Street: Fighting to Replace America's Water Pipes." *The New York Times.* 10 Nov. 2017. Accessed Mar. 2020 <www.nytimes.com>.

10 "The Aging Water Infrastructure: Out of Sight, Out of Mind?" Deloitte Insights. 21 Mar. 2016. Accessed Mar. 2020 <www2.deloitte.com>.

11 *S.3021, 2018. America's Water Infrastructure Act of 2018.* U.S. Congress. 3 January, 2018. Accessed Mar. 2020 <www.congress.gov>.

12 *2019 Data Breach Investigations Report.* Verizon. 2019.

13 "Our States." Aqua America Inc.. N.D. Accessed Mar. 2020 <www.aquaamerica.com>.

14 "United Water in the United States." United Water Federal Services. 2015. Accessed Mar. 2020 <www.unitedwater.com>.

15 Brum, Robert, and Nancy Cutler. "Rockland's Stinky Water: Suez Vows Upgrades amid Protest." Lohud.com, Rockland/Westchester Journal News. 16 Nov. 2019. Accessed Mar. 2020 <www.lohud.com>.

16 "State Sues Aqua Illinois After Lead Found In Chicago Suburb's Water." Illinois Public Media. Aug. 2019.

17 Jehl, Douglas. "As Cities Move to Privatize Water, Atlanta Steps Back." *The New York Times.* 10 Feb. 2003. Accessed Mar. 2020 <www.nytimes.com>.

18 Lam, James. "Operational Risk Management." *Enterprise Risk Management: from Incentives to Controls.* John Wiley & Sons, Inc., 2014, pp. 207-233.

19 Corasaniti, Nick. "18 Water Main Breaks Flood Hoboken, Pitting Mayor Against Water Company." *The New York Times.* 29 Aug. 2018. Accessed Mar. 2020 <www.nytimes.com>.

---

[20] "Summary of the Clean Water Act." Environmental Protection Agency. 11 Mar. 2019. Accessed Mar. 2020 <www.epa.gov>.
[21] "Overview of the Safe Drinking Water Act." Environmental Protection Agency. 14 Jan. 2020. Accessed Mar. 2020 <www.epa.gov
[22] Philip, Agnel, et al. "63 Million Americans Exposed to Unsafe Drinking Water." *USA Today*. 15 Aug. 2017. Accessed Mar. 2020 <www.usatoday.com>.
[23] *2018 Environmental Performance Index*. Yale Center for Environmental Law & Policy, Yale University. Jan. 2018. Accessed Mar. 2020 <epi.yale.edu>.
[24] Wood, Chris, et al. "Trump Weakens the Nation's Clean Water Efforts." *The New York Times*. 10 Feb. 2020.
[25] Davenport, Coral. "Trump Removes Pollution Controls on Streams and Wetlands." *The New York Times*. 23 Jan. 2020.

A Need for Increased Support of Cybersecurity Education

[1] Cabaj, Krzysztof et al. "Cybersecurity education: Evolution of the discipline and analysis of master programs." *Computers & Security*, vol. 75. June 2018. Accessed 26 Feb. 2019 <https://www.sciencedirect.com/science/article/pii/S0167404818300373>.
[2] Jontz, Sandra. "Cybersecurity Education Receives a Makeover." *AFCEA*. April 1 2015. Accessed 19 March 2019 <https://www.afcea.org/content/Article-cybersecurity-education-receives-makeover>.
[3] https://www.nist.gov/itl/applied-cybersecurity/nice/about
[4] https://www.nist.gov/itl/applied-cybersecurity/nice/about/strategic-plan
[5] Adams, Bernadette et al. "CHARTING A COURSE FOR SUCCESS: AMERICA'S STRATEGY FOR STEM EDUCATION." *National Science and Technology Council*. Dec. 2018. Accessed 19 March 2019 <https://www.whitehouse.gov/wp-content/uploads/2018/12/STEM-Education-Strategic-Plan-2018.pdf>.
[6] Manson, Daniel and Pike, Ronald. "The Case for Depth in Cybersecurity Education." *ACM Inroads*. March 2014. Accessed 15 March 2019 <https://dl.acm.org/citation.cfm?doid=2568195.2568212>.
[7] "National K-12 Cybersecurity Education Implementation Plan." Accessed 19 March 2019

<https://www.nist.gov/sites/default/files/documents/2017/04/26/nice_k12_implementation_plan.pdf>.

[8] Estrin, Daniel. "In Israel, teaching kids cyber skills is a national mission." *The Times of Israel.* 4 Feb. 2017. Accessed 19 March 2019 <https://www.timesofisrael.com/in-israel-teaching-kids-cyber-skills-is-a-national-mission/>.

[9] https://www.gen-cyber.com/about/

[10] Delaney, Melissa. "High Schools Prep Students to Fill Cybersecurity Skills Shortage." *EdTech.* 2 July 2018. Accessed 19 March 2019 <https://edtechmagazine.com/k12/article/2018/07/high-schools-prep-students-fill-cybersecurity-skills-shortage>.

[11] White, Sarah K. "Top U.S. universities failing at cybersecurity education." *CIO.* 25 April 2016. Accessed 15 March 2019 <https://www.cio.com/article/3060813/top-u-s-universities-failing-at-cybersecurity-education.html>.

[12] Schneider, Fred B. "Cybersecurity Education in Universities." *IEEE Security & Privacy.* 1 Aug. 2013. Accessed 20 Feb. 2019 <https://ieeexplore.ieee.org/document/6573305>.

[13] Austin, Greg. *Cybersecurity in China : The Next Wave.* Springer. 15 May 2018. Accessed 18 March 2019 <https://ebookcentral.proquest.com/lib/washington/detail.action?docID=5394735>.

[14] Siqi, Cao. "China to build world-class cyber security schools within 10 years." *Global Times.* 15 Aug. 2017. Accessed 18 March 2019 <http://www.globaltimes.cn/content/1061480.shtml>.

[15] *Ibid.*

[16] Press, Gil. "6 Reasons Israel Became A Cybersecurity Powerhouse Leading The $82 Billion Industry." *Forbes.* 18 July 2017. Accessed 18 March 2019 <https://www.forbes.com/sites/gilpress/2017/07/18/6-reasons-israel-became-a-cybersecurity-powerhouse-leading-the-82-billion-industry/#5e51081d420a>.

[17] Pressley, Alix. "Israel becomes 'breeding ground' for cybersecurity tech talent." *Intelligent CIO.* 22 Aug 2018. Accessed 18 March 2019 <http://www.intelligentcio.com/eu/2018/08/22/israel-becomes-breeding-ground-for-cybersecurity-tech-talent/>.

[18] Dark, Melissa et al. "Evaluating Cybersecurity Education Interventions: Three Case Studies." *IEEE Security & Privacy.* 4 June 2015. Accessed 18 March 2019 <https://ieeexplore.ieee.org/document/7118092>.

[19] Zurkus, Kacy. "How Can Industry Leaders and Academia Help Improve Cybersecurity Education?." *SecurityIntelligence.* 14 Nov. 2018. Accessed 18 March 2019 <https://securityintelligence.com/how-can-industry-leaders-and-academia-help-improve-cybersecurity-education/>.

[20] Morello, John. "We Need To Modernize Cybersecurity Education To Include Vital Skills." *Forbes.* 3 Dec. 2018. Accessed 18 March 2019 <https://www.forbes.com/sites/forbestechcouncil/2018/12/03/we-need-to-modernize-cybersecurity-education-to-include-vital-skills/#1f0e63595529>.

[21] Stone, Adam. "Cybersecurity Education Goes Broad." *Security Magazine.* 4 Jan. 2019. Accessed 19 March 2019 <https://www.securitymagazine.com/articles/89723-cybersecurity-education-goes-broad>.

[22] Dark, Melissa et al. "Advancing Cybersecurity Education." *IEEE Security & Privacy.* Nov.-Dec. 2014. Accessed 17 March 2019 <https://ieeexplore.ieee.org/document/7006436>.

[23] Morrow, Susan. "Minorities in Cybersecurity: The Importance of a Diverse Security Workforce." *InfoSec.* 29 May 2018. Accessed 19 March 2019 <https://resources.infosecinstitute.com/minorities-in-cybersecurity-the-importance-of-a-diverse-security-workforce/#gref>.

Cybersecurity in the Pharmaceutical Industry

[1] "Players in the Pharmaceutical Industry (Big Pharma)." *Desert Hope*, 2 Oct. 2019, https://deserthopetreatment.com/addiction-guide/drug-industry-trends/.

[2] "Johnson & Johnson - 49 Year Stock Price History: JNJ." *Macrotrends*, 2019, https://www.macrotrends.net/stocks/charts/JNJ/johnson-johnson/stock-price-history.

[3] "How Long a New Drug Takes to Go through Clinical Trials." *Cancer Research UK*, 22 Feb. 2019, https://www.cancerresearchuk.org/find-a-clinical-trial/how-clinical-trials-are-planned-and-organised/how-long-it-takes-for-a-new-drug-to-go-through-clinical-trials.

[4] Williams, Sean. "7 Facts You Probably Don't Know About Big Pharma." *The Motley Fool*, The Motley Fool, 19 July 2015, https://www.fool.com/investing/value/2015/07/19/7-facts-you-probably-dont-know-about-big-pharma.aspx.

---

5 5 Spyd3r April 8, et al. "The History Of Hacking." Help Net Security, 11 Mar. 2019, https://www.helpnetsecurity.com/2002/04/08/the-history-of-hacking/.
6 "Players in the Pharmaceutical Industry (Big Pharma)."
7 "What Is the Value of Stolen Digital Data?" Keeper Blog, 27 Apr. 2018, https://www.keepersecurity.com/blog/2017/05/12/what-is-the-value-of-stolen-digital-data/
8 Spyd3r April 8, et al.
9."What Is the Value of Stolen Digital Data?"
10 Spyd3r April 8, et al.
11 Douthwaite, Andrew. "How Can Pharma Protect Itself from Cyber Attacks?" *EPM Magazine*, 30 Sept. 2019, https://www.epmmagazine.com/opinion/how-can-pharma-protect-itself/.
12 Souza, Chris. "The State Of IT Security In The Pharma Industry Today." *Www.lifescienceleader.com*, 12 Oct. 2018, https://www.lifescienceleader.com/doc/the-state-of-it-security-in-the-pharma-industry-today-0001.
13 "Cost of a Data Breach Study." *IBM*, 2019, https://www.ibm.com/security/data-breach?ce=ISM0484&ct=SWG&cmp=IBMSocial&cm=h&cr=Security&ccy=US.
14 "What Is the Value of Stolen Digital Data?"
15 Cybercrimemag. "Cybercrime Damages $6 Trillion by 2021." *Cybercrime Magazine*, 9 Dec. 2018, https://cybersecurityventures.com/hackerpocalypse-cybercrime-report-2016/.
16 Spyd3r April 8, et al.
17 Souza, Chris. "What has Pharma Learned from the Merck Attack." *PharmaExec*, PharmaExec, 18 November 2017, http://www.pharmexec.com/what-has-pharma-learned-merck-cyber-attack.
18 Arif, Arsalan. "Merck Was Hit Hard by a Vicious Cyberattack Yesterday. Here Is What We Know." *Endpoints News*, Endpoints News, 28 June 2017, https://endpts.com/merck-was-hit-hard-by-a-vicious-cyberattack-yesterday-here-is-what-we-know/.
19 *Ibid.*
20 "The State of Cybersecurity in the Pharmaceutical Industry: Cyware Hacker News." *Cyware*, Home Hacker News Threat Intel & Info

Sharing The State of Cybersecurity in the Pharmaceutical Industry, 25 Nov. 2019, https://cyware.com/news/the-state-of-cybersecurity-in-the-pharmaceutical-industry-42835bac.

[21]"Merck Cyber Attack May Cost Insurers $275 Million: Verisk's PCS." *Reuters*, Thomson Reuters, 19 Oct. 2017, https://www.reuters.com/article/us-merck-co-cyber-insurance/merck-cyber-attack-may-cost-insurers-275-million-verisks-pcs-idUSKBN1CO2NP.

[22] Souza, Chris.

[23] Kathyberardi. "Merck Cyber Attack: The Aftermath of a 135 Million Dollar Data Breach." *IT Security Central - Teramind Blog*, 30 May 2018, https://itsecuritycentral.teramind.co/2017/11/10/merck-cyber-attack-the-aftermath-of-a-135-million-dollar-data-breach/.

[24] "The State of Cybersecurity in the Pharmaceutical Industry: Cyware Hacker News."

[25] Kathyberardi.

[26] "The State of Cybersecurity in the Pharmaceutical Industry: Cyware Hacker News."

[27] *Ibid.*

[28] *Ibid.*

[29] *Ibid.*

[30] Morris, Matt. "Industrial Cybersecurity Defenses Essential for Pharma Companies." *Pharma Manufacturing*, 15 Nov. 2017, https://www.pharmamanufacturing.com/articles/2017/industrial-cybersecurity-defenses-essential-for-pharma-companies/.

[31] *Ibid.*

[32] Donnelly, Conor. "Johnson & Johnson Data Breach Affects Hundreds of Irish Customers." *IT Governance Blog*, 29 May 2019, https://www.itgovernance.eu/blog/en/johnson-johnson-data-breach-affects-hundreds-of-irish-customers.

[33] Palmer, Eric. "Roche, like Bayer, Was Hit in Winnti Cyberattack ." *FiercePharma*, 24 July 2019, https://www.fiercepharma.com/manufacturing/roche-like-bayer-was-targeted-winnti-cyber-attack.

[34] Morris, Matt.

[35] Douthwaite, Andrew. "How Can Pharma Protect Itself from Cyber Attacks?" *EPM Magazine*, 30 Sept. 2019, https://www.epmmagazine.com/opinion/how-can-pharma-protect-itself/.

[36] Donnelly, Conor.

---

[37] The Future of Cyber Survey. (2019). [ebook] Available at: https://www2.deloitte.com/us/en/pages/advisory/articles/future-of-cyber-survey.html [Accessed 29 Nov. 2019].

[38] *Ibid.*

[39] Pytlik, Walter. "Healthcare Industry." *Cybersecurity Is an Important Issue for the Pharmaceutical Industry - Healthcare Industry*, 16 Jan. 2019, https://www.gesundheitsindustrie-bw.de/en/article/news/cybersecurity-is-an-important-issue-for-the-pharmaceutical-industry.

[40] Palmer, Eric.

Following Up on the Internet Bill of Rights

[1] Lewallen, Jonathan. "3 Key Takeaways from the Zuckerberg Hearings." *Washington Post.* 12 Apr 2018. Accessed Mar. 2019 <www.washingtonpost.com>.

[2] Swisher, Kara. "Introducing the Internet Bill of Rights" *The New York Times.* 4 Oct. 2018. Accessed Mar. 2019. <nytimes.com>

[3] "The World Wide Web: The Invention That Connected The World." Google Arts & Culture. Accessed Mar 2019. <artsandculture.google.com>

[4] Khanna, Ro. "Release: Rep. Khanna Releases 'Internet Bill Of Rights' Principles, Endorsed By Sir Tim Berners-Lee." House of Representatives. 4 Oct 2018. Accessed Mar. 2019. <khanna.house.gov>.

Khanna, Ro. "Rep Ro Khanna: Why we need an 'Internet Bill of Rights'" CNBC. 11 Apr 2018. Accessed 10 Mar 2019. <cnbc.com>.

[5] U.S. Reports: Katz v. United States, 389 U.S. 347 (1967).

[6] Berkman and Couts, "Title II is the key to net neutrality–so what is it?" The Daily Dot. 20 May 2014. Accessed Mar. 2019. <www.dailydot.com>

[7] *Compare Broadband Availability in Different Areas.* Federal Communication Commission. Accessed Mar. 2019. <broadbandmap.fcc.gov>

[8] "About the California Consumer Privacy Act" Californians for Consumer Privacy. Accessed Feb. 2019. <www.caprivacy.org>

Nickelsburg, Monica. "Washington State Considers New Privacy Law to Regulate Data Collection and Facial Recognition Tech" GeekWire. 22 Jan 19. Accessed Feb. 2019. <www.geekwire.com>.

[9] "Consumer Data Privacy in a Networked World." The White House. Feb 2012. Accessed Mar. 2019 <www.obamawhitehouse.archives.gov>.
[10] Khanna, Ro. "Facebook's and Google's Breaches Show It's Time for an Internet Bill of Rights." Time. 11 Oct 2018. Accessed 2 May 2019. <www.time.com>
[11] Presentation by Ashley Farley. "Open for Difference: Making knowledge a Public Good." World IA Day. Seattle, Washington. 23 Feb. 2019.
[12] Madden, Mary and Rainie, Lee. "Americans' Views About Data Collection and Security." *Pew Research Center."* 20 May 2015. Accessed Mar. 2019. <pewinternet.org>.
[13] Zakrzewski, Cat. "The Technology 202: Apple's Tim Cook wants Congress to rein in data brokers" *The Washington Post.* 17 Jan. 2019. Accessed Jan. 2019. <washingtonpost.com>.
[14] "Communications & Technology Subcommittee." House Committee on Energy & Commerce. N.D. Accessed Mar. 2019. <energycommerce.house.gov>.
[15] "GovTrack.us." Science, Technology, Communications Bills in the 116th Congress. Accessed 9 Mar 2019. <www.govtrack.us>.
[16] Arbel, Tali. "Democrat Bill Seeks to Restore Obama-era Net Neutrality Regs." *Associated Press.* 6 Mar 2019. Accessed Mar. 2019. <washingtonpost.com>.
[17] "Communications, Technology, Innovation and the Internet." U.S. Senate Committee on Commerce, Science & Transportation. N.D. Accessed Mar 2019. <commerce.senate.gov>.
[18] Cruz, Ted (@SenTedCruz) ""Net Neutrality" is Obamacare for the Internet; the Internet should not operate at the speed of government." 10 Nov 2014, 7:43 am. Tweet. Accessed Mar. 2019.
[19] Cruz, Ted and O'Reilly, Michael. "Opinion: Stop the Next Internet Power Grab." *Roll Call.* 21 Nov 2017. Accessed Mar. 2019. <www.rollcall.com>.
[20] Collier, Kevin. "Senators Fighting Online Privacy Rules Take Money from Industry." *Vocativ.* Mar 2017. Accessed Mar. 2019. <www.vocativ.com>.
[21] *Exec. Order No. 13821: Streamlining and Expediting Requests To Locate Broadband Facilities in Rural America.* Executive Office of the President. 11 Jan. 2018. Accessed Mar. 2019 <www.federalregistrer.gov>.
[22] "NTIA Seeks Comment on New Approach to Consumer Data Privacy" National Telecommunications and Information Administration. 25 Sept 2018. Accessed Mar. 2019. <ntia.doc.gov>

[23] Moore, Adam. *Privacy Rights: Moral and Legal Foundations.* The Pennsylvania State University Press. 2008.

From Fintech Darling to Bankruptcy: Control Failures of Wirecard

[1] Dan McCrum, "Wirecard's Suspect Accounting Practices Revealed," *Financial Times,* October 15, 2019, https://www.ft.com/content/19c6be2a-ee67-11e9-bfa4-b25f11f42901.

[2] Ibid.

[3] Lionel Laurent, "Wirecard Fraud Scandal Could Give Fintech a Bad Name," *Bloomberg.com* (Bloomberg, June 23, 2020), https://www.bloomberg.com/opinion/articles/2020-06-23/wirecard-fraud-scandal-could-give-fintech-a-bad-name?sref=oQfaxV65.

[4] Ibid.

[5] Ibid.

[6] Paul J. Davies, "Wirecard Says Missing $2 Billion Probably Doesn't Exist," *The Wall Street Journal* (Dow Jones & Company, June 22, 2020), https://www.wsj.com/articles/wirecards-missing-2-billion-probably-doesnt-exist-board-says-11592802732.

[7] Ibid.

[8] Dan McCrum and Stefania Palma, "Wirecard's Problem Partners," *Financial Times,* March 29, 2019, https://www.ft.com/content/cd12395e-4fb7-11e9-b401-8d9ef1626294.

[9] Dan McCrum, "KPMG Was Engaged as Auditor to Group Used in Suspicious Wirecard Deals," *Financial Times* (Financial Times, October 19, 2020), https://www.ft.com/content/2c1a79e6-8cb0-4895-9005-9515e24c8677.

[10] Ibid.

[11] Paul J. Davies, "Wirecard Says Missing $2 Billion Probably Doesn't Exist," *The Wall Street Journal* (Dow Jones & Company, June 22, 2020), https://www.wsj.com/articles/wirecards-missing-2-billion-probably-doesnt-exist-board-says-11592802732.

[12] Ibid.

[13] Paul J. Davies, "How Wirecard Went From Tech Star to Bankrupt," *The Wall Street Journal* (Dow Jones & Company, July 2, 2020), https://www.wsj.com/articles/wirecard-bankruptcy-scandal-missing-$2billion-11593703379.

[14] Stefania Palma and Dan McCrum, "Executive at Wirecard Suspected of Using Forged Contracts," *Financial Times*, January 30, 2019, https://www.ft.com/content/03a5e318-2479-11e9-8ce6-5db4543da632.
[15] Dan McCrum, "Wirecard's Suspect Accounting Practices Revealed," *Financial Times*, October 15, 2019, https://www.ft.com/content/19c6be2a-ee67-11e9-bfa4-b25f11f42901.
[16] Ibid.
[17] Dan McCrum and Stefania Palma, "Wirecard's Problem Partners," *Financial Times*, March 29, 2019, https://www.ft.com/content/cd12395e-4fb7-11e9-b401-8d9ef1626294.
[18] Ibid.
[19] Ibid.
[20] Ibid.
[21] Dan McCrum, "Wirecard's Suspect Accounting Practices Revealed," *Financial Times*, October 15, 2019, https://www.ft.com/content/19c6be2a-ee67-11e9-bfa4-b25f11f42901.

Wash Your Hands and Update Your Software

[1] Searle, Annie. "Pandemic Readiness in the US Financial Services Sector: When Failture is Not an Option." *Journal of Business Continuity & Emergency Planning.* Volume 2 Number 4. 7 Mar. 2008. Accessed Mar. 2020 <www.anniesearle.com>.
[2] "Bill Gates on the Next Great Epidemic." *CBS News.* 18 Jan. 2017. Accessed Mar. 2020 <www.cbsnews.com/video/bill-gates-on-the-next-great-epidemic>.
[3] Hautala, Laura. "As Coronavirus Crisis Worsens, Hacking Is Increasing, Security Experts Say." *CNET.* 19 Mar. 2020, Accessed Mar. 2020 <www.cnet.com/news/as-coronavirus-crisis-worsens-hacking-is-increasing-security-experts-say>.
[4] Ogée, Andrien & Guinard, Dominique. "Blockchain is not a magic bullet for security. Can it be trusted?" World Economic Forum. 19 Aug. 2019. Accessed Mar. 2020 <www.weforum.org/agenda/2019/08/blockchain-security-trust>.
[5] Van Eecke, Patrick & Haie, Anne-Gabrielle. "Practitioner's Corner · Blockchain and the GDPR: The EU Blockchain Observatory Report." *European Data Protection Law Review.* Volume 4 (2018), Issue 4. Apr. 2018. Accessed Mar. 2020 https://doi.org/10.21552/edpl/2018/4/18>.
[6] *Ibid.*

7 *Ibid.*

8 Thompson, Clive. "How to Teach Artificial Intelligence Some Common Sense." *Wired.* 13 Nov. 2018. Accessed Mar. 2020 <www.wired.com/story/how-to-teach-artificial-intelligence-common-sense>.

9 *Ibid.*

10 *Ibid.*

11 *Ibid.*

12 Richardson, Rashida & Schultz, Jason M. & Crawford, Kate. "Dirty Data, Bad Predictions: How Civil Rights Violations Impact Police Data, Predictive Policing Systems, And Justice." *New York University Law Review.* Volume 94, Issue 1. May 2019. Accessed Mar. 2020 <www.nyulawreview.org/wp-content/uploads/2019/04/NYULawReview-94-Richardson_etal-FIN.pdf>.

13 *Ibid.*

14 *Ibid.*

15 Thompson.

16 Searle.

17 Rundle, James, and Catherine Stupp. "Hackers Target Companies With Coronavirus Scams." *The Wall Street Journal.* 4 Mar. 2020, Accssed Mar. 2020 <www.wsj.com/articles/hackers-target-companies-with-fake-coronavirus-warnings-11583267812>.

18 *Ibid.*

19 *Ibid.*

20 *Ibid.*

21 Hautala.

22 *Ibid.*

23 *Ibid.*

24 *Ibid.*

25 Rundle.

26 *Ibid.*

27 Thompson.

28 Angelou, Maya. "Quotes by Maya Angelou." Goodreads. N.D. Accessed Mar. 2020 <www.goodreads.com/quotes/13397-be-present-in-all-things-and-thankful-for-all-things>.

A Consequentialist Argument For A Centralized Genetic Databank

[1] Santa Clara University. "A Framework for Ethical Decision Making." *Markkula Center for Applied Ethics*, www.scu.edu/ethics/ethics-resources/ethical-decision-making/a-framework-for-ethical-decision-making/.

[2] Sinnott-Armstrong, Walter. "Consequentialism." Stanford Encyclopedia of Philosophy, Stanford University, 22 Oct. 2015, plato.stanford.edu/entries/consequentialism/.

[3] Johnson, Robert, and Adam Cureton. "Kant's Moral Philosophy." Stanford Encyclopedia of Philosophy, Stanford University, 7 July 2016, plato.stanford.edu/entries/kant-moral/.

[4] Sinnot-Armstrong, Walter.

[5] Laestadius, Linnea I., Jennifer R. Rich, and Paul L. Auer. "All Your Data (Effectively) Belong to Us: Data Practices among Direct-to-Consumer Genetic Testing Firms." Genetics In Medicine 19 (2016): 513. Print.

[6] Regalado, Antonio, and Antonio Regalado. "2017 Was the Year Consumer DNA Testing Blew Up." MIT Technology Review, MIT Technology Review, 13 Feb. 2018, www.technologyreview.com/s/610233/2017-was-the-year-consumer-dna-testing-blew-up/.

[7] Khan, Razib, and David Mittelman. "Consumer Genomics Will Change Your Life, Whether You Get Tested or Not." *Genome Biology* 19.1 (2018): 120. Print.

[8] Stoeklé, Henri-Corto, et al. "23andme: A New Two-Sided Data-Banking Market Model." BMC Medical Ethics 17.1 (2016): 19. Print.

[9] Allyse, Megan A., et al. "Direct-to-Consumer Testing 2.0: Emerging Models of Direct-to-Consumer Genetic Testing." Mayo Clinic Proceedings 93.1 (2018): 113-20. Print.

[10] Bunnik EM, Janssens ACJW, Schermer MHN Personal utility in genomic testing: is there such a thing? Journal of Medical Ethics 2015;41:322-326.

[11] *Ibid.*

[12] Spector-Bagdady, Kayte. ""the Google of Healthcare." Enabling the Privatization of Genetic Bio/Databanking." Annals of Epidemiology 26.7 (2016): 515-19. Print.

[13] Ramage, Michael S. (2018). "Chapter 15: Forensic Specialization". In Shown Mills, Elizabeth. Professional Genealogy, Preparation, Practice & Standards. Genealogical Publishing Co. p. 337. ISBN 9780806320724

[14] Jakman, Alan. "Forensic Genealogy-The Real Story." Forensic Magazine, 13 Dec. 2016, www.forensicmag.com/article/2016/12/forensic-genealogy-real-story.

[15] "CODIS - NDIS Statistics." FBI, FBI, 8 June 2016, www.fbi.gov/services/laboratory/biometric-analysis/codis/ndis-statistics.

[16] *Ibid.*

[17] Corbyn, Zoë. "How Taking a Home Genetics Test Could Help Catch a Murderer." The Guardian, Guardian News and Media, 1 Dec. 2018, www.theguardian.com/science/2018/dec/01/how-home-dna-tests-are-solving-cold-cases-golden-state-killer.

[18] *Ibid.*

[19] Stoekle, Henri-Corto, et al.

[20] Spector-Bagdady, Kayte.

[21] Barbara Prainsack, Ph.D. (2011) Voting with their Mice: Personal Genome Testing and the "Participatory Turn" in Disease Research, Accountability in Research, 18:3, 132-147, DOI: 10.1080/08989621.2011.575032

[22] Lussier, Alexandre A., and Alon Keinan. "Crowdsourced Genealogies and Genomes." Science 360.6385 (2018): 153. Print.

[23] "New Genetic Associations for Parkinson's Disease Identified." 23andMe Blog, 11 Sept. 2017, blog.23andme.com/23andme-research/new-genetic-associations-parkinsons-disease-identified/.

[24] Molteni, Megan. "23andMe Is Digging Through Your Data for a Parkinson's Cure." Wired, Conde Nast, 13 Sept. 2017, www.wired.com/story/23andme-is-digging-through-your-data-for-a-parkinsons-cure/.

[25] "Study Finds New Genetic Associations for Depression." 23andMe Blog, 19 Apr. 2018, blog.23andme.com/23andme-research/study-finds-new-genetic-associations-for-depression/.

[26] "CODIS - NDIS Statistics."

[27] Gearty, Robert. "DNA, Genetic Genealogy Made 2018 the Year of the Cold Case: 'Biggest Crime-Fighting Breakthrough in Decades'." Fox News, FOX News Network, www.foxnews.com/us/dna-genetic-

genealogy-made-2018-the-year-old-the-cold-case-biggest-crime-fighting-breakthrough-in-decades.

[28] Zhang, Sarah. "How a Tiny Website Became the Police's Go-To Genealogy Database." The Atlantic, Atlantic Media Company, 1 June 2018, www.theatlantic.com/science/archive/2018/06/gedmatch-police-genealogy-database/561695/.

[29] Murphy, Erin E. "The Dark Side of DNA Databases." The Atlantic, Atlantic Media Company, 8 Oct. 2015, www.theatlantic.com/science/archive/2015/10/the-dark-side-of-dna-databases/408709/.

[30] Spector-Bagdady, Kayte.

[31] "CODIS - NDIS Statistics."

[32] "Law Enforcement DNA Databases Draw Scrutiny, Controversy." Public Radio International, www.pri.org/stories/2016-09-16/law-enforcement-dna-databases-draw-scrutiny-controversy.

[33] "After The Golden State Killer, The Ethics Of Genetic Testing." Science Friday, www.sciencefriday.com/segments/after-the-golden-state-killer-the-ethics-of-genetic-testing/.

[34] Murphy, Heather. "How an Unlikely Family History Website Transformed Cold Case Investigations." The New York Times, The New York Times, 15 Oct. 2018, www.nytimes.com/2018/10/15/science/gedmatch-genealogy-cold-cases.html.

[35] Zhang, Sarah. "Most People of European Ancestry Can Be Identified From a Relative's DNA." *The Atlantic*, Atlantic Media Company, 11 Oct. 2018, www.theatlantic.com/science/archive/2018/10/golden-state-killer-genealogy/572545/.

[36] Erlich, Yaniv, et al. "Identity Inference of Genomic Data Using Long-Range Familial Searches." *Science* 362.6415 (2018): 690. Print.

[37] Murphy, Heather.

[38] Zhang, Sarah.

[39] Spector-Bagdady, Kayte.

[40] Gymrek, Melissa, et al. "Identifying Personal Genomes by Surname Inference." *Science* 339.6117 (2013): 321. Print.

[41] Price, W. Nicholson, et al. "Shadow Health Records Meet New Data Privacy Laws." *Science* 363.6426 (2019): 448. Print.

[42] "CODIS - NDIS Statistics."

[43] Naomi Elster. "How Forensic DNA Evidence Can Lead to Wrongful Convictions." *JSTOR Daily*, JSTOR, 6 Dec. 2017, https://daily.jstor.org/forensic-dna-evidence-can-lead-wrongful-convictions/

[44] Konkel, Lindsey. "Racial and Ethnic Disparities in Research Studies: The Challenge of Creating More Diverse Cohorts" *Environmental health perspectives* vol. 123,12 (2015): A297-302.

[45] "Diversity Matters in Research." *23andMe Blog*, 6 Mar. 2019, blog.23andme.com/23andme-research/diversity-matters-in-research/.

[46] 23andMe. "Roots into the Future®." *23andMe*, www.23andme.com/roots/.

[47] "Diversity Matters in Research."

[48] Naomi Elster.

[49] Manrai, Arjun K., et al. "Genetic Misdiagnoses and the Potential for Health Disparities." *New England Journal of Medicine* 375.7 (2016): 655-65. Print.

[50] Johnson, Robert, and Adam Cureton.

AI and Policing: Bias, Failures, and A Path Forward

[1] Rigby, Michael J. "Ethical Dimensions of Using Artificial Intelligence in Health Care." *AMA Journal of Ethics*. Feb. 2019. Accessed 13 March 2019 <www.journalofethics.ama-assn.org>.

[2] "An Act to Promote Transparency, the Public's Welfare, Civil Rights, and Civil Liberties." *ACLU*. Oct. 2018. Accessed 27 Feb. 2019 <www.aclu.org>.

[3] Williams, Mary-Anne. "Risky Bias in Artificial Intelligence." *Australasian Science, 39, 43.* Jul. 2018. Accessed 27 Feb. 2019 <www.search.proquest.com>.

[4] Lohr, Steve. "Facial Recognition Is Accurate, if You're a White Guy." *The New York Times*. 9 Feb. 2018. Accessed 27 Feb. 2019 <www.nytimes.com>.

[5] Dastin, Jeffrey. "Amazon scraps secret AI recruiting tool that showed bias against women." *Reuters*. 9 Oct. 2018. Accessed 27 Feb. 2019 <www.reuters.com>.

[6] Buolamwini, Joy. "Amazon's Symptoms of FML—Failed Machine Learning—Echo the Gender Pay Gap and Policing Concerns." *MIT Media Lab.* 19 Oct. 2018. Accessed 27 Feb. 2019 <www.medium.com>.

[7] Snow, Jacob. "Amazon's Face Recognition Falsely Matched 28 Members of Congress with Mugshots." *ACLU.* 26 July 2018. Accessed 3 March 2019 <www.aclu.org>.

[8] Buolamwini, Joy. "Re: Audit of Amazon Rekognition Uncovers Gender and Skin-Type Disparities." 25 June 2018. Accessed 28 Feb. 2019 <www.uploads.strikinglycdn.com>.

[9] Cagle, Matt and Ozer, Nicole. "Amazon Teams Up with Government to Deploy Dangerous New Facial Recognition Technology." *ACLU.* 22 May 2018. Accessed 3 March 2019 <www.aclu.org>.

[10] Williams, Timothy. "Study Supports Suspicion That Police Are More Likely to Use Force on Blacks." *The New York Times.* 7 July 2016. Accessed 4 March 2019 <www.nytimes.com>.

[11] Bedoya, Alvaro, et al. "The Perpetual Line-Up." *Georgetown Law Center on Privacy & Technology.* 18 Oct. 2016. Accessed 27 Feb. 2019 <www.perpetuallineup.org/>.

[12] Crawford, Kate, et al. "Dirty Data, Bad Predictions: How Civil Rights Violations Impact Police Data, Predictive Policing Systems, and Justice." *New York University Law Review Online.* 13 Feb. 2019.

[13] Chen, Alex. "The Threat of Artificial Intelligence to POC, Immigrants, and War Zone Civilians." *Towards Data Science.* 6 Feb. 2019. Accessed 27 Feb. 2019 <www.towardsdatascience.com>.

[14] Koepke, Logan and Robinson, David. "Stuck in a Pattern: Early evidence on "predictive policing" and civil rights." *Upturn.* Aug. 2016. Accessed 27 Feb. 2019 <www.upturn.org>.

[15] Malik, Nikita. "The Problems with Using Artificial Intelligence and Facial Recognition in Policing." *Forbes.* 29 Oct. 2018. Accessed 3 March 2019 <www.forbes.com>

[16] Lloyd, Kirsten. "Bias Amplification in Artificial Intelligence Systems." *Cornell University*. 20 Sept. 2018. Accessed 28 Feb. 2019 <www.arxiv.org>.

[17] "Criminal Law Reform." *ACLU*. Accessed 5 March 2019 <www.aclu.org>.

[18] Smith, Brad. "Facial recognition technology: The need for public regulation and corporate responsibility." *Microsoft*. 13 July 2018. Accessed 3 March 2019 <www.blogs.microsoft.com>.

[19] Crawford, Kate et al. "AI Now Report 2018." *AI Now Institute*. Dec. 2018. Accessed 24 Feb. 2019 <www.ainowinstitute.org>.

[20] Joh, Elizabeth. "Artificial Intelligence and Policing: First Questions." *Seattle University Law Review*. 2018.

[21] Buolamwini, Joy. "How I'm fighting bias in algorithms." *TED*. Nov. 2016. Accessed 24 Feb. 2019 <www.ted.com>.

[22] "Community Control Over Police Surveillance." *ACLU*. Accessed 3 March 2019 <www.aclu.org>.

An Analysis of the Indian Adoption Project and Current Migrant Family Separation Policies

[1] *National Indian Law Library*. n.d. 07 Dec 2018. <narf.org/nill/documents/icwa/faq/access.html>

[2] Herrera, Jack. "A New Report Reveals How Family Separation Led Border Officials to Break the Law." *Pacific Standard* 04 Oct. 2018. Accessed 07 Dec. 2018. <psmag.com/news/a-new-report-reveals-how-family-separation-led-border-officials-to-break-the-law>.

[3] Jacobs, Margaret D. "Remembering the "Forgotten Child": The American Indian Child Welfare Crisis of the 1960s and 1970s." *The American Indian Quarterly* 37.1-2 (2013): 136-159.

[4] Krol, Debra. "Inside the Native American Foster Care Crisis Tearing Families Apart." *Vice* 08 Feb 2018. Accessed 07 Dec 2018. <vice.com/en_us/article/a34g8j/inside-the-native-american-foster-care-crisis-tearing-families-apart>.

[5] O'Sullivan, Meg Devlin. ""More Destruction to These Family Ties": Native American Women, Child Welfare, and the Solution of Sovereignty." *Journal of Family History* 41.1 (2016): 19-38

---

[6] Willis, Cheryl D and Donna M Norris. "Custodial Evaluations of Native American Families: Implications for Forensic Psychiatrists." *Journal of the American Academy of Psychiatry and the Law* 38.4 (2010): 540-546.

[7] *National Indian Child Welfare Association.* n.d. Accessed 06 Dec. 2018. <nicwa.org/>.

[8] Flynn, Meagan. "Court strikes down Native American adoption law, saying it discriminates against non-Native Americans." *The Washington Post* 10 Oct 2018. Accessed 07 Dec. 2018. <washingtonpost.com/news/morning-mix/wp/2018/10/10/court-strikes-down-native-american-adoption-law-saying-it-discriminates-against-non-native-americans/?utm_term=.cf74306272e4>.

[9] Lind, Dara. "The Trump administration's separation of families at the border, explained." 15 Jun. 2018. Accessed 07 Dec 2018. <vox.com/2018/6/11/17443198/children-immigrant-families-separated-parents>.

[10] Miroff, Nick, Amy Goldstein and Maria Sacchetti. "'Deleted' families: What went wrong with Trump's family-separation effort." *The Washington Post* 28 Jul 2018. Accessed 07 Dec. 2018. <washingtonpost.com/local/social-issues/deleted-families-what-went-wrong-with-trumps-family-separation-effort/2018/07/28/54bcdcc6-90cb-11e8-8322-b5482bf5e0f5_story.html?noredirect=on&utm_term=.392191ddcdc9>.

[11] Domonoske, Camila and Richard Gonzales. "What We Know: Family Separation And 'Zero Tolerance' At The Border." National Public Radio 19 Jun 2018. Accessed 07 Dec. 2018. <npr.org/2018/06/19/621065383/what-we-know-family-separation-and-zero-tolerance-at-the-border>.

[12] Semple, Kirk. "For Families Split at Border, an Anguished Wait for Children's Return." *The New York Times* 01 Sep 2018. Accessed 07 Dec. 2018. < nytimes.com/2018/09/01/world/americas/immigrant-families-separation-border.html>.

[13] Lind, Dara. "The executive order Trump claims will end family separation, explained." *Vox* 20 Jun 2018. Accessed 07 Dec. 2018. <vox.com/2018/6/20/17485488/executive-order-immigration-trump-families-together>.

[14] Jordan, Miriam. "'Why Did You Leave Me?' The Migrant Children Left Behind as Parents Are Deported." *The New York Times* 28 Jul 2018. Accessed 07 Dec. 2018. <nytimes.com/2018/07/27/us/migrant-

families-
deportations.html?action=click&module=RelatedCoverage&pgtype=Article®ion=Footer>.

[15] Detlor, B. "Information Management". *International Journal of Information Management* 30.2 (2010), 103-108

[16] Floridi, Luciano. *Information: A Very Short Introduction.* Oxford: Oxford University Press, 2010.

[17] Burke, Garance. "AP Investigation: Deported parents can lose custody of kids." *Associated Press* 09 Oct 2018. Accessed 07 Dec. 2018. <apnews.com/795a71655ebd4803b6742d1306555986>.

[18] Joyce, Kathryn. "The Threat of International Adoption for Migrant Children Separated From Their Families." *The Intercept* 01 Jul 2018. Accessed 07 Dec. 2018. <theintercept.com/2018/07/01/separated-children-adoption-immigration/>.

[19] *American Indian Adoptees.* n.d. Accessed 06 Dec. 2018. <blog.americanindianadoptees.com/p/how-to-open-closed-adoption-records-for.html>.

[20] Becker-Green, Jody. "Developing One's Self: Adoption and Identity Formation Through the Eyes of Transracially Adopted Native American Adults." *Dissertations and Theses* (2009): Paper 2792.

[21] Palmiste, Claire. "From the Indian Adoption Project to the Indian Child Welfare." Indigenous Policy Journal 22.1 (2011): 1-11.

[22] LaRoche, James. "I Only Speak For Myself." IMT 500C Student Paper. 2016.

[23] Barnhardt, Ray and Oscar Kawagley Angayuqaq . "Indigenous Knowledge Systems and Alaska Native Ways of Knowing." *Anthropology and Education Quarterly* 36.1 (2005): 8-23.

[24]Cleek, Ashley. "The government says Border Patrol agents in the Southwest speak Spanish - but many migrants speak Indigenous languages." *Public Radio International* 03 Jul 2018 Accessed 07 Dec. 2018. <pri.org/stories/2018-07-03/government-says-border-patrol-agents-southwest-speaks-spanish-many-migrants-speak>

[25] Fishman, Joshua. *Reversing Language Shift.* Clevedon: Multilingual Matters, 1991.

[26] Crawford, James. "Endangered Native American Languages: What Is To Be Done and Why?" *The Bilingual Research Journal* 19.1 (1995): 17-38

B Corporations: Purpose-Driven Business for the Good of All

[1] "Maryland First State in Union to Pass Benefit Corporation Legislation." CSR Wire. 14 April 2010. Accessed June 2020. <www.csrwire.com/press_releases/29332>.

[2] "Maryland First State in Union to Pass Benefit Corporation Legislation." CSR Wire. 14 Apr. 2010. Accessed June 2020. <www.csrwire.com/press_releases/29332>.

[3] "State by State Status of Legislation." *B Lab.* Accessed June 2020. <www.benefitcorp.net>.

[4] "Annual Benefit Report." Pennsylvania Department of State Bureau of Corporations and Charitable Organizations. February 2017. Accessed June 2020. <www.dos.pa.gov/BusinessCharities/Business/RegistrationForms/Documents>.

[5] Melia, Thomas O. "The Corporate Conscience." *The American Interest.* 21 Mar. 2018. Accessed June 2020. < www.the-american-interest.com>.

[6] Leighton, Mara. "B Corps are businesses committed to using their profit for good — these 14 are making some truly great products." *Business Insider.* 23 Mar. 2020. Accessed June 2020. <www.businessinsider.com>.

[7] Mishel, Lawrence and Wolfe, Julie. "CEO compensation has grown 940% since 1978." *Economic Policy Institute.* 14 Aug. 2019. Accessed June 2020. <www.epi.org>.

[8] Meacham, James D. "Ethics in Business: Theory and Practice." Information Management IMT550 Presentation. 16 Apr. 2020.

[9] "A Global Community of Leaders." *B Lab.* Access June 2020. < www.bcorporation.net>.

[10] "About B Corps." *B Lab.* Access June 2020. < www.bcorporation.net-about-B-corps>.

[11] "Business Roundtable Redefines the Purpose of a Corporation to Promote 'An Economy That Serves All Americans.'" *Business Roundtable.* 19 Aug. 2019. Accessed June 2020. <businessroundtable.org>.

[12] Hackenberg, Jonquil. "2020 Will Be The Year Of Sustainable Business: Here's Why." *Forbes.* 28 Nov. 2019. Accessed June 2020. <www.forbes.com>.

[13] "Why Companies Certify." *B Lab.* Access June 2020. < www.bcorporation.net/certification>.

Instagram and Mental Health — Profits or Positivity?

[1] Gesenhues, Amy. "Time Spent on Facebook, Snapchat Remains Flat, but Instagram Sees Growth." *Marketing Land*, 28 May 2019, Accessed 30 Nov. 2019 <www.marketingland.com/time-spent-on-facebook-snapchat-remains-flat-but-instagram-sees-growth-261705>.

[2] "Our Story." Instagram, 26 Mar. 2019, Accessed 30 Nov. 2019 <www.instagram-press.com/our-story/>.

[3] Clement, J. "Preferred Social Networks of U.S. Teens 2019." Statista, 15 Oct. 2019, Accessed 30 Nov. 2019 <www.statista.com/statistics/250172/social-network-usage-of-us-teens-and-young-adults/>.

[4] MacMillan, Amanda. "Why Instagram Is the Worst Social Media for Mental Health." *Time.* 25 May 2017, Accessed 30 Nov. 2019 <www.time.com/4793331/instagram-social-media-mental-health/>.

[5] So, Adrienne. "Instagram Will Test Hiding 'Likes' in the US Starting Next Week." *Wired.* 16 Nov. 2019, Accessed 30 Nov. 2019 <www.wired.com/story/instagram-hiding-likes-adam-mosseri-tracee-ellis-ross-wired25/>.

[6] Leventhal, Jamie. "How Removing 'Likes' from Instagram Could Affect Our Mental Health." *PBS*. 25 Nov. 2019, Accessed 30 Nov. 2019 <www.pbs.org/newshour/science/how-removing-likes-from-instagram-could-affect-our-mental-health>.

[7] Wagner, Kurt. "Instagram Will Remove 'Likes' From Posts for Some U.S. Users." *Bloomberg.* 8 Nov. 2019, Accessed 1 December, 2019 <www.bloomberg.com/news/articles/2019-11-09/instagram-will-remove-likes-from-posts-for-some-u-s-users>.

[8] King, Jacob. "How to Measure Mental Health." Centre for Urban Design and Mental Health, UD/MH, Accessed 1 Dec. 2019 <www.urbandesignmentalhealth.com/how-to-measure-mental-health.html>.

[9] Clement, J. "Instagram Sponsored Influencer Content Volume 2020." Statista, 11 Apr. 2019 Accessed 1 Dec. 2019

<www.statista.com/statistics/693775/instagram-sponsored-influencer-content/>.

[10] Carbone, Lexie. "This Is How Much Instagram Influencers Really Cost." *Later Blog.* 10 Apr. 2019, Accessed 1 Dec. 2019 <www.later.com/blog/instagram-influencers-costs/>.

[11] Iqbal, Mansoor. "Instagram Revenue and Usage Statistics (2019)." *Business of Apps.* 6 Nov. 2019, Accessed 1 Dec. 2019 <www.businessofapps.com/data/instagram-statistics/#4>.

[12] Leskin, Paige. "Influencers Are Fighting for Attention as Instagram Tests Removing Likes from Its Platform: 'There's No Audience Applause at the End of a Performance'." *Business Insider.* 5 Sept. 2019. Accessed 1 Dec. 2019 <www.businessinsider.com/instagram-influencers-removing-likes-impact-2019-9>.

[13] Hamilton, Isobel Asher. "It Looks like Facebook, Instagram, and YouTube Want to Kill the Popularity Metrics They Invented." *Business Insider.* 3 Sept. 2019. Accessed 3 Dec. 2019 <www.businessinsider.com/facebook-instagram-youtube-killing-like-subscribers-2019-9>.

The Global Paradox of Digital Divides in a Shrinking Village

1 McLuhan, Marshall. The Gutenberg Galaxy: The Making of Typographic Man. 1962.

2 McLuhan, Marshall. Understanding Media: The Extensions of Man. 1964.

3 van Dijk, Jan A. G. M. The Deepening Divide: Inequality in the Information Society. 2005.

4 Hazeley, Del. "Bridging the Digital Divide – The African Condition." ASA Institute for Risk and Innovation. 2013. Accessed 3 June 2020. <https://static1.squarespace.com/static/5d34d73f43d37a0001d73dcf/t/5eb030181d97446802ca00fa/1588604953214/ASAResearchNote_2013_Hazeley_BridgingDigitalDivide.pdf>.

5 Hazeley, D. Page 2.

6 Singh, Manish. "Facebook, Telcos to build huge subsea cable for Africa and Middle East." Tech Crunch. 14 May 2020. Accessed 2 June 2020. <https://techcrunch.com/2020/05/14/2africa-africa-middle-east-facebook-subsea-cable/>.

7 Singh, M.

8 Google Cloud. "Expanding our global infrastructure with new regions and subsea cables." Google. Accessed 3 June 2020. <https://www.blog.google/products/google-cloud/expanding-our-global-infrastructure-new-regions-and-subsea-cables/>.

9 United Nations. "The Millennium Development Goals Report 2015." 2015. Accessed 2 June 2020 https://www.un.org/millenniumgoals/2015_MDG_Report/pdf/MDG%202015%20rev%20(July%201).pdf

10 United Nations. 2015. P. 7.

11 United Nations. 2015. P. 7.

12 United Nations. 2015. P. 67.

13 Chinn, M., & Fairlie, R. "The Determinants of the Global Digital Divide: A Cross-Country Analysis of Computer and Internet Penetration." Oxford Economic Papers, 59(1). 2007. Accessed 3 June 2020. < https://doi.org/10.1093/oep/gpl024>.

14 Chinn, M., & Fairlie, R. Page 38.

15 Chinn, M., & Fairlie, R. Pgs. 38-40.

16 United Nations. "About the Sustainable Development Goals." United Nations. Accessed 3 June 2020. <https://www.un.org/sustainabledevelopment/sustainable-development-goals/>.

17 United Nations. 2020. Accessed 3 June 2020.

18 United Nations. "Goal 9: Build resilient infrastructure, promote sustainable industrialization and foster innovation" United Nations. Accessed 3 June 2020. <https://www.un.org/sustainabledevelopment/infrastructure-industrialization/>.

19 Economic and Social Council. "Progress Towards the Sustainable Development Goals." United Nations. Accessed 3 June 2020 <https://sustainabledevelopment.un.org/content/documents/26158Final_SG_SDG_Progress_Report_14052020.pdf>. Page 22.

20 Garrido, M. and Fellows, M. "Access to Information and the Sustainable Development Goals." Technology & Social Change Group, University of Washington. 2017. Page 11. Accessed 3 June 2020. <https://da2i.ifla.org/sites/da2i.ifla.org/files/uploads/docs/da2i-2017-introduction.pdf>. Page 11.

21 Garrido, M. and Fellows, M. Pgs. 11-12.

22 van Dijk, J. Pgs. 13-14.

23 van Dijk, J. Page 13.

---

24 van Dijk, J. Page 10.
25 Google Cloud. "Infrastructure: Introducing Equiano, a subsea cable from Portugal to South Africa." Google. n.d. Accessed 3 June 2020. < https://cloud.google.com/blog/products/infrastructure/introducing-equiano-a-subsea-cable-from-portugal-to-south- africa>.
26 Hazeley, D. P. 6.
27 Hazeley, D. P. 6.
28 Hazeley, D. P. 7.
29 Norbrook, N., Soumaré, M., et al. "HUBS NOT HYPE: Tech hubs across Africa to incubate the next generation." The Africa Report. 14 February 2020. Accessed 3 June 2020. <https://www.theafricareport.com/23434/tech-hubs-across-africa-to-incubate-the-next- generation/>.
30 Toyama, K. (2010). "Can Technology End Poverty? " Boston Review 36(5). 1 November 2010. Accessed 3 June 2020. <http://www.bostonreview.net/forum/can-technology-end-poverty>.
31 Toyama, K.
32 Ruge, TMS. "CELEBRITY STUNTS OF ALTRUISM ARE KILLING LIVELIHOODS IN AFRICA." 16 April 2009. Accessed 3 June 2020. <http://tmsruge.com/2009/04/16/celebrity-stunts-of-altruistism-are-killing-livelihoods-in-africa/>.
33 Ruge, TMS.

The Dubious Merits of Meritocracy

[1] Booker, Cory. "Cory Booker: It's Time for The Next Step in Criminal Justice Reform." *The Washington Post.* 10 Mar. 2019. Accessed Mar. 2019 <www.washingtonpost.com>.

[2] Breuninger, Kevin. "Ex-Trump campaign boss Paul Manafort's light sentence in Mueller case could soon become much longer." *CNBC.* 8 Mar. 2019. Accessed Mar. 2019 <www.cnbc.com>.

[3] Booker, Cory.

[4] *Ibid.*

[5] Ziedenberg, Jason and Vincent Schiraldi. *Costs and Benefits? The Impact of Drug Imprisonment in New Jersey.* Justice Policy Institute. Oct. 2003. Accessed Mar. 2019 <www.justicepolicy.org>.

[6] Bell, Jamaal. "Mass Incarceration: A Destroyer of People of Color and Their Communities." *HuffPost.* Dec. 2017. Accessed Mar. 2019 <www.huffpost.com>.

[7] Graham, Sandra and Lowery, Brian. "Priming Unconscious Racial Stereotypes About Adolescent Offenders." *Law And Human Behavior.* Oct. 2004. Accessed Mar. 2019.;
David C. Baldus, George Woodworth, David Zuckerman, and Neil Alan Weiner. "Racial Discrimination and the Death Penalty in the Post-Furman Era: An Empirical and Legal Overview with Recent Findings from Philadelphia." *Cornell Law Review.* 1998. Accessed Mar. 2019 <scholarship.law.cornell.edu>.

[8] Cheney-Rice, Zak. "One-Third of the World's Women in Prison Have One Striking Thing in Common." *Mic.* 28 Sep. 2014. Accessed Mar. 2019 <www.mic.com>.

[9] Correll, Joshua, Bernadette Park, Charles Mosley Judd, Bernd Wittenbrink, Melody S. Sadler and Tracie Lynn Keesee. "Across The Thin Blue Line: Police Officers And Racial Bias In The Decision To Shoot." *Journal of Personality and Social Psychology.* 2007.

[10] Mina Cikara, Rachel A. Farnsworth, Lasana T. Harris, and Susan T. Fiske. "On The Wrong Side Of The Trolley Track: Neural Correlates Of Relative Social Valuation." *Social Cognitive And Affective Neuroscience,* 5(4), 404-413. 2010.;
Fiske, S. T., Cuddy, A. J. C., Glick, P., & Xu, J. "A Model of (Often Mixed) Stereotype Content: Competence and Warmth Respectively Follow from Perceived Status and Competition." *Journal of Personality and Social Psychology,* 82(6), 878902. 2002.;
Moreira, W. "O impacto da meritocracia nas decisoes socialmente criticas (Master's Thesis)." Universidade de Lisboa, Lisboa, Portugal. 2016.

[11]Blair, I. V., Havranek, E. P., Price, D. W., Hanratty, R., Fairclough, D. L., Farley, T., & Steiner, J. F. "Assessment of Biases Against Latinos and African Americans Among Primary Care Providers and Community Members." *American Journal Of Public Health,* 103(1), 92-98. 2013.;
Cooper, L. A., Roter, D. L., Carson, K. A., Beach, M. C., Sabin, J. A., Greenwald, A. G., & Inui, T. S. "The Associations of Clinicians' Implicit Attitudes About Race With Medical Visit Communication and Patient Ratings of Interpersonal Care." *American Journal Of Public Health,* 102(5), 979-987. 2012;

Green, A. R., Carney, D. R., Pallin, D. J., Ngo, L. H., Raymond, K. L., Iezzoni, L. I., & Banaji, M. R. "Implicit Bias Among Physicians And Its Prediction of Thrombolysis Decisions For Black And White Patients." *Journal Of General Internal Medicine*, 22(9), 1231-1238. 2007.;
Haider, A. H., Sexton, J., Sriram, N., Cooper, L. A., Efron, D. T., Swoboda, S., & Lipsett, P. A. "Association of Unconscious Race and Social Class Bias with Vignette-Based Clinical Assessments by Medical Students." *JAMA*, 306(9), 942-951. 2011.;
Haider, A. H., Schneider, E. B., Sriram, N., Dossick, D. S., Scott, V. K., Swoboda, S. M., & Lipsett, P. A. "Unconscious Race and Social Class Bias Among Acute Care Surgical Clinicians and Clinical Treatment Decisions." *JAMA Surgery*, 150(5), 457464. 2015.;
Haider, A. H., Schneider, E. B., Sriram, N., Scott, V. K., Swoboda, S. M., Zogg, C. K., & Freischlag, J. A. "Unconscious Race and Class Biases Among Registered Nurses: Vignette-Based Study Using Implicit Association Testing." *Journal of the American College of Surgeons*, 220(6), 1077-1086. 2015.;
Stepanikova, I. "Racial-Ethnic Biases, Time Pressure, and Medical Decisions." *Journal of Health and Social Behavior*, 53(3), 329-343. 2012.

[12] Bilhim, J. O Mérito nos Processos de Seleção da Alta Direção da Administração Pública Portuguesa: mito ou realidade? XVII Congresso Internacional do CLAD sobre a Reforma do Estado e da Administração Pública, 57-78. 2012;
Sealy, Ruth. "Changing Perceptions of Meritocracy In Senior Women's Careers." *Gender in Management: An International Journal.* May 2010.

[13] Freitas, Gonçalo Santos.

Everest-Philipps, Max. "Meritocracy and Public Service Excellence." *International Journal of Civil Service Reform and Practice*, Astana Civil Service Hub. Nov. 2015. Accessed Mar. 2019 <www.astanahubjournal.org>.

[14] Isaacs, Julia. International Comparisons of Economic Mobility. *The Brookings Institution.* Jul. 2016. Accessed Mar. 2019 <www.brookings.edu>;
Everest-Philipps, Max.

[15] Isaacs, Julia.

[16] "British Social Attitudes." *NatCen Social Research.* 2009. Accessed Mar. 2019 <www.bsa.natcen.ac.uk>.

---

[17] "A Framework for Thinking Ethically." Markkula Center for Applied Ethics, Santa Clara University (SCU). May 2009. Accessed Mar. 2019 <www.scu.edu>.

[18] Freitas, Gonçalo Santos.;
Furnham, Adrian. "The Protestant Work Ethic and Attitudes Towards Unemployment." *Journal of Occupational Psychology*, 55(4), 277-285. 1982;
Ziedenberg, Jason and Vincent Schiraldi.;
McCoy, Shannon K. and Brenda Major. "Priming Meritocracy and the Psychological Justification of Inequality." *Journal of Experimental Social Psychology*, 43(3), 341. 2007.;
Vala, J., Lima, M., & Lopes, D. "Social Values, Prejudice and Solidarity in the European Union." *In European Values at the End of the Millennium*, eds. Wil Arts, & Loek Halman. Leiden: Brill. 2004;
Costa-Lopes, R., Wigboldus, D., & Vala, J. Priming meritocracy increases implicit prejudice. Lisboa: Colecção Working Papers ICS. 2017.

[19] Freitas, Gonçalo Santos.;
Wellman, Joseph D, Xi Liu and Clara L. Wilkins. "Priming Status-Legitimizing Beliefs: Examining The Impact On Perceived Anti-White Bias, Zero-Sum Beliefs, and Support For Affirmative Action Among White People." *British Journal of Social Psychology*, 55(3), 426–437. 2015.

[20] Vostroknutov, Alexander. "Merit and Justice: An Experimental Analysis of Attitude to Inequality." *PLoS*. Dec. 2014. Accessed Mar. 2019 <www.journals.plos.org>.

[21] Feng, C., Luo, Y., Gu, R., Broster, L., Shen, X., Tian, T., Luo, Y., Krueger, Frank. "The Flexible Fairness: Equality, Earned Entitlement, and Self-Interest." *PLoS*. Sep. 2013 <www.journals.plos.org>.

[22] Castilla, Emilio and Stephen Benard. "The Paradox of Meritocracy in Organizations." *Administrative Science Quarterly*. Dec. 2010. Accessed Mar. 2019 <www.journals.sagepub.org>.

[23] *Ibid.*

[24] Freitas, Gonçalo Santos.

[25] Freitas, Gonçalo Santos.;
Hagan, J. "Extralegal Attributes And Criminal Sentencing: An Assessment of a Sociological Viewpoint." *Law and Society Review*, 8, 357–383. 1974.;

Johnson, S. L. "Black Innocence and the White Jury." *Michigan Law Review*, 83, 1611–1708. 1985.

[26] Freitas, Gonçalo Santos.

[27] Castilla, Emilio and Stephen Benard.

[28] Freitas, Gonçalo Santos.

Von Mises, Ludwig. *Bureaucracy*. Yale University Press. 1944. Accessed Mar. 2019 <www.mises.org>.

Regan, Tom. "Introduction to Moral Reasoning." *In Information Ethics: Privacy, Property, and Power*, edited by Adam D. Moore, University of Washington Press, 2005.

Rosas & Ferreira, 2014

[29] Freitas, Gonçalo Santos.;

Jost, J. T., & Hunyady, O. "Antecedents and Consequences of System-Justifying Ideologies." *Current Directions in Psychological Science.* 14(5), 260-265. 2005.;

McCoy, S. K., & Major, B. Priming meritocracy and the psychological justification of inequality. Journal of Experimental Social Psychology, 43(3), 341. 2007.

[30] Medina, Jennifer., Benner, K.atie., and Taylor, Kate. "Actresses, Business Leaders and Other Wealthy Parents Charged in U.S. College Entry Fraud." *The New York Times.* Mar. 2019. Accessed Mar. 2019 <www.nytimes.com>.

[31] Zimmer, Ben. "A 'Meritocracy' Is Not What People Think It Is." *The Atlantic.* 14 Mar. 2019. Accessed Mar. 2019 <www.theatlantic.com>.

[32] *Ibid.*

[33] de Botton, Alain. "A Kinder, Gentler Philosophy of Success." TEDGlobal. Jul. 2009. Accessed Mar. 2019 <www.ted.com>.

[34] *Ibid.*

[35] "A Framework for Thinking Ethically."

[36] Malachowski, Alan. "Rorty's Political Turn." *Aeon Media Group.* 6 Mar. 2019. Accessed Mar. 2019 <www.aeon.co>.

Accenture's Technology Vision 2020 for Innovation DNA

[1] Michael Blitz, et. al, "Technology Vision 2020: We, the Post-Digital People Full Report." Accenture, 2020. p. 111. https://www.accenture.com/us-

en/insights/technology/_acnmedia/Thought-Leadership-Assets/PDF-2/Accenture-Technology-Vision-2020-Full-Report.pdf.
[2] Jocelyn Aqua, et. al. "Consumer Intelligence Series: Protect.me, " PWC United States. Accessed May 30, 2020, https://www.pwc.com/us/en/services/consulting/library/consumer-intelligence-series/cybersecurity-protect-me.html.
[3] Michael Blitz, et. al, "Technology Vision 2020: We the Post-Digital People," Accenture Research, Accenture, Accessed May 24, 2020. https://www.accenture.com/us-en/insights/technology/technology-trends-2020.
[4] Michael Blitz, et. al, "Technology Vision 2020: We, the Post-Digital People Full Report." Accenture, 2020. p. 117.
[5] Jennifer Langston, "Project Silica proof of concept stores Warner Bros. 'Superman' movie on quartz glass," *Microsoft Innovation Stories*, November 4, 2019, https://news.microsoft.com/innovation-stories/ignite-project-silica-superman/.
[6] Michael Blitz, et. al, "Technology Vision 2020: We the Post-Digital People."
[7] Michael Blitz, et. al, "Technology Vision 2020: We the Post-Digital People."
[8] Adam Burden, et. al, "Full Value. Full Stop. Full Report" *Accenture Into the New*. Accessed May 27, 2020 .https://www.accenture.com/us-en/insights/future-systems/future-ready-enterprise-systems.
[9] Adam Burden, et. al, "Full Value. Full Stop. Full Report."
[10] James Wilson, "Why You Should Mind the Innovation Achievement Gap." Accenture Research Blog. October 25, 2019, https://www.accenture.com/us-en/blogs/accenture-research/innovation-achievement-gap.
[11] James Wilson, "Why You Should Mind the Innovation Achievement Gap."
[12] United States Securities and Exchange Commission. "Starbucks Corporation Form 10-K."
[13] David G.W. Birch, "Introduction," *Digital Identity Management: Perspectives on Technological, Business, and Social Implications*, Gower Publishing Ltd., 2007. Page 6.
[14] Jeff Stone, "Starbucks CISO Explains Security Outsourcing Model," The Wall Street Journal, October 12, 2018, https://www.wsj.com/articles/starbucks-ciso-explains-security-outsourcing-model-1539377251
[15] Michael Blitz, et. al, "Technology Vision 2020: We, the Post-Digital People Full Report." Accenture, 2020. p. 120.
[16] Michael Blitz, et. al, "Technology Vision 2020: We, the Post-Digital People Full Report." Accenture, 2020. p. 115.
[17] "Harnessing Nature to Brew a More Sustainable Beer." Indigo Agriculture. Accessed May 30, 2020. https://www.indigoag.com/anheuser-busch.

---

[18] Michael Blitz, et. al, "Technology Vision 2020: We, the Post-Digital People Full Report." Accenture, 2020. p. 119.
[19] "AI in 2019: A Year in Review." *Medium*. Accessed May 27, 2020. https://medium.com/@AINowInstitute/ai-in-2019-a-year-in-review-c1eba5107127.
[20] Summary of Annie Searle's INFO 415 Spring 2020 quarter takeaways
[21] Jeff Stone, "Starbucks CISO Explains Security Outsourcing Model."

Amazon Prime Air: A Disaster Waiting to Happen?

[1]Navellier, L. (2020, October 16). *Is Amazon Stock a Good Buy After Prime Day?* Retrieved from INVESTORPLACE:
https://investorplace.com/2020/10/is-amazon-stock-a-good-buy-after-prime-day/

[2] Saleh, K. (n.d.). *The Importance of Same Day Delivery – Statistics and Trends.* Retrieved from invesp: https://www.invespcro.com/blog/same-day-delivery/

[3] Rose, C. (2013, December 1). *Amazon's Jeff Bezos looks to the future.* Retrieved from 60 Minutes:
https://www.cbsnews.com/news/amazons-jeff-bezos-looks-to-the-future/

[4] Searle, A. (2020, November 30). *Final Paper(5 pages).* Week 10A Autumn 2020 INFO 312 FINAL, lecture slide.

[5] Korman, R. (2019, February 22). *What is 'safe enough' for drone deliveries?* Retrieved from Seattle Times:
https://www.seattletimes.com/business/boeing-aerospace/what-is-safe-enough-for-drone-deliveries/

[6] Captain, S. (2020, May 14th). *Minnesota man shoots down drone with shotgun.* Retrieved from DroneDJ:
https://dronedj.com/2020/05/14/minnesota-man-shoots-down-drone-with-shotgun/

[7] Mann, J. (2015, December). The Internet of Things: Opportunities and Applications across Industries. (I. I. Analytics, Interviewer)

[8] FAA. (2016, June 27). *What we do.* Retrieved from Federal Aviation Administration: https://www.faa.gov/about/mission/activities/

[9] Palmer, A. (2020, August 31). *Amazon wins FAA approval for Prime Air drone delivery fleet.* Retrieved from CNBC:
https://www.cnbc.com/2020/08/31/amazon-prime-now-drone-delivery-fleet-gets-faa-approval.html

[10] FAA. (2020, April 1). *14 CFR Part 135 Certification Process.* Retrieved from Federal Aviation Administration :

---

https://www.faa.gov/licenses_certificates/airline_certification/135_certification/cert_process/

[11] FAA. (2020, May 12). *Package Delivery by Drone (Part 135).* Retrieved from Federal Aviation Administration : https://www.faa.gov/uas/advanced_operations/package_delivery_drone/

[12] Searle, A. (2020, October 19). *Using RACI Model for Clarity.*Week 4A Autumn 2020 INFO 312 FINAL, lecture slide.

[13] Sheetz, M. (2019, December 21). *INVESTING Analysts say Alphabet, UPS have early edge in delivery's next frontier: drones.* Retrieved from CNBC: https://www.cnbc.com/2019/12/21/analysts-alphabet-ups-have-edge-in-deliverys-next-frontier-drones.html

[14] Bowman, J. (2020, September 3). *Delivery Drones Could Save Amazon Billions.* Retrieved from The Motley Fool: https://www.fool.com/investing/2020/09/03/delivery-drones-could-save-amazon-billions/

Apple's Security & Privacy Practices

[1] Apple Inc. (2020). Privacy Governance. Retrieved March 10, 2020, from Apple: https://www.apple.com/legal/privacy/en-ww/governance/

[2] Siri Team. (2018, April 16). Personalized Hey Siri, Vol. 1, Issue 9. (Apple Inc.) Retrieved March 10, 2020, from Apple's Machine Learning Journal: https://machinelearning.apple.com/2018/04/16/personalized-hey-siri.html

[3] Siri Team. (2017, October 1). Hey Siri: An On-device DNN-powered Voice Trigger for Apple's Personal Assistant, Vol. 1, Issue 6. (Apple Inc.) Retrieved March 10, 2020, from Apple's Machine Learning Journal: https://machinelearning.apple.com/2017/10/01/hey-siri.html

[4] Hardy, E. (2018, April 16). More goes into 'Hey Siri' than you might think. (Cultomedia) Retrieved March 10, 2020, from Cult of Mac: https://www.cultofmac.com/542121/hey-siri-apple-machine-learning-journal-april-2018/

[5] Apple Inc. (2019, July 10). If Siri or "Hey Siri" isn't working. Retrieved March 10, 2020, from Apple Support: https://support.apple.com/en-us/HT207489

[6] Apple Inc. (2020, February 26). About Face ID advanced technology. Retrieved March 10, 2020, from Apple Support: https://support.apple.com/en-us/HT208108

[7] Brewster, T. (2018, December 18). We Broke Into A Bunch Of Android Phones With A 3D-Printed Head. (Forbes Media, LLC; Forbes

family) Retrieved March 10, 2020, from Forbes: https://www.forbes.com/sites/thomasbrewster/2018/12/13/we-broke-into-a-bunch-of-android-phones-with-a-3d-printed-head/#1d5682fb1330

[8] Apple Inc. (2020). Hardware microphone disconnect in Mac. Retrieved March 10, 2020, from Apple Platform Security: https://support.apple.com/guide/security/hardware-microphone-disconnect-in-mac-secbbd20b00b/1/web/1

[9] Lowell, K. G. (2017). Civil Liberty or National Security: The Battle Over iPhone Encryption. Georgia State University Law Review, 33, 485-517.

[10] Cox, J. (2018, April 12). Cops Around the Country Can Now Unlock iPhones, Records Show. Retrieved February 21, 2020, from Vice: https://www.vice.com/en_us/article/vbxxxd/unlock-iphone-ios11-graykey-grayshift-police

[11] Welch, C. (2018, July 10). Apple's USB Restricted Mode: how to use your iPhone's latest security feature. (Vox Media) Retrieved March 10, 2020, from The Verge: https://www.theverge.com/2018/7/10/17550316/apple-iphone-usb-restricted-mode-how-to-use-security

[12] Kelly, G. (2019, November 26). Privacy and Security Evaluation of the Apple HomePod smart speaker. (Common Sense) Retrieved March 10, 2020, from Common Sense Education: https://www.commonsense.org/education/articles/privacy-and-security-evaluation-of-the-apple-homepod-smart-speaker

[13] Apple Inc. (2020, January 28). Apple Platform Security Fall 2019. Retrieved February 1, 2020, from Apple Platform Security: https://support.apple.com/guide/security/welcome/web

[14] Apple Inc. (2020). Privacy Features. Retrieved March 10, 2020, from Apple: https://www.apple.com/privacy/features/

[15] Apple Inc. (2019, September). Photos Tech Breif. Retrieved March 10, 2020, from Apple: https://www.apple.com/ios/photos/pdf/Photos_Tech_Brief_Sept_2019.pdf

[16] Apple Inc. (2019, November). Safari Privacy Overview. Retrieved March 10, 2020, from Apple: https://www.apple.com/safari/docs/Safari_White_Paper_Nov_2019.pdf

[17] Apple Inc. (2019, July). Transparency Report. Retrieved February 5, 2020, from Apple: https://www.apple.com/legal/transparency/

[18] Nicas, J. (2019, October 9). Apple Removes App That Helps Hong Kong Protesters Track the Police. (The New York Times Company) Retrieved March 10, 2020, from The New York Times:

https://www.nytimes.com/2019/10/09/technology/apple-hong-kong-app.html

[19] Menn, J. (2020, January 21). Exclusive: Apple dropped plan for encrypting backups after FBI complained - sources. (Thomson Reuters Corporation) Retrieved March 10, 2020, from Reuters: https://www.reuters.com/article/us-apple-fbi-icloud-exclusive/exclusive-apple-dropped-plan-for-encrypting-backups-after-fbi-complained-sources-idUSKBN1ZK1CT

[20] Apple Inc. (2019, November 18). iCloud Security Overview. Retrieved March 12, 2020, from Apple Support: https://support.apple.com/en-us/HT202303

[21] Lewis, P. (2020, March 2). iOS 14 release date and new feature rumours. (Mac Publishing) Retrieved March 20, 2020, from Mac World: https://www.macworld.co.uk/news/apple/ios-14-release-date-3779520/

[22] Gartenberg, C. (2019, May 7). Google reveals that 10 percent of devices are using Android 9 Pie, nine months after its release. (Vox Media) Retrieved March 10, 2020, from The Verge: https://www.theverge.com/2019/5/7/18535811/google-android-9-pie-usage-numbers-10-percent-ios-comparison-io-2019

Deepfakes on Instagram: Mitigating Event and Process Risk

[1] "Threat Horizon 2019." Information Security Forum. Mar. 2017. Accessed Feb. 2020 <www.securityforum.org>.

[2] Mueller, Robert S. *Report on the Investigation Into Russian* Interference *In the 2016 Election, Vol. I.* U.S. Department of Justice. Mar. 2019. Accessed Feb. 2020 <www.documentcloud.org>.

[3] Rusli, Evelyn M. "Facebook Buys Instagram for $1 Billion." *New York Times.* 9 Apr. 2012. Accessed Feb. 2020 <www.dealbook.nytimes.com>.

[4] Smith, Allan. "Facebook's Instagram poised to be 2020 disinformation battleground, experts say." *NBC News.* 19 Oct. 2019. Accessed Feb. 2020 <www.nbcnews.com>.

[5] Lam, James C. "An Animal Kingdom of Disruptive Risk." NACD *Directorship.* Feb. 2019. Accessed Feb. 2020 <boardleadership.nacdonline.org>.

[6] "Rise of the Deepfakes." *The Week.* 9 Jun. 2018. Accessed Feb. 2020 <www.theweek.com>.

[7] Barrett, Paul M. "Disinformation and the 2020 Election: How the Social Media Industry Should Prepare." NUY Stern Center for Business and Human Rights. Sep. 2019. Accessed Feb. 2020 <www.stern.nyu.edu>.

[8] Ibid.
[9] DiResta, Renee et al. "The Tactics and Tropes of the Internet Research Agency." *New Knowledge Organization.* Dec. 2018. Accessed Feb. 2020 <www.nyt.com>.
[10] Lam, James. "Operational Risk Management." *Enterprise Risk Management.* Wiley. 2003.
[11] "Community Guidelines." Instagram. N.d. Accessed 4 Feb. 2020 <www.instagram.com>.
[12] Zuckerberg, Mark. "Standing for Voice and Free Expression." Facebook. 17 Oct. 2019. Accessed Feb. 2020 <www.facebook.com>.
[13] Bickert, Monica. "Enforcing Against Manipulated Media." Facebook. 6 Jan. 2020. Accessed Feb 2020 <www.facebook.com>.
[14] *Ibid.*

GDPR Enforcement and Google's €50 Million Fine

[1] *DLA Piper GDPR Data Breach Survey: February 2019.* DLA Piper. Feb 19. 2019. Accessed 20 Feb. 2019. <www.dlapiper.com>. Pg. 3.
[2] "Regulation (EU) 2016/679 of the European Parliament and of the Council of 27 April 2016 on the protection of natural persons with regard to the processing of personal data and on the free movement of such data, and repealing Directive 95/46/EC (General Data Protection Regulation)." *Official Journal of the European Union.* 4 May. 2016. Vol. L119. pp. 1-88. Pg 33.
[3] Calder, Alan. *EU GDPR: A Pocket Guide.* European 2nd Ed. IT Governance Publishing. Accessed 1 Mar. 2019. <www.oreilly.com>. Pg. 34-35.
[4] Cobb, Stephen. *Data Privacy and Data Protection: US Law and Legislation.* ESET. 2016. Accessed 9 Mar. 2019. <www.welivesecurity.com>. Pg. 6.
[5] General Data Protection Regulation. 2016. Pg. 34.
[6] General Data Protection Regulation. 2016. pg. 33.
[7] General Data Protection Regulation. 2016. pg. 65.
[8] General Data Protection Regulation. 2016. pg. 34.
[9] Beard, Stephen. "For Ireland, Multinational Companies are a Blessing and a Curse." *Marketplace.* 20 Jun. 2018. Accessed Mar. 2019. <www.marketplace.org>.
[10] Calder. 2018. Pg. 24.
[11] Calder. 2018. Pg. 9.
[12] General Data Protection Regulation. 2016. pg. 80.
[13] *GDPR in numbers.* European Commission. 25 Jan. 2019. Accessed 7 Mar. 2019. <https://ec.europa.eu/>.
[14] General Data Protection Regulation. 2016. pg. 55.
[15] General Data Protection Regulation. 2016. pg. 82.

[16] Monteiro, Ana M. "First GDPR Fine in Portugal Issued Against Hospital for Three Violations." 3 Jan. 2019. *iapp.org*. Accessed Mar. 2019. <iapp.org>., General Data Protection Regulation. 2016. pg. 35.

[17] Monteiro, Ana M. 2019.

[18] *Annual report: 25 May - 31 December 2018*. Data Protection Commission. 28 Feb. 2019. Accessed 3 Mar, 2019. <https://www.dataprotection.ie>. Pg. 52.

[19] Mulligan, Stephen P. "Google Fined for Violation of EU Data Protection Law." *Congressional Research Service*. 22 Feb. 2019. Accessed Mar. 2019. <fas.org>. Pg. 3.

[20] Commission Nationale de l'Informatique et des Libertés. "The CNIL's Restricted Committee Imposes a Financial Penalty of 50 Million Euros Against GOOGLE LLC." *CNIL*. 21 Jan. 2019. Accessed Mar. 2019. <www.cnil.fr>.

[21] Commission Nationale de l'Informatique et des Libertés. 2019.

[22] Commission Nationale de l'Informatique et des Libertés. 2019.

[23] La Quadrature du Net. "First Sanction Against Google Following Our Collective Complaints." *La Quadrature du Net*. 21 Jan. 2019. Accessed Feb. 2019. <www.laquadrature.net>.

[24] noyb. "GDPR: Complaint by Noyb Leads to € 50 Mio Penalty Against Google Over Invalid Consent." *noyb*. 21 Jan. 2019. Accessed Mar. 2019. <noyb.eu>.

[25] General Data Protection Regulation. 2016. pg. 81.

[26] General Data Protection Regulation. 2016. pg. 81.

[27] La Quadrature du Net. 2019.

[28] General Data Protection Regulation. 2016. pg. 40

[29] Commission Nationale de l'Informatique et des Libertés. 2019.

[30] Commission Nationale de l'Informatique et des Libertés. 2019.

[31] Commission Nationale de l'Informatique et des Libertés. 2019.

[32] Kramer Levin Naftalis & Frankel LLP. "Google's Fine and the French Data Protection Authority's Far-Reaching GDPR Compliance Measures." *JDSUPRA.com*. Feb 28. 2019. Accessed Mar. 2019. <www.jdsupra.com>.

[33] General Data Protection Regulation. 2016. pg. 39.

[34] General Data Protection Regulation. 2016. pg. 50.

[35] Haynes, Allyson H. "Online privacy policies: Contracting away control over personal information?" *Penn State Law Review*. 2007. Vol. 111, No. 3. Pg. 605-606.

[36] General Data Protection Regulation. 2016. pg. 36.

[37] Commission Nationale de l'Informatique et des Libertés. 2019.

[38] Commission Nationale de l'Informatique et des Libertés. 2019.

[39] Commission Nationale de l'Informatique et des Libertés. 2019.

[40] Commission Nationale de l'Informatique et des Libertés. 2019., General Data Protection Regulation (2016) pg. 6., Kramer Levin Naftalis & Frankel LLP (2019).
[41] noyb. "Complaint Under Article 77(1) GDPR." *noyb.* 25 May. 2018a. Accessed Mar. 2019. <noyb.eu>. Pg. 6-7.
[42] Noyb. 2018a. pg 6-7.
[43] Rosen, Jeffrey. "The Deciders: Facebook, Google and the Future of Privacy and Free Speech." 2011. In *Constitution 3.0: Freedom and Technological Change.* Rosen, Jeffrey, & Wittes, Benjamin. Eds. 2011. Brookings Institution Press. Pg. 79.
[44] Commission Nationale de l'Informatique et des Libertés. 2019.
[45] Katell, Michael. "Algorithmic Profiling as Reputation." 2018. Unpublished Manuscript, Information School, University of Washington, Seattle, Washington. Pg. 10.
[46] Calder. 2018. Pg. 30.
[47] Kanter, Jake and Hamilton, Isobel Asher. "Google fined $1.7 billion over a 3rd breach of EU antitrust rules in 3 years." *Business Insider.* 20 Mar. 2019. Accessed Apr. 2019. <www.businessinsider.com>.
[48] Kramer Levin Naftalis & Frankel LLP. 2019., Mulligan. 2019. Pg. 3.
[49] Bastone, Nick, and Ghosh, Shona. "Google Confirms It Will Appeal Its Recent $57 Million Fine for Breaching Europe's Strict New Privacy Rules." *Business Insider.* 23 Jan. 2019. Accessed Feb. 2019. <www.businessinsider.com>.
[50] Commission Nationale de l'Informatique et des Libertés. 2019.
[51] La Quadrature du Net. "It's Time to Tackle GAFAM and Their World." La Quadrature du Net. 18 Apr. 2018. Accessed Feb. 2019. <www.laquadrature.net>., noyb. "GDPR: noyb.eu Filed Four Complaints Over "Forced Consent" Against Google, Instagram, WhatsApp and Facebook." 25 May, 2018b. Accessed Mar. 2019. <noyb.eu>.
[52] La Quadrature du Net. 2019.
[53] *Annual report: 25 May - 31 December 2018.* 2019. Pg. 50-51.
[54] *Annual report: 25 May - 31 December 2018.* 2019. Pg. 50.
[55] Carswell, Simon. "Decisions on Alleged Big Tech Data Breaches Due this Summer." *The Irish Times.* 28 Feb. 2019. Accessed Mar. 2019. <www.irishtimes.com>.
[56] *DLA Piper GDPR Data Breach Survey: February 2019.* 2019. Pg. 4.

Huawei Company Risk Management

[1] "Huawei Investment & Holding Co., Ltd. 2018 Annual Report." Huawei Investment & Holding Co., Ltd. 29 Mar. 2019. Accessed Dec. 2019 <www.huawei.com>.

2 "Our Vision, Mission, and Strategy." Huawei. 3 Apr. 2019. Accessed Dec. 2019 <www.huawei.com>.
3 Searle, Annie. 25 Sept. 2019, Seattle.
4 "Huawei's Views and Strategy Regarding Talent." *Huawei People.* 31 Mar. 2018. Accessed Dec. 2019 <www.huawei.com>.
5 新华网. "任正非签发内部文：华为面临一些问题就是中年危机." _新浪财经_新浪网, 20 May 2018, http://finance.sina.com.cn/chanjing/gsnews/2018-05-20/doc-ihaturft0744803.shtml.
6 Hoffmire, John & Zhu, Zhibiao & Wang, Fusheng. "Employee Stock Ownership Plans and Their Effect on Productivity: The Case of Huawei." 2013
7 Tao, David De CremerTian. "Huawei: A Case Study of When Profit Sharing Works." *Harvard Business Review.* 24 Sept. 2015. Accessed Dec. 2019 <www.hbr.org>.
8 Lindvall, Nora. "Huawei Faces Average 21.8 Percent Resignation Rate from PhD Employees Leaving." Pandaily, 26 Feb. 2019. Accessed Dec. 2019 <www.pandaily.com>.
9 Almond, Kyle. "A Rare Look inside Huawei, China's Tech Giant." CNN. May 2019. Accessed Dec. 2019 <www.cnn.com>.
10 Wakabayashi, Daisuke, and Alan Rappeport. "Huawei C.F.O. Is Arrested in Canada for Extradition to the U.S." The New York Times, The New York Times, 5 Dec. 2018, https://www.nytimes.com/2018/12/05/business/huawei-cfo-arrest-canada-extradition.html.
11 Proctor, Gordon. "Http://Onlinepubs.trb.org/Onlinepubs/Nchrp/Docs/NCHRP08-93_QuickGuide.Pdf." Http://Onlinepubs.trb.org/Onlinepubs/Nchrp/Docs/NCHRP08-93_QuickGuide.Pdf, The StarIsis Corporation, June 2016.
12 IBID
13 "Identifying Emerging Risks." Protiviti, Protiviti Board Perspectives, https://www.protiviti.com/US-en/insights/bpro-issue-70.

Kyoto Animation Arson Attack Risk Analysis

1 京アニ火災　スプリンクラー義務ない建物." Nippon TV (in Japanese). 19 July 2019. Accessed Dec.2019

<https://web.archive.org/web/20190722035349/http://www.news24.jp/articles/2019/07/19/07467552.html>.

[2] Kyoto Animation Co., Ltd. "Corporate Philosophy - About Us." Kyoto Animation Website. Accessed December 4, 2019. <https://www.kyotoanimation.co.jp/en/company/philosophy/>.

[3] IBID

[4] "提40公升汽油去纵火！京都动画浩劫 嫌动机？-李四端的云端世界." 六度新聞（in Chinese）. Accessed December 4, 2019. <https://6do.news/article/1182913>.

[5] IBID

[6] Cook, Tim. "Kyoto Animation Is Home to Some of the World's Most Talented Animators and Dreamers - the Devastating Attack Today Is a Tragedy Felt Far beyond Japan. KyoAni Artists Spread Joy All over the World and across Generations with Their Masterpieces. 心よりご冥福をお祈りいたします。." Twitter. Twitter, July 18, 2019. <https://twitter.com/tim_cook/status/1151875113903542272?lang=en>.

[7] "Board Oversight of Reputation Risk." Protiviti. Accessed Dec. 2019. <https://www.protiviti.com/sites/default/files/united_states/insights/board_perspectives_-_risk_oversight_-_issue_83_-_board_oversight_of_reputation_risk.pdf>.

[8] SoraNews24. "Kyoto Animation Confirms It Received Novel from Writer with Same Name, Address as Arson Suspect." Japan Today. Accessed 4 December 2019. <https://japantoday.com/category/crime/kyoto-animation-confirms-it-received-novel-from-writer-with-same-name-address-as-arson-suspect>.

[9] "アニメ会社放火 男が会社に一方的に恨み募らせた可能性も." NHKニュース (日本放送協会). Accessed Dec. 2019. <https://web.archive.org/web/20190721145500/https://www3.nhk.or.jp/news/html/20190720/k10011999691000.html >.

[10] Adeosun, Ladipo. "Corporate Reputation as a Strategic Asset." International Journal of Business and Social Science Feb. 2013. Accessed Dec. 2019. <https://pdfs.semanticscholar.org/2875/be7bc48bab39af45c817fe9f3c6d109b2beb.pdf >.

[11] Searle, Annie. "Enterprise Risk Management." University of Washington. 25 Sept. 2019, Seattle.

[12] Zixiao Chen. “京都动画纵火案细节曝光：楼顶逃生门本可打开，但因浓烟弥漫未能及时逃生.” 环球网.環球時報 (in Chinese). Accessed Dec. 2019. < http://world.huanqiu.com/exclusive/2019-07/15181009.html?agt=15422>.

[13] Mukai, Daisuke. “Reaching Veranda Vital for Survival in Kyoto Animation Arson：The Asahi Shimbun.” The Asahi Shimbun, 17 Aug. 2019. <http://www.asahi.com/ajw/articles/AJ201908170029.html>.

[14] “一気に燃える「爆燃」か、吹き抜け「火の回り早い」.” 読売新聞オンライン. Accessed Dec. 2019. <https://web.archive.org/web/20190719110800/https://www.yomiuri.co.jp/national/20190719-OYT1T50109/>.

[15] "京アニ" 代理人弁護士 第1スタジオの防犯対策を説明. NHKニュース. 日本放送協会. 23 July 2019. Accessed 4 Dec 2019. <https://web.archive.org/web/20190824041042/https://www3.nhk.or.jp/news/html/20190723/k10012005391000.html>.

[16] Proctor, Gordon. “Managing Risk Across the Enterprise: Final Quick Guide for State Departments of Transportation.” TRANSPORTATION RESEARCH BOARD OF THE NATIONAL ACADEMIES. Accessed Dec. 2019 <http://onlinepubs.trb.org/onlinepubs/nchrp/docs/NCHRP08-93_QuickGuide.pdf>.

[17] Adeosun, Ladipo. “Corporate Reputation as a Strategic Asset.” International Journal of Business and Social Science Feb. 2013. Accessed Dec. 2019. <https://pdfs.semanticscholar.org/2875/be7bc48bab39af45c817fe9f3c6d109b2beb.pdf >.

[18] IBID

[19] “33人の死亡確認、平成以降最悪 京都アニメーション火災」.”京都新聞』京都新聞社. Accessed Dec. 2019. < https://www.kyoto-np.co.jp/articles/-/9338>.

[20] IBID

[21] "ご支援の御礼とご案内（初出7月24日、改訂9月13日）" ご支援の御礼とご案内（初出7月24日、改訂9月13日）. Kyoto Animation (in Japanese). 13 September 2019. <https://www.kyotoanimation.co.jp/information/?id=3075 >.

---

[22] Kyoto Animation Co., Ltd. "Corporate Philosophy - About Us." Kyoto Animation Website. Accessed December 4, 2019. <https://www.kyotoanimation.co.jp/en/company/philosophy/>.

NASDAQ's Exploration into Blockchain Technology

[1] Kennon, J. (2019, December 08). What to Know About the NASDAQ, the World's Second-Largest Stock Market. Retrieved March 14, 2020, from https://www.thebalance.com/what-is-the-nasdaq-356343

[2] Simpson, S. (2020, January 29). The Death Of The Trading Floor. Retrieved March 14, 2020, from https://www.investopedia.com/financial-edge/0511/the-death-of-the-trading-floor.aspx

[3] C. (2020). NDAQ. Retrieved March 14, 2020, from https://money.cnn.com/quote/profile/profile.html?symb=NDAQ

[4] CNN, NDAQ.

[5] Simpson, S.

[6] Ibid.

[7] Manual, B. (2012, November 09). What is NASDAQ? Retrieved March 14, 2020, from https://www.businessnewsdaily.com/3403-nasdaq.html

[8] Ibid.

[9] Amadeo, K. (2020, March 13). How the Stock Market Works. Retrieved March 14, 2020, from https://www.thebalance.com/how-does-the-stock-market-work-3306244

[10] Ibid.

[11] Hayes, A. (2020, March 14). A Breakdown on How the Stock Market Works. Retrieved March 14, 2020, from https://www.investopedia.com/articles/investing/082614/how-stock-market-works.asp

[12] Kenton, W. (2020, February 29). Centralized Market. Retrieved March 14, 2020, from https://www.investopedia.com/terms/c/centralizedmarket.asp

[13] Elijah, J. (2019, September 11). The perils of centralized databases. Retrieved March 14, 2020, from https://projecthydro.org/blog/the-perils-of-centralized-databases/

[14] Ibid.

[15] Popper, N. (2018, June 28). What is the Blockchain? Explaining the Tech Behind Cryptocurrencies. Retrieved March 14, 2020, from

https://www.nytimes.com/2018/06/27/business/dealbook/blockchains-guide- information.html?action=click
[16] Ibid.
[17] Marr, B. (2018, November 21). A Complete Beginner's Guide To Blockchain. Retrieved March 14, 2020, from https://www.forbes.com/sites/bernardmarr/2017/01/24/a-complete-beginners-guide-to-blockchain/
[18] Ervin, E. (2018, August 17). Blockchain Technology Set To Revolutionize Global Stock Trading. Retrieved March 14, 2020, from https://www.forbes.com/sites/ericervin/2018/08/16/blockchain-technology-set-to- revolutionize-global-stock-trading/
[19] Schwab.com. (2019, March 08). Stock Settlement: Why You Need to Understand the T+2 Timeline. Retrieved March 14, 2020, from https://www.schwab.com/resource-center/insights/content/stock-settlement-why-you- need-to-understand-t2-timeline
[20] Ervin, E.
[21] Cointelegraph. (2017, December 06). How Blockchain Technology Works. Retrieved March 14, 2020, from https://cointelegraph.com/bitcoin-for-beginners/how-blockchain-technology-works-guide-for-beginners
[22] Ibid.
[23] Vitus, A. (2018, February 08). What's needed to unlock the real power of blockchain and distributed apps. Retrieved March 14, 2020, from https://techcrunch.com/2018/02/08/whats-needed-to-unlock-the-real-power- of-blockchain-and-distributed-apps/
[24] Ibid.
[25] Finance. (n.d.). Retrieved March 14, 2020, from https://consensys.net/blockchain-use-cases/finance/
[26] Tena, M. (2017, January 16). 7 regulatory challenges facing blockchain: BBVA. Retrieved March 14, 2020, from https://www.bbva.com/en/7-regulatory-challenges-facing-blockchain/
[27] International legal business solutions - Global Legal Insights. (n.d.). Retrieved March 14, 2020, from https://www.globallegalinsights.com/practice-areas/blockchain-laws-and-regulations/usa
[28] Tena, M.
[29] French, J. (2018, April 23). Nasdaq exec says exchange is 'all-in' on using blockchain technology. Retrieved March 14, 2020, from https://www.thestreet.com/investing/nasdaq-all-in-on-blockchain-technology-14551134

---

[30] Rizzo, P. (2015, November 27). Inside Linq, Nasdaq's Private Markets Blockchain Project. Retrieved March 14, 2020, from https://www.coindesk.com/hands-on-with-linq-nasdaqs-private-markets-blockchain-project

[31] Ibid.

[32] Nasdaq Ventures. (n.d.). Retrieved March 14, 2020, from https://www.nasdaq.com/nasdaqventures

[33] Ibid.

[34] Castillo, M. (2019, January 25). Nasdaq Leads $20 Million Investment In Enterprise Blockchain Startup Symbiont. Retrieved March 14, 2020, from https://www.forbes.com/sites/michaeldelcastillo/2019/01/23/exclusive-nasdaq-leads-20-million-investment-in- enterprise-blockchain-startup-symbion

---

The Evolution of Aadhar in India

[1] Drumm, C., Pandey, N., Young, C., Wong, J., Koswin, K., & Sardesai, S. "Case study: Aadhar-providing proof of identity to one billion". *Toronto: Munk School of Global Affairs.* 2017.

[2] HK, V. "SC's Aadhar Verdict | Privacy vs Identity". *Deccan Herald.* 20 Sep 2018. Accessed May 2019 <www.deccanherald.com>

[3] "Around 10 lakh people enrol, update Aadhaar every day: UIDAI". *ET Online.* 11 Jul 2018. Accessed May 2019 < www.economictimes.indiatimes.com>

[4] Gordon Proctor & Associates; The Starlsis Corporation; Jeff Roorda and Associates, Inc. "Managing Risk across the Enterprise: Final Quick Guide for State Departments of Transportation." *Transportation Research Board.* p-16. 21 May 2015.

[5] Bhardwaj, K. "Explainer: Aadhaar is vulnerable to identity theft because of its design and the way it is used". *Scroll.in.* 2 Apr 2017. Accessed May 2019 <www.scroll.in>

[6] Sachdev, V. "Aadhaar Authentication for Govt Services Fails 12% of Time: UIDAI". *The Quint.* 27 Mar 2018. Accessed May 2019 <www.thequint.com>

[7] Suhag, R., & Chaturvedi, A.. "Comparison of the 2010 and the 2016 Aadhaar Bills" . *PRS Legislative Research.* 2016. Accessed May 2019 <www.prsindia.org>

[8] Green, P. E.. "Enterprise Risk Management: A Common Framework for the Entire Organization". *Elsevier.* p-67.2016.

---

[9] Kumar, A. P.. "Lessons from the World's Largest e-Identity Program – India's Aadhaar". *Procivis.* 13 Feb 2018. Accessed May 2019 www.procivis.ch

www.ingramcontent.com/pod-product-compliance
Lightning Source LLC
Chambersburg PA
CBHW060834280326
41934CB00007B/785

* 9 7 9 8 9 8 5 0 1 0 1 0 7 *